BEYOND THE
WATER'S EDGE:
AMERICA'S FOREIGN POLICIES

THE LIPPINCOTT SERIES IN AMERICAN GOVERNMENT

Under the editorship of William C. Havard,

Virginia Polytechnic Institute and State University

Howard Bliss *Vassar College*
M. Glen Johnson *Vassar College*

BEYOND THE WATER'S EDGE:

AMERICA'S FOREIGN POLICIES

J.B. Lippincott Company
Philadelphia New York Toronto

ISBN 0-397-47316-8

Library of Congress Card Number 74-17408

Printed in the United States of America

1 3 5 7 9 8 6 4 2

Library of Congress Cataloging in Publication Data

Bliss, Howard
   Beyond the water's edge.

   Includes bibliographical references.
   1. United States—Foreign relations—1945-
I. Johnson, Maurice Glen, joint author.
II. Title.
JX1417.B54   327.73   74-17408
ISBN 0-397-47316-8

To our parents,
who have encouraged
us to value debate.

Table of Contents

Preface

To write about American foreign policy in the mid-1970s is a perplexing task. The signs of fundamental change in the principles and procedures of decision-making are abundant. Yet, many of the older, historically sanctioned patterns persist. It is an era of rapid change and not insignificant experimentation. Yet patterns of action, deeply rooted in the habits developed during the Cold War, reappear with sometimes alarming strength. It is therefore proper and desirable that far-ranging debate should currently characterize discussion about foreign policy.

We have made that debate the focus of our analysis because we believe it to be a watershed in the understanding of American foreign policy, if not in foreign policy itself. If for no other reason, it is a watershed which divides the young from the old. Those who reached maturity after 1965—which includes the overwhelming majority of today's college students—have been conditioned to think of debate over fundamental issues and assumptions of foreign policy and foreign policy-making as omnipresent and legitimate. Such debate—always vociferous, often strident, and sometimes violent—constitutes their introduction to awareness of American foreign policy. The apparent placidity of the debate at the time of the overwhelming victory of President Nixon in the 1972 election—an event which, we believe, merely papered over a deep uneasiness sometimes bordering on despair among many Americans, especially the young—did not mark its end. Debate merely shifted from the streets to the Congress, from the campuses to the scholarly journals, from demonstration to discussion.

To those who are older, the current debate is seen in a different light. Their formative experience in foreign affairs goes back to the postwar consensus. They accepted the assumptions which guided foreign policy in that period. They gained maturity in an era in which debate over the fundamentals of foreign policy was not really a legitimate activity. Politics, for them, was something which was supposed to stop "at the water's edge." Parties and politicians might argue at length about domestic policy but foreign policy, at least the fundamental assumptions which guided American actions in the world beyond our shores, was formerly considered to be beyond the proper range of partisan or public debate.

Both attitudes retain a powerful hold over their respective generations. They help to explain the tendencies of Presidents Johnson and Nixon to equate criticism of their foreign policies by American youth with giving aid and comfort to the enemy, and the disdainful reactions of the young to such charges. We believe this divergence of perception is one of the major impediments to understanding and communication in the current debate. For this reason also, we have made that debate one of the major perspectives from which we approach the making of foreign policy.

In doing so, we do not hide our view that debate over the fundamental issues and assumptions of United States foreign policy is healthy, too long suppressed by the uniformity of consensus politics, and also one of the most effective ways of encouraging restraints on the excessive and often indiscriminate use of American power by policy-makers.

Because we believe debate over fundamental issues is healthy, we have not shrunk from controversial interpretations and assertions about the major issues in the current debate. If such assertions stimulate further inquiry into American foreign policy and foreign policy-making, one of our major purposes will have been achieved. Thus, we have tried to cite useful sources to which the reader can turn for further analysis of these topics or for contrary points of view.

In addition to the focus on the current debate, this book has several other particular perspectives of which the reader should be aware and which we, therefore, set out explicitly here.

First, we believe that the interaction between policy and process is crucial to an understanding of foreign policy. Too much of the literature treats foreign policy and policy-making as if they were fully separable entities, doubtless a result of the tendency of historians to focus on policy and of political scientists to focus on process. Fortunately such a separation is rapidly becoming a casualty of a more concerted interdisciplinary approach to foreign policy.

Second, we believe there is a much greater continuity over the whole sweep of American experience in foreign policy than is generally recognized. Only in some ways does World War II provide the sharp dividing line which is attributed to it. In other ways—as we try to show explicitly in Chapter 3 and implicitly throughout the book—it represents only a speeding up of tendencies which are firmly rooted in American history.

Third, we believe the primacy of the President in making American foreign policy cannot be overemphasized. The President makes foreign policy! All of the factors which limit his freedom of action and to which we devote considerable attention throughout the book should not be allowed to obscure the overwhelming role of the President in the foreign policy process. Experience, culture, Congress, organizational and bureaucratic politics, even the foreign policy debate itself—in which we place so much faith—affect foreign policy primarily by influencing the President. Watergate and the accompanying forced resignation of President Nixon in no way alter this emphasis. Indeed, success in foreign policy was repeatedly invoked by former President Nixon and some Congressmen to offset the startling disclosures of corruption in the domestic political process. More importantly, despite often expressed fears, there is little evidence that former President Nixon's troubles diminished his ability to work his will in the foreign policy sphere even while he was severely weakened domestically by the Watergate scandals. The entire Watergate experience seems to confirm our emphasis on the dominant role of the President in foreign policy by demonstrating the disinclination of the American people (and their representatives in Congress as well) to recognize an intimate connection between the values and perceptions which inform foreign policy and those which inform domestic policy. (The existence of this connection is directly addressed in Chapters 2 and 4.) Throughout Watergate, foreign policy was held to be separate and the President was considered worthy of support in that field no matter how corrupt and discredited in the domestic field. Whether the President should be at the center of foreign policy-making is a separate issue we discuss in the final chapter.

The authors of a book which attempts to synthesize and interpret a field as broad as American foreign policy incur wide-ranging debts of gratitude. Happily, a book also provides a welcome opportunity to acknowledge those debts.

Intellectually, our primary debt is to each other. The book is jointly authored in both conception and execution. We have discussed, argued, and occasionally battled over every idea; we have edited, rewritten, and supplemented each other's drafts; and we have both learned in the process.

Most of our other intellectual debts are acknowledged in footnotes. But we cannot fail to mention several generations of students in our classes at Vassar. They have questioned, debated with us, and brought refreshing ideas to challenge those shaped primarily by scholarly writing. Our colleagues at Vassar have been unstinting in their willingness to react to our ideas and to share theirs with us. We have profited from the opportunity to discuss some of the interpretations in this book with selected individuals at the Department of State during our participation in State's Scholar-Diplomat Seminar program and in return visits of Foreign Service officers to Vassar.

We are indebted to Vassar College for academic leaves spent in Europe and the research facilities in London and Brussels that were used during the early stages of preparing the manuscript.

William Havard read the manuscript and offered valuable suggestions. John B. Hoey, Elaine Terranova, and the staff of J. B. Lippincott provided help and encouragement whenever it was needed. The Vassar Committee on Faculty Research helped to defray the financial burden of research and manuscript preparation. Our research assistants, Sandy Edwards, Sloane Elman, and Mary Young have tracked down innumerable facts and dug out many references. As always, Mrs. Mildred Tubby was especially helpful and accurate in typing the manuscript. For errors of fact, we, of course, accept responsibility.

1.   America's Foreign Policies in the 1970s: The Challenge to Consensus

"The postwar period in international relations has ended."
—Richard M. Nixon, 1970

"The era of the Cold War is over."
—Leonid Brezhnev, 1973

Since 1965, discussion of American foreign policy has taken place in the context of great controversy over the fundamental role of the United States in world affairs. All the principles cherished as guidelines for foreign policy in earlier years; all the perceptions about America's purposes in the world; all the procedures, painstakingly developed, for making foreign policy decisions; and all the individuals and institutions responsible for those decisions have been subjected to searching analysis and criticism. The controversy is unique because it comes hard on the heels of a pervasive consensus which enveloped foreign policy from the late 1940s to 1965—the Cold War consensus. The dramatic shift from consensus to controversy is interesting enough in itself but, more importantly, it is crucial to analysis of foreign policy in the 1970s. It forces a change in emphasis from description of the structural details of foreign policy machinery and routine acceptance of standard justifications for the enormous American involvement in the affairs of other nations. It compels a critical look at how American foreign policy is made and who makes it; the role of American experience, values and culture in guiding foreign policy decisions; and the future conduct of American foreign policy.

The United States stands at one of those rare crossroads in foreign policy. It is clear that the country will not continue on the road well marked by the post-World War II consensus but less clear to which one of several alternative paths it will turn. It is evident that choice is now open in a way it has not been since the close of World War II.

After taking office, President Nixon correctly asserted that "the postwar period in international relations has ended."[1] One careful observer cited the significance of the new "period":

The consensus underlying the constancy in foreign policy from Truman to Johnson was at an end. On January 20, 1969, there was no basic foreign policy to be handed over intact to the Nixon Administration.

The period when policy changes could be attributed to changes in reliance on various tools of power, as distinct from changes in national interests and objectives, seemed to call for an analysis of contending programs and strategies. For the period we are now entering the analysis of foreign policy choices will have to cut deeper, to the debate over contending concepts of national purpose and international order.[2]

In the post-1965 period, controversy has often been expressed in wide-ranging debate which has helped to clarify fundamental choices for Americans. In succeeding chapters, we will turn to the principal influences on those choices: the American experience and culture; the international setting of American foreign policy; the role of the President, the military, the Congress, the public, and pressure groups including the military-industrial complex in policy-making. First, it is necessary to examine the way in which debate has emerged and the issues it has raised for foreign policy-making. These are our objectives in this chapter.

BASIC ASSUMPTIONS OF THE POSTWAR CONSENSUS

The postwar consensus was composed of seven main assumptions about the nature of the postwar world, American interests, the threats to those interests, and the most appropriate method of formulating American policy. These seven assumptions,[3] widely shared by policy-makers and the general public, conditioned the interpretation of specific events in the postwar international environment in ways we shall examine in Chapter 3. Here, we will only identify and describe these assumptions.

The first and the most significant of these assumptions was a belief that:

1. *In the aftermath of World War II, Communism was an aggressive and expansionist ideology, both dangerous and threatening in combination with Soviet power.* The Soviet Union was seen as intent on expanding its own political and military spheres of influence by incorporating as many countries and as much territory as possible into its orbit. Though the American impression of Soviet strategy admitted the fact of changing tactics during the two postwar decades, the central goal of expansionism was considered constant. Thus, American policy-makers recognized that the immediate postwar policy of the Soviet Union was one of forcible establishment by the Red Army of satellite regimes controlled from Moscow and possessing only the flimsiest facade of independence. This policy could gradually evolve to include the more subtle diplomatic and economic courting of regimes which had come to power with considerable independence, such as the Castro regime in Cuba. The first basic

assumption of postwar American policy, however, allowed Americans to see all increases in Soviet influence, whatever their form, as part of the drive toward territorial and ideological expansionism.

There was also general agreement that the Soviet Union had the capability of acting on its intentions throughout the postwar period. It is clear that the United States overestimated Soviet capabilities at various times during the postwar era.[4] Nevertheless, the salient fact is that the United States—virtually all relevant segments of public and official opinion—believed the Soviet Union not only was intent on expanding its sphere of influence and control wherever the opportunity presented itself *but possessed the capability of doing so.* Viewed from the American perspective, Soviet expansionism would eventually affect the balance of power. The security of the United States—won at such high cost in two world wars—would be difficult to sustain in a world in which Soviet power, coupled with an ideology alien to dominant American beliefs, controlled increasingly large and strategic areas of the globe.[5] Thus, in its simplest formulation, the United States operated in the postwar world on the assumption that Soviet intentions and capabilities were hostile to the interests of the United States.

2. *The Communist threat is global in nature.* Americans viewed Soviet-American relations as a zero-sum game; any gain for them was a loss for us. Thus, the United States could not view with equanimity the development of a Communist political system in any country, however small or however remote. Such an event would have to be viewed as a gain for "them" and a loss for "us." In this view, there could be no common interests between these two super powers; international Communism had to be fought at every step, regardless of where it was. Most Americans viewed peace and world order as indivisible.

3. *The United States is the only country with both the will and the capacity to resist the Soviet-Communist threat.*

Americans believed that the role of bulwark against international Communism was thrust upon them. They considered themselves compelled to accept an unwanted role. The economic and military exhaustion experienced by most countries during World War II supported this assumption.

4. *Soviet-American relations are the central feature of international politics.* The centrality of the Soviet threat and the uniqueness of the American capacity to meet it converge toward a major assumption on which the postwar consensus was built, the belief that *the contest between the Americans and the Russians was the decisive conflict of international politics; the major conflict of world politics was a bipolar one.* Three important perspectives follow from this assumption: first, a view on the nature of the Communist sphere of influence; second, a perspective on the so-called Third World, the underdeveloped countries of Asia, Africa, and Latin America which during the postwar period were throwing off the yoke of colonial rule; and, third, a perspective about relations with allies, especially in the North Atlantic area. A unified bloc controlled from Moscow was the central assumption of the first perspective. Americans assumed that Communist leadership, highly motivated to expand its sphere of influence, would take steps to perpetuate exclusive control over the areas brought under its hegemony.

More ambiguity was involved in the perspective which guided American policy in relation to the Third World than in the case of American perceptions of the Communist bloc. Consequently, more shifts of policy and more intensive debate over appropriate policy toward the Third World took place during the period of consensus than was characteristic of reactions to the Soviet Union. None of the fluctuations reflected any alteration in the basic assumption that American relations with the Third World were inextricably conditioned by the far more important two-sided conflict between the United States and the Soviet Union. A similar predicament characterized American policies within the Atlantic alliance. Although they were seen differently by successive American administrations, as we shall see in Chapter 3, alliance policies were uniformly considered to be largely conditioned, if not dictated, by the priority of the Soviet-American contest.

5. *The United States is benevolent, fair, and objective.* In reluctantly accepting the role of bulwark against international Communism, Americans believed that they were making enormous sacrifices in the interests of other states. Motives of self-interest were assumed to be secondary. Americans sought no territory, no special privileges, no empire; America sought only to protect the "free" countries of the world from a Communist threat. Americans were startled, therefore, when other states began to display suspicion of American motives. They attributed it to ignorance on the part of these states of what was in their own interest and continued to assume that America's role in the world was benevolent and disinterested.

6. *Politics should stop at the water's edge.* Since the nature of the enemy was clear and the United States had reluctantly accepted a role thrust upon it by circumstances, foreign policy should receive the united support of all the people. Partisan debate, however prized in domestic affairs, was illegitimate in foreign policy. Bipartisanship was considered the correct approach to foreign policy. Like two small brothers who fight interminably between themselves but unite to fend off the attacks of the neighborhood bully, American partisans were to submerge their differences in the confrontation with the international Communist bully. Those who had the temerity to dissent from the assumptions on which foreign policy was based were either ignored or vilified. Harry Truman put this approach clearly in a letter to his successor, Dwight Eisenhower:

> *What I've always had in mind was and is a continuing foreign policy. You know that is a fact because you had a part in outlining it.*

Partisan politics should stop at the boundaries of the United States. I'm extremely sorry that you have allowed a bunch of screwballs to come between us.[6]

7. *The President makes American foreign policy.* The Founding Fathers may have separated the powers of government and created a system of checks and balances, but they could not have realized the unprecedented demands the postwar threat would place on American government. In a time of extreme danger, the more leisurely pace of formulating policy and arguing out policy differences had to give way to acceptance of more unified support of presidential leadership. The appropriate role for Congress and the courts, the press and the public, was to help the President meet this challenge. Congressional criticism or negations of presidential action afforded protection for the Republic in the domestic sphere. They prevented the concentration of political power in the hands of the Executive, but only in the domestic sphere. Although the Founding Fathers separated the powers of government to prevent a concentration of power, in foreign affairs the Republic could no longer afford such a luxury.

These foregoing assumptions were the basic elements of the postwar consensus. For nearly 20 years—the late 1940s to 1965—the Cold War consensus was the foundation for American foreign policy. Though no longer supported by a massive consensus, these assumptions continue to exercise a powerful influence on policy-making.

THE COSTS OF CONSENSUS

No powerful dogma can hold a people in its grip for long without leaving an influential legacy; the postwar foreign policy consensus is no exception. The legacy of consensus bedevils contemporary efforts to construct a rational dialogue over future issues of foreign policy.

The first casualty of consensus was debate itself. For nearly 20 years, critics who challenged the fundamental assumptions on which foreign policy was based were unable to obtain a serious hearing. So widely shared were these assumptions that debate was reduced to a question of method, of the means of implementing the goals of policy. Only rarely were the goals of policy and the assumptions which shaped these goals subjected to scrutiny, evaluation, or reassessment. They were continually reaffirmed, of course, but in a manner more akin to the reaffirmation of faith contained in the recitation of an accepted litany than as an act of inquiry and assessment, more as ritual than rigorous analysis. Cant phrases such as "Communist aggression," "responsibility for the Free World," and "Sino-Soviet threat" justified most policies pursued by the United States and symbolized the ideas shaping the world view of those who made policy.

The second casualty of consensus was the reputation of people who questioned the assumptions on which it was based. Consensus was pervasive and dissenters so few that they were either ignored or persecuted. The set of assumptions undergirding consensus *seemed* an accurate reflection of reality and, in some respects, was confirmed by events. When American policy *seemed* to be successful, there was no need to take the dissenters seriously. This was the experience of Walter Lippmann when he systematically criticized the containment policy from the outset.[7]

When policy *seemed* to go wrong, consensus provided a basis for the persecution of the dissenter. The explanation for persecution, in the McCarthy period especially, can be traced to the basic Cold War consensus. To those who shared in the consensus, it was inconceivable that they could be wrong; that possibility was not admissible among Americans grown unaccustomed to questioning fundamental assumptions. Policy failure was more easily ascribed to incompetence or disloyalty among those who make or influence policy. What better candidates to be assigned the responsibility for failure than those who dissented, however mildly, from the dogma of the day; those who wondered aloud about the realism of assuming eternal and implacable hostility between capitalism and Communism; those who wondered aloud about the universality of beneficent effects of American military intervention; those who suggested that justice and progress might one day have to be won at the price of stability. Such people were the obvious targets of a consensus-dominated society.

The period of the Cold War consensus brought just such an attack upon dissenters. Its most extreme form is associated with the early 1950s and the name of Senator Joseph McCarthy. But it was not confined to that period nor to that Senator. School boards, business corporations, state legislatures, and private citizens joined in the hunt for subversives throughout the land. Few were found but, on the basis of accusation, some suffered loss of job, livelihood, pension rights, friends, and, sometimes, even home and family. Among those most vilified were a group of China specialists in the Department of State. They were held responsible for the alleged failure of America's China policy in the late 1940s. They were hounded out of their jobs by charges of incompetence and disloyalty and some were even forced into "voluntary" exile. To this day, the Department of State has not been able to re-establish the level of competence and expertise lost in that purge. Moreover, the lessons of the McCarthyite charges were not lost on those who were not its direct victims. Clearly, dissent and debate were not approaches to foreign policy tasks while consensus reigned. Whatever debate was not suppressed by consensus itself was more systematically suppressed by the charges of incompetence and disloyalty which it fostered.

These casualties of consensus were most pronounced, of course, during the high period of the postwar consensus during the early 1950s. But intellectual and political habits are slow to change. These legacies of consensus continue to be seen today.

On all sides of the current foreign policy debate, issues of personality and charges of incompetence and disloyalty seem easier to come by than serious discussion of fundamental issues. Two examples from opposite sides of the political spectrum will illustrate the point. Some revisionist historians, about whom we will have more to say later, offer the alleged "evil" anti-Soviet biases of Harry S. Truman as an explanation for the origins of the Cold War.[8] On the other hand, Spiro Agnew's charge that those who dissented from President Nixon's Vietnam policy were giving "aid and comfort to the enemy" reflects the worst McCarthy tactics.[9]

THE CHALLENGE TO CONSENSUS

In the 1960s the consensus which had supported American foreign policy since the end of the Second World War began to break down. It was first undermined by the challenges to fundamental American assumptions in the domestic sphere. The rise of the civil rights movement forced Americans to examine their commitment to equality of opportunity and equality before the law. Scholars and publicists focused attention on problems of poverty, health care, planned obsolescence, pollution of all kinds, and the apparent unwillingness or inability of American society to address these problems successfully. Americans became vulnerable to profound doubts about the basic traits of their collective life—their faith in progress, their optimism, their egalitarianism, their sense of political virtue—in an unprecedented way. A society which, for nearly 200 years, had a general belief that it was politically unique in its commitment to resolving the age-old problems of injustice, poverty, and racism, discovered that it had many of the problems of older polities and, furthermore, had created a great many new ones as well. Far worse, Americans seemed no longer confident that they would find solutions around the next corner.

To this domestic crisis of confidence was added the sustained agony of Vietnam. The consensus which had supported American foreign policy for 20 years received its most serious challenge. That challenge unleashed the greatest debate over foreign policy in the history of the Republic. Of course, there had been great debates before, but the only ones to rival that of the late 1960s and early 1970s were the imperialist/anti-imperialist conflict following the Spanish-American War in 1898, and the League of Nations controversy after World War I. The new debate exceeded even those great conflicts in intensity, scope of participation, duration, and fundamental issues raised.[10]

The story is an all too familiar one: with each successive escalation of American commitment and American casualties between 1965 and 1968, the vocal, voluminous, and vehement criticism of American policy reached a new crescendo. With the de-escalation of American participation and the shortening of American casualty lists following the election of President Nixon in 1968, criticism became muted and less strident but no less direct in its attack on the assumptions which had sustained the consensus of the postwar period.

At a more fundamental, but less familiar level, the initial critiques of American policy in Vietnam, which held the United States to be overcommitted and endangering its essentially successful and benevolent role in world affairs, were replaced by criticisms of the United States as malevolent, not only in Vietnam, but throughout the whole range of its foreign policies.[11] While the war escalated under President Johnson and then as it shifted from the ground to the air and sea under President Nixon, the critique mounted by the opponents of the war both deepened and broadened. It broadened to include a whole range of other issues which dot the landscape of American foreign policy. Issues such as military intervention, support of military regimes, and Asian versus European commitments were tied to the general American stance in the world of which the

Vietnam disaster was only a symptom. The critique deepened to question not just the American effort in Vietnam and elsewhere but the whole set of assumptions and values upon which the postwar consensus had been so carefully built. In the words of one critic, "Vietnam was no mistake."[12] Instead, it was the logical outgrowth of the set of assumptions—the world view, if you will—which had guided American policy-makers throughout the postwar era. If American motives as well as American methods, if American intent as well as American ingenuity, if America's commitment to benevolent values as well as America's capability to achieve them—if all these were called into question in Vietnam, it seemed reasonable to question former inviolate assumptions in all policy arenas in which the United States was active.

Foreign policy debate, submerged by consensus politics, broke into the open after 1965, at first with an intensity which yielded more heat than light but subsequently settling into a steady and often illuminating flame of criticism. Many critics concentrated their heaviest attacks on policies of the past, those which had characterized the building and maintaining of consensus. They undertook to revise the traditional interpretation of American policy throughout the postwar period. They questioned the orthodox interpretations of the origins of the Cold War and America's role in it. They further questioned American involvement in the Korean War, in the Dominican Republic, and in the whole of the Third World.[13] These exercises in historical reinterpretation soon spilled over into the analysis of more contemporary and continuing issues. Critics began to question the balance between congressional and presidential power in foreign policy-making; the role of the military in American policy-making and the interlocking nature of military and industrial requirements; American economic power and the role of American based multinational corporations;[14] American policies of arms control; alliance management; foreign aid; and American policy in Latin America, Southeast Asia and the Middle East.

The debate soon revealed three major schools of thought about American foreign policy:[15]

1. *The "traditionalists."*[16] Architects and supporters of postwar American policy, the traditionalists accept the assumptions on which the postwar consensus was forged. They were the creators and sustainers of consensus. Their ranks were swelled in the early postwar years by almost the entire foreign-policy community. Every postwar President and Secretary of State may be counted among the traditionalists, though some of them occasionally voiced doubts about basic consensus assumptions, as President Eisenhower did in his farewell address, President Kennedy did in his American University speech in June, 1963, and in his Declaration of Interdependence speech of July 4, 1962, and President Nixon did in the Guam exposition of the Nixon doctrine. All of them have acted primarily on the assumptions of the postwar consensus.

In brief, traditionalists see the United States as standing for the forces of good in the world, compelled to accept the burden of defending the "Free World" against the world-wide aggressive ambitions of the Communist powers. They see the United States as striving through economic aid and technical and political advice and example, to assist less fortunate nations to achieve a better life. They are prepared to admit that the United States has made mistakes in foreign policy over the last thirty years (some traditionalists are even prepared to label the Vietnam War a mistake) but, in their view, these were mistakes of tactics, not mistakes of will, motive, purpose, or values.

2. *The "limitationists."*[17] In general the limitationists accept the basic thrust of the assumptions which underlie the postwar consensus. In the main, they can be counted as a part of that consensus until the mid-1960s. With the escalation of the Vietnam War, they began to view the United States as overcommitted and to press for self-imposed limits on American commitments abroad.

Limitationists vary in their reasons for urging greater restraint. Some argue that scarce resources are more urgently needed to meet pressing domestic needs. Others suggest that excessive commitments abroad ignored unfortunate side-effects of American intervention, effects that were sometimes worse than the evil which American intervention had been designed to combat in the first place. Still others argue that the world situation has so changed that heavy American commitments appropriate in the early Cold War days are no longer required. In this view, the Communist threat has moderated, at least on a global scale if not in certain specific geographic arenas. These limitationists generally support the commitments of the Truman and Eisenhower years, though some think the rhetoric with which they were presented was excessive, but feel the time has come for greater restraint. Other limitationists feel the time has come for other countries to shoulder some of the burden the United States has been carrying for so long.

The limitationists also urge alterations in the way in which foreign policy is made, for they rightly see the substance of policy and the process of policy-making as being inextricably linked. Two major aspects of the policy-making process have received major attention from the limitationists. First, they are concerned about excessive power being placed in the hands of the President. Since many of the most politically active limitationists are members of Congress, it is not surprising that they have become increasingly concerned about the apparent inability of that body to place effective restraints on presidential action. A second area which worries many limitationists, both in Congress and outside, is the excessive role of military considerations in foreign policy decisions. Limitationists are not only concerned about the prevalence of military people in the councils of decision but what they see as the tendency of even civilian decision-makers to place undue emphasis on military factors.

3. *The "revisionists."*[18] As the Vietnam War became more unpopular and the protests against it more vehement, revisionists received an increasingly attentive hearing.

Revisionist criticism of American foreign policy is more comprehensive than that of limitationists. Revisionists reject the assumptions which supported the postwar consensus. They picture the United States as a modern imperialist power, engaging in global intervention in pursuit of self-serving interests. They reject the view—shared in varying degrees by the traditionalists and limitationists alike—that there is any serious objective Communist threat to American or "Free World" (a term they see as meaningless) interests. Moreover, they reject the notion that there has been any such threat at any time since the end of World War II. They often picture the United States as a more serious threat to the freedom and independence of other states. They hold the United States at least jointly responsible for starting and perpetuating the Cold War.

As with the limitationists, there are a variety of views among the revisionists. Some see the United States as motivated by the narrow economic self-interest of capitalism.[19] In this view, the United States is engaged in almost classic economic imperialism. Other revisionists focus on ideological anti-Communism (though this, of course, is not unrelated to the first view) which they consider has become an all-consuming crusade.[20] These revisionists see the doctrine of militant anti-Communism uniting foreign policy and the domestic witchhunts of the McCarthy era. Other revisionists give less emphasis to the economic and ideological elements in American policy. They see the United States acting as great powers customarily act, intervening in the affairs of other states largely because the development of preponderant power logically compels its use. Revisionists do agree in rejecting the notion that the United States can play the role of objective arbiter in the world.

Revisionists like limitationists view policy and policy-making as being intimately connected. In addition, revisionists see preponderant presidential and military power as symptomatic of a larger malaise in foreign policy-making. They emphasize the ways in which policy-makers are drawn from the milieu of American corporate power representing liberal capitalist values. Specifically, they find that top decision-makers are drawn from the ranks of business and the corporate legal fraternity.[21] Their liberal capitalist values allegedly inform deliberations about American policy and determine policy outcomes; revisionists find those values wanting.

FOUNDATIONS OF DEBATE ON AMERICAN FOREIGN POLICY

A public and official consensus on basic principles of American foreign policy no longer exists. Instead, old assumptions are directly challenged by limitationists and, often dramatically, by revisionists. As debate grew in intensity, focusing on Vietnam but raising much broader questions, it became clear that it reflected widely divergent views on a number of basic areas of United States policy, views long submerged by the consensus on which policy had rested for nearly twenty years. There are four fundamental areas of debate: (1) major forces of change in world affairs; (2) the responsibility of the United States to other states; (3) the role of the United States in maintaining international order; and (4) the question of who should make foreign policy. Together, these four areas establish the foundation for the debate which has succeeded the consensus of the first two postwar decades.

1. *Major forces of change in world affairs: nationalism and Communism.* Two doctrines remain potent forces in international politics. Nationalism is the older of the two, being a product of the modern nation-state system. Centered first in Europe where the nation-state system evolved, nationalism has been transformed during the twentieth century, and spread to the four corners of the globe.[22] Nationalism involves a feeling that one's destiny is intimately bound up with the destinies of one's own

particular nation, with the mythic symbolism of the nation-state itself. It implies that supreme political loyalty is due the cause of one's nation—at the very least, maintenance of political independence and territorial integrity of the nation or achievement of those attributes if they do not yet exist.

Communism, as an ideology, rests on a completely contrary set of beliefs. It expresses, not the supremacy of the national group, but the prime importance of economic class. Communism is an internationalist ideology. Marx and Engels called on the workers of the world to unite, not the Frenchmen or the Irish or the Jews or the Catholics or the Muslims or the dark-skinned peoples or any other national, racial, or religious group. In this classical sense, Marxism runs directly counter to nationalism.[23]

Of course, neither nationalism nor Communism is often seen in its pure form. Both are modified and bent to serve the needs of the state or political movement in which they are embodied at any given moment. Communism, in particular, has repeatedly demonstrated its compatibility with nationalist movements.[24]

Americans have a long history of sympathy to nationalist aspirations of people in all areas of the globe. Woodrow Wilson's emphasis on self-determination reflected this basic sympathy. United States pressure on European allies during and after World War II to grant independence and self-government to their colonies was based on the same attitude. But Hitler's National Socialism cast the phenomenon of nationalism into disrepute. The chaos which Hitler created in the old nation-states of Europe seemed to presage the decline of nationalism. Analyses of the interdependence of nation-states brought on by the pace of industrialization strengthened this point of view. Concurrently, those economic ills of capitalism, dramatically illustrated by the depression of the 1930s combined with the World War of the 1940s, appeared during the postwar era to foreshadow the triumph of Communism.

There is little doubt that Americans saw the version of Communism practiced in the Soviet Union, and later in China, as the major force with which they would have to contend in the postwar international system. This did not mean that they ignored nationalism. Quite the contrary; they sought to foster it wherever possible, provided it was not a xenophobic and anti-Western variety. Thus, Americans created real difficulties with allied powers by espousing the cause of colonial independence and incurred the hostility of the Arab world by supporting Jewish nationalism in Israel. Close ties with the nationalist-Communist regime of Yugoslavia were also established. But Americans remained preoccupied with Communism; support of nationalism was always seen in the context of its implications for the struggle with Communism. Thus, support for colonial independence was never carried to the point of weakening the Atlantic alliance against Communism; it was an irritant but was never carried to the point of risking a rupture of the alliance. Similarly, cooperation with Yugoslavia was fostered as a device for weakening the vastly more powerful and, it was thought, more aggressive Communist power of the Soviet Union.

Many critics have argued that the United States overemphasized the role of Communism and underemphasized the importance of nationalism in the postwar world.[25] With a rhetoric supporting nationalist causes, these critics claim, the United States managed to suppress genuinely nationalistic movements because they also happened to be Communist-dominated or Communist-supported. In Greece, in Guatemala, in the Dominican Republic, in Laos and, most dramatically, in Vietnam, America fought the national aspirations of oppressed peoples while loudly proclaiming the right of these peoples to determine their own future. In China and in Cuba, the same effort was made without success. This confusion of genuine nationalism and Communism has contributed significantly to the image of the United States as an imperialist power—indeed, as the imperialist power par excellence—in spite of a very genuine anti-imperialist and pro-nationalist set of beliefs.

More recently, the examination of the United States as an imperialist power has been challenged by scholars who perceive a basic trend toward a "transnational" world order (at least among the developed nations). Characterized by technological demands and the organization of business enterprise on multinational principles, both nationalism and Communism are seen to be increasingly anachronistic because of fundamental changes in modern industrial society that inexorably lead to increasing interdependence. In this view, the United States remains the most powerful economic unit in the evolution of a transnational world, but is affected by the policies of oil producers, business interests, other non-governmental interests, and the activities of international organizations which weaken the authority of American policy-makers' decisions.

2. *The responsibility of the United States to other states: An American "Mission"?* Americans have long prided themselves on being a force for progress in world affairs. The example of the American political system—the first major representative democracy—provided the foundation of this belief. The relative success of the American economic system enhanced it. The idealism of Wilson; the mission of the Atlantic Charter; the altruism of the Marshall Plan; the sacrifice for postwar foreign aid programs; the Alliance for Progress; the key role of the United States in the United Nations and its support for the rule of law—all of these provided evidence of the American stand for the progressive development of an international system grounded on justice, peace, and economic well-being. The rhetoric of American policy extolls American virtue in all these areas. There is no doubt that most Americans, including American decision-makers, are genuinely committed to a more humane and just world for all people.

But critics of American policy have begun to charge that the United States' commitment to progress is decisively undermined by a much stronger emphasis on stability; the United States, they say, is a status quo power, resisting change by all means at her command.[26] The assumption, characteristic of postwar American policy, that stability is to be preferred to disruptive change, has caused the United States to ally itself with many oppressive and reactionary regimes. The United States has supported authoritarian regimes in much of Latin America, on Taiwan and in Korea, in Spain and Greece, and, of course, in Vietnam. The emphasis on stability and the tendency to support the status quo accounts in large part for American support of the brutally genocidal regime in Pakistan in 1971 against the nationalist aspirations of the people of Bangladesh aided by India, the largest democracy in the world. It explains why so much of American foreign aid, given with a very genuine desire to improve the economic well-being of millions of poverty-stricken people, is permitted to find its way into the pockets of supporters of a repressive regime and why much of the expenditure goes for military aid which improves the capacity of such regimes to defend themselves (i.e., maintain stability), often against their own people.

There can be little doubt (though some of the revisionist critics have voiced such doubt) that the American desire to play a progressive role in world affairs is authentic and that Americans are genuinely perplexed when so many of their policies seem to have just the opposite effect. They are uneasy and unhappy in their alliance with oppressive regimes. They are frustrated when progress is not brought about by foreign aid expenditures. They are puzzled when their country is seen by others as a conservative and even reactionary power. This paradoxical situation, say the critics, results from the fact that Americans have placed a disproportionate emphasis on stability and have failed to recognize that instability is often the price of progress.

3. *The role of the United States in maintaining international order.* The current debate has made intervention an evil

word. But those who call for a halt to American interventionism in the affairs of other states sacrifice reality for simplicity. Neither the architects of postwar American policy nor most of their sophisticated critics make that mistake. It is no more possible for a large, wealthy, industrialized country like the United States to eschew intervention in the affairs of other states than it is for such a country to eschew an industrial economy and return to an agrarian one (another irrelevant plea of some "New Left" critics of American society). The question is not whether America will intervene, but how and where, and under what guidelines; when and for what purpose. For simply by existing, producing and trading industrial goods and agricultural products, maintaining a large defense force, supporting industrial and scientific research and development, consuming natural resources, and maintaining a society relatively open to ideas and immigration, the United States is led to some types of intervention in the affairs of other countries.[27]

In the aftermath of World War II, Americans assumed that they alone were able to protect the world from aggressive Communist powers; they alone stood as barriers to international law violators; they alone possessed the primary means to implement the United Nations Charter against those who would transgress the letter and spirit of this pillar of international law. In short, Americans considered the United States to be thrust into the role of global policeman. Some Americans even used such imagery.[28]

Some critics claim that American acceptance of a global police role, especially since it involved primary reliance on military force, encouraged military intervention by the United States far in excess of what was necessary or appropriate. Many observers have urged a more restricted view of appropriate guidelines for intervention. International institutions which would preferably make judgments on alleged violations of international law were still claimed to be in their infancy and, all too often, dominated by the United States and her allies. For the United States to assume the role of judge, jury, and executioner was an act of arrogance both inappropriate and self-defeating. Eventually it would evoke the charge of lawlessness by those whose judgment of the facts differed. A more appropriate guideline for American intervention, in the critics' view, was a narrow interpretation of self-interest.[29] Guidelines of national interest would restrict American military intervention to cases in which there was a clear and direct threat to the United States. The global policeman guideline, they said, encouraged indiscriminate military intervention and substituted an almost reflex action for the more subtle political judgments implied by a narrower conception of national interest.

4. *Who should make foreign policy?* Critics of the Cold War consensus questioned the way in which foreign policy was made. Though their criticism often bordered on attacks on personality, in its most sophisticated form it was more serious than that. It represented a challenge to the interests which the critics said controlled American foreign policy.

At its most popular level this criticism revolved around alleged excessive influence of the military in foreign policy decision-making. There are many dimensions to this question. At one level it simply reflects the long-standing American inclination to turn decisions over to the military in time of war and the concern of the critics of American foreign policy that the Cold War was no exception.[30]

At a more subtle level, it represents a concern about whether any nation can devote so large a proportion of its resources to military preparedness and create so large a military establishment without creating a major source of power over decisions. In its extreme form, this argument becomes the garrison-state hypothesis, long ago ably argued by Harold Lasswell,[31] in which a state devotes so much of its resources to military pursuits that its entire existence becomes subordinated to military considerations. According to this view, it does not matter whether decisions are made by civilians or by the military; they are "militarized" in either case.

A related criticism—popularized by the notion of a "military-industrial complex"—argues that development of a mutual interest in certain military policies, especially the development and procurement of "bigger" and "better" weapons systems, between the military and a large segment of American corporate enterprise predetermines policy in this area. It does not usually matter to these critics whether or not such control over policy is the result of explicit planning intentionally pursued or the inadvertent by-product of the existence of mutual interests; the effect, they argue, is the same—the subversion of genuine freedom to set foreign policy without undue influence of military considerations.

Not all critics of foreign policy-making focus on military considerations. Others argue that policy-making is dominated by the capitalist frame of reference of the American corporate world and serves their interests. Their dominance, these critics argue, insures that the substantive decisions of American foreign policy will be designed to protect the interest of American liberal capitalism.

Not even the defenders of American foreign policy would argue that the processes for making foreign policy are ideal. But in accordance with their defense of consensus politics, their criticisms tend to be much less fundamental. They see problems of foreign policy-making to be essentially problems of management and organization.

These four areas of discussion central to the current debate—the relative roles of nationalism and Communism in international politics, the nature of long-term American interests in the world, the appropriate guidelines for American intervention in world politics, and the question of control over the making of American foreign policy—are woven together.

Basically, the divergent answers given to them reflect different political orientations to the nature and extent of perceived threats to American interests. Defenders of American policy give relatively greater weight to Communism, xenophobic nationalism, Soviet and/or Chinese military power, guerilla movements, and the like than do more vociferous critics. Critics argue that policy-makers tend to overemphasize all threats to American interests from other states, especially military threats. In their most extreme statements, critics claim a more serious threat emanates from the United States than is directed against it. Insofar as critics do see threats to the United States, they are more apt to emphasize those related to the widening gap between the rich nations and the poor, the economic drain and accident potential of the arms race, and the possibility of economic and social upheaval at home caused by the over-expenditure of resources abroad.

Stripped to the most elementary form, these differences between defenders and critics of American policy represent a fundamental and enduring disharmony in their perceptions of the American national interest.

CONCLUSION:
THE COMING ISSUES OF FOREIGN POLICY

It is, of course, impossible to predict the precise form of future issues that will constitute the basic subjects of debate over foreign policy. Even the most general issues cannot be identified with certainty. These issues will be determined as much by forces beyond the control of American policy-makers and would-be policy-makers as by conscious decision. This is especially true of the specific geographical arenas in which new issues will arise. Nevertheless, it is possible to hazard an informed guess about the issues which will arise in the late 1970s and early 1980s. These issues will reappear throughout this book and we will return to a consideration of them in the final chapter. The reader should see their relationship to the areas of debate we have just discussed and keep them in mind while examining, in subsequent chapters, the factors conditioning the formulation of United States foreign policy.

Actually, there are a variety of issues which cluster around the basic areas of debate already described. These issues are identified in Table 1. Although no priority is established among them, together they represent a likely agenda for the continuation of the debate on foreign policy already begun with the breakdown of the Cold War consensus. We will return to a discussion of these often-overlapping issues in the final chapter.

TABLE 1
FOREIGN POLICY ISSUE CLUSTERS, 1970s TO 1980s

Area of Debate	Issue Cluster
I. Major forces of change	Conflict and coexistence with USSR, China
	Types and amounts of military expenditures (Further development of antiballistic missile system MIRV)
	Degree of support for independent European community
	Ordering priorities for domestic needs versus external goals
	Control of multinational corporations
	Reform of the international monetary system

TABLE 1–Continued
FOREIGN POLICY ISSUE CLUSTERS, 1970s TO 1980s

Area of Debate	Issue Cluster
II. Responsibility to other states	Foreign aid: amount, direction Support of economic aid through international organizations Economic interdependence Trade policies
III. Role of the United States in maintaining order	Support for United Nations Criteria for intervention Alliances, especially NATO Overseas bases Military assistance programs
IV. Who should make foreign policy	Military-industrial complex: accountability Congressional-Executive relations Accountability of Executive Branch Secrecy Freedom of Press State vs. White House

It is too early to say whether these issues will be considered in the context of a clearly articulated awareness of the basic areas of debate outlined above. The challenge to consensus has been a fundamental one; what its enduring features will be is not yet clear.[32] Nonetheless, the challenge to consensus will require choices in matters of foreign policy by all interested citizens. In succeeding chapters, we will discuss many of the elements that bear directly on the choices that ensue from the substitution of debate for the Cold War consensus.

2. What Is Foreign Policy?

*"Effective freedom in foreign affairs
. . . is the capacity to choose
between relatively few options."*
—F. S. Northedge

Some scholars and commentators treat foreign policy as if it were made in isolation and unrelated to other types of governmental policy. The powers of government to conduct foreign policy often differ sharply from their powers in other areas.[1] The Executive Branch is customarily more dominant in foreign policy than in other spheres. Even after parliamentary control of the executive became established practice in England in the 16th and 17th centuries, parliamentarians continued to concede the exclusive right of the king to make foreign policy. The notions of bipartisan foreign policy and presidential predominance which we discuss in Chapters 5 and 7 are a significant expression of this view. Colleges and universities confirm the special character of foreign policy; they offer courses on American diplomatic history and the formulation of American foreign policy separated from other public policy courses (all other public policy is often lumped together) as if the process of foreign policy-making differed in some clear-cut way from the making of other policy.

On the other hand, some scholars emphasize the way in which foreign policy is the outgrowth of domestic politics.[2] Furthermore, many able critics of the contemporary American scene picture a seamless web of American political and cultural attitudes and values reflected in both domestic and foreign policy choices. Some argue that the Vietnam War was but an extension of American attitudes of exploitation clearly seen in the domestic arena of race relations.

Why should foreign policy be treated separately rather than in the same way as any other policy-making by government? Is making foreign policy really different from making welfare policy, penal policy, environmental policy, and educational policy? Aren't the same forces at work; the same interests operative; the same processes activated?

SIMILARITY OF DOMESTIC AND FOREIGN POLICY

In both formulation and execution, foreign and domestic policies and politics are inextricably linked in so many ways that a distinction between the two seems artificial. A moment's reflection makes it clear that foreign policy often grows out of domestic policy priorities and domestic political considerations.

1. *The consequences of a domestic or foreign policy decision often spill over from one area to the other.* The intimate connections in economic matters between domestic and foreign policies are especially illustrative of this difficulty. A decision to alter the Federal Reserve discount or domestic interest rate, for example, normally taken to alter the rate of domestic investment or influence the domestic rate of inflation, will have an important impact on the decisions of American business firms to invest abroad and the decisions of foreign firms to invest in the United States. Eventually, it will have a significant effect on the international competitive position of firms and the countries in which they are based. Behind the complexity of the international monetary discussions of 1972-1973 was the crucial fact that these decisions, made in an international forum, were possible only after weighing crucial domestic considerations in the various states concerned. Frequently, negotiators found that domestic and international considerations pointed them in contradictory

directions. During the prolonged "energy crisis" that began to emerge in 1973, contradictory interests of oil producers and consumers, American political objectives in the Middle East and economic objectives at home also illustrate the interrelationship of domestic and international factors.

Similarly, decisions in the realm of defense policy are usually considered part of foreign policy. The decision to build or not to build a particular defense system such as the Anti-Ballistic Missile System (ABM) or the Multiple Independently-Targetable Re-entry Vehicle (MIRV) has consequences at home as well as abroad. It affects the whole range of disarmament negotiations, number and use of foreign military bases, the prospects for settlement of outstanding disputes such as the Berlin question, and the general atmosphere of Soviet-American relations. Such decisions also have significant impact on many American corporations which depend in varying degrees on defense contracts. Quite apart from defense and foreign policy considerations, a decision to cancel an important contract for a weapons system will be difficult to take if the contracting corporation is in financial difficulties or if the decision threatens large numbers of workers with unemployment.

Even an issue apparently confined to the domestic sphere such as civil rights—so strongly under the influence of state governments—spills over into the foreign policy sphere more often than most people realize. The attitudes of Africans and other nonwhites toward the United States, both at the individual and governmental levels, is sharply influenced by the rhetoric and policies of states and private citizens toward black Americans. There was a time, during the Eisenhower administration, when the President offered an almost regular White House breakfast to African diplomats who had been refused service in "white only" restaurants along U.S. 40 in Maryland between New York and Washington.

2. *Domestic party, group, and individual conflict influences foreign policy choices.* There is little doubt that Senator Taft's

criticisms of President Truman's foreign policies in the late 1940s were at least partially determined by the struggle between him and Governor Thomas E. Dewey for control of the Republican Party. Personal incompatibility between Senator Lodge and President Wilson was at least partly responsible for Wilson's failure to include Lodge in the delegation to the Paris Peace Conference in 1919 and, hence, for Lodge's subsequent vigorous opposition to the League of Nations and Wilson's obstinate refusal to compromise with the Senate forces led by Lodge. No one can reflect on President Truman's decision to recognize the new State of Israel in the election year of 1948, or President Nixon's decision to veto a UN resolution condemning Israeli retaliatory raids in Lebanon in the election year of 1972 without realizing the importance for foreign policy of the Jewish vote and its concentration in populous, pivotal northeastern states. Balance in American Middle East policy can be partly attributed to the countervailing influence of other domestic groups who have a vested interest in continuing access to the oil resources controlled by the Arab countries of the area, a major element in the rapidly developing energy crisis in the United States. The timing and justifications of President Nixon's Vietnam peace negotiations, even some features of the policy position, gave the appearance of being designed to cut the ground from under his Democratic opponent in the 1972 elections. If intended, the maneuvering clearly succeeded!

There is a larger sense, too, in which foreign policy grows out of the domestic setting of American politics. The values and beliefs which condition the policy choices of American policy-makers are shaped to a greater degree by their experience in domestic politics than by their experience in international affairs. Yet those values and beliefs will determine, in large measure, the perception of the intentions and actions of policy-makers in other nations and the limits within which American policy-makers can react to the actions of others. President Johnson once said, "The overriding rule which I want to affirm is that our foreign policy must always be an extension of our domestic policy. Our safest guide to what we do abroad is always what we do at home."[3] In a general fashion, the American belief that the national prosperity of the United States is somehow hinged to the "private enterprise" nature of its economy has helped to "guide" many aspects of foreign policy including the judgment about the acceptability of other regimes as allies of the United States, the suitability of various projects for American assistance, the prospects for economic development in various countries and hence the degree to which they qualify for loans from the United States or various international lending institutions in which the United States commands the major voice. Often, the relationship between such guiding values and foreign policy decisions is ambiguous and obscure but no less crucial. We shall examine this relationship in greater detail in Chapter 3 when we assess the legacy of history and in Chapter 4 when we discuss national character.

DIFFERENCES BETWEEN DOMESTIC AND FOREIGN POLICY

The distinction between domestic and foreign policy remains an analytically useful one. It points to differences between the two spheres which, though usually matters of degree, are significant and often crucial to an understanding of the behavior of policy-makers. Furthermore, there is evidence that, in the American setting, foreign policy activates a set of political attitudes which are in significant ways separate from those which inform discussions of domestic policy questions.[4] Foreign policy-makers must operate within a different frame of reference from their domestic policy-making colleagues. Four major factors differentiate the foreign policy sphere from that of domestic policy: (1) knowledge of the foreign sphere is usually more limited; (2) information is more difficult to obtain; (3) situations are more complex; and (4) policy-makers have less control. These factors overlap and reinforce each other and contribute to the analytic distinction between foreign and domestic policy.

1. *Limited background knowledge.* In the domestic context, decision-makers start with a fund of knowledge which is usually absent when they are dealing with a foreign policy issue. They have a "feel" for the circumstances surrounding an issue and the personalities involved in it which even the best-informed and most cosmopolitan statesman cannot have when dealing with a foreign problem. On a domestic issue such as race relations, for example, the President and his advisors start with vast knowledge and considerable experience. They have likely visited the areas where the issue is crucial; they probably know many of the protagonists personally; they are aware of the legal, political, and social background of the issue because it has been woven into the fabric of American politics for generations.

When dealing with a foreign policy issue, the President and his advisors operate under the handicap of a much more limited fund of knowledge and experience. This is less true of the professional diplomat but even he is disadvantaged by the formality of his position from knowing as much as the political conciliator for domestic problems. If the issue of foreign policy involves a specific country or area, the high-level decision-maker may have visited it, but probably on a semi-official or official visit when his contact with the major protagonists was severely limited. He probably knows few of them personally and is likely to be relatively unfamiliar with the political, social and historical context of the conflict.

Furthermore, officials possess an intuitive capacity born of cultural affinity and shared values to predict the reactions of the participants in domestic conflict. This is not to say officials have values which are identical to those of the protagonists. On the contrary, there are wide differences in cultural affinity and value systems within the United States, but these differences are minimal when compared to the gulf which often separates the cultural assumptions and values of most Americans from those of the people of other nations, especially nations whose cultural heritage is non-Western.[5] Briefing papers prepared for the President and his advisors include as thorough a description as possible of information of this nature, but the problem of assimilating this information is far more difficult in the foreign as compared to the domestic sphere. Such data are not part of that body of information which is so internalized that it becomes second nature in the consideration of domestic policy.

Failure to take into account cultural and value differences often leads to unexpected foreign policy backlash. Barbara Tuchman records numerous instances when American disregard for the Chinese concern with "face" led to the failure of American policy in China during World War II.[6] President Truman acted with a surer hand and at least initial success in the Greek-Turkish crisis of 1947 partly because he had a grasp of the historical and cultural factors involved in that crisis—a grasp acquired by extensive study of the area as a young man. But the sure hand was conspicuously missing when he sought to assess the probable Chinese reaction to the American decision to wage the Korean War north of the 38th parallel.

2. *Limited information sources.* Similarly, reliable information is much easier to come by in domestic situations than in foreign ones. First, raw information such as census and economic data is more readily available in the United States, which has an enviable capability for record-keeping and data collection. Few other countries even approach the United States in the range and accuracy of data resources. Furthermore, it is easier to acquire reliable information about developments in a domestic crisis than in a foreign one. On the foreign scene, the movement of data collectors, such as American diplomats and newsmen, may be severely restricted, and information sources may be dominated by

foreign countries which want to manipulate information for their own purposes. In the area of intentions and motives, the difficulty of gathering information abroad is even more pronounced, especially in authoritarian political systems. Of course, reliable information, especially information about motives and intentions, is never complete in the domestic political sphere, but it is often far easier to acquire.

The problem, however, is not always one of lack of reliable information. Often decision-makers are plagued by a surfeit of information and the problem becomes one of sorting out what is relevant. Inability to identify relevant information is the same thing, from a policy-making point of view, as not having that information. An excellent example of this problem is found in the fact that the American government apparently possessed numerous bits of evidence that the Japanese were preparing to attack Pearl Harbor on December 7, 1941, but the governmental policy-making machinery seemed unable to interpret these bits of information correctly.[7] Misreading data can be as serious as not having the information at all and is more likely to occur in foreign policy than in domestic.

3. *More complexity.* Foreign policy discussions tend to be more complex than their domestic counterparts. Domestic policy involves a wealth of parties, economic and social institutions, interest groups of all kinds, bureaucratic and legal considerations, and a host of other variables. In the foreign sphere, these complexities are multiplied by similar considerations for each of the numerous countries involved in or affected by a given decision. Consider, for example, President Nixon's decision to visit Communist China in 1972. That decision could not have been made in a reasonable manner without a thorough exploration of both domestic and foreign implications. On the domestic front, there was the obvious consideration of the 1972 elections and the visit's effect on the various factions which would be choosing the Republican nominee, as well as the effect on the

relationship between the Republicans and each of the several candidates for the Democratic presidential nomination. Beyond that, the President had to consider the reactions and influence of the pro-Chiang China lobby; American business interests in Asia; the Congress, especially the Senate Foreign Relations Committee; various rivalries within the Executive Branch, especially those relating to the Departments of State and Defense; the National Security Council machinery; and many other factors. If this had been a question dominated by domestic factors, his decision could have been made on the basis of these considerations alone.

Because the decision was a foreign policy question with consequences for many countries, numerous other considerations were involved. What, for example, would be the likely effect on U.S.-Soviet relations and on the relative power of "hawks" and "doves" among Soviet decision-makers? How would the Japanese react, and what effect would their reaction have on the political future of the pro-Western government in Japan and on U.S.-Japanese relations, including the effort to secure Japanese cooperation in restricting competitive exports from Japan to the United States? What would a decision to visit Communist China imply about American freedom of action with respect to arms shipments to Pakistan at a time of internal disruption in that country and how would possible restrictions on arms shipments affect U.S. relations with India? To what extent would this decision alter the bargaining position of the U.S. in Vietnam peace talks; what effect would it be likely to have on China's relations with North Vietnam, and how would that affect Hanoi's bargaining position? How would China's chances of United Nations representation be affected and what would be the implications for American policy in the United Nations? This listing only scratches the surface of the issues involved in this and many other less sensational foreign policy decisions whose complexity is measured by the range of consequences which confront American policy-makers.

4. *Lack of Control.* Finally, foreign policy decision-makers are far less able to control the outcome of their decisions and the political environment in which those decisions are implemented than are domestic decision-makers. Political leaders are always subjected to circumstances in which they lack full control, even in the domestic sphere. Indeed, the American system of government is designed to prevent the concentrated exercise of control. The constitutional provisions of federalism and checks and balances, the loosely disciplined party system, and the economic system of private enterprise combine to frustrate efforts at centralizing control of the society. Sometimes policy-makers seem impotent to cope with serious domestic problems. These impediments pale into insignificance, however, when one considers the near total lack of control over events in other countries and the international environment.

The United States, with all its power, seems able to exercise little direct control over the policies of other states, even such near-client states as South Vietnam. Policy-makers must feel enormous frustration at their inability to influence more completely such governments as that of President Thieu in South Vietnam. This government owes its genesis and continued existence to American policy, yet defies repeated American demands for free elections by laws which effectively foreclose genuine competitive elections, thus frustrating American desires for a peace settlement for a period of months and even years. Of course, the case of South Vietnam also illustrates ways in which American policy-makers can work their will, as when President Nixon persuaded President Thieu to withdraw some of his objections to the peace settlement reached in early 1973. The striking thing about this relationship, however, is the near equality of the negotiating process in the face of wide disparities in power.

Limitations on American ability to control events and policies in other countries, even relatively weak ones, are dramatically evident in many areas of recent United States foreign policy. Indeed, that the United States has wielded as much influence as it has in the face of such limits is a credit to the skill and persistence of American diplomats and policy-makers.

In sum, foreign policy has to operate in the arena of international politics in which there is no sovereign authority to make binding procedural or substantive rules enforceable on the participants. American foreign policy must be made in an international setting of far more fragmented authority than the domestic setting. It is, therefore, more difficult to execute the policy.

FOREIGN POLICY DEFINED

It should now be apparent that the often implicit conception of foreign policy is simply not accurate. The very term "policy" implies rational choice among a comprehensive list of alternatives, a choice based on full knowledge and information and one which can be implemented with available resources to achieve a desired and predictable end. There is unity and coherence in the concept of "policy."

The reality tends to be far different, especially in the field of foreign policy. Because information and knowledge are often incomplete, because situations are so complex, because decision-makers exercise only marginal control over events, and because interest in and authority over foreign policy decisions are so fragmented, the practical world of policy tends to lack the unity and coherence which the abstract concept implies.

It is often preferable to abandon the notion of *a foreign policy decision*. Foreign policy can be usefully conceived as a *continuous process* involving incremental change in existing relations with other states. A decision-maker does not start with a clean slate. The idealized model of policy-making in which an actor assembles all the relevant information, takes a decision, and goes on to the next problem is rarely, if ever, found in foreign policy. Every decision must grow out of past decisions; every decision will require further decisions. Moreover, many decisions are being taken simultaneously at many levels of government; these decisions overlap and often contradict one another, sometimes deliberately but more often inadvertently.

At any given point in time, the United States, through various institutions and individuals, is articulating and acting upon a whole range of divergent—and sometimes contradictory—policies. Rarely does the United States speak with one voice in foreign policy. The press, academic commentators, the parties, the Congress and its committees all contribute to making foreign policy and often it is not the same foreign policy the President is "making." Even the Executive Branch has different conceptions of what its "policy" is. The Departments of State and Defense, the White House, and subunits of each are constantly acting on their own interpretation of what policy is or their own assessment of what it ought to be. Each is engaged in a constant struggle to see that its particular version of "policy" prevails.

Such struggles are not often won or lost permanently. In foreign policy-making, defeats tend to be temporary; the protagonist often continues to fight for his "foreign policy." He may shift his tactics; he may try to mobilize support in another department or agency; he may bide his time and wait for a more opportune moment; he may use his operational authority to undermine the decision taken and implement his own conception of the appropriate foreign policy; he may resign and attempt to mobilize public, press, academic, or pressure group support for his position. Moreover, he will find it difficult to know whether he has won or lost, for the consequences of foreign policy decisions are not often clear-cut. Their incremental nature means that they are often composites of the positions advocated by the various protagonists. A decision-maker may carry the day on one aspect of policy but lose his argument on another. Thus the governmental "doves" in the Johnson administration might lose the argument for a more flexible negotiating position in the peace talks but win the argument for troop reductions.

Foreign policy in the United States, then, is most often the result of the interaction of myriad forces, competing and bargaining with each other. The outcome reflects this. It usually partakes of all of the often contradictory positions and is rarely fixed for any length of time. The United States does not produce a foreign *policy*; it produces foreign *policies*! Louis J. Halle, who served in the Department of State before going into academia, describes the policy-making process as "chaos," "unordered, a succession of accidents," upon which coherent order and, hence, understanding is imposed after the fact by participants, scholars, and observers.[8]

The traditional distinction between foreign policy and foreign relations adds to the lack of coherence and order which characterizes foreign policy. According to the typical form of this distinction, foreign policy deals with the central questions of national existence and is virtually synonymous with national security policy, a conception to which we shall return several times in the course of this book. Foreign policy, in this sense, is the normal preoccupation of the higher echelons of government; the President, the secretary of state, and their chief lieutenants. Foreign relations refers to both the routine transactions which the United States has with other states—consular and cultural activities and the like—and the foreign activities of non-governmental institutions including trade and investment activities of American business and efforts of internationally active interest groups such as the AFL-CIO and the World Council of Churches.[9] The involvement of many divergent groups in foreign relations complicates the foreign policy picture for it will be immediately apparent that their activities often impinge very directly on "higher" foreign policy. The distinction inevitably becomes blurred. Consular decisions on the granting of visas, the decisions of cultural affairs officers to sponsor a particular entertainment group, corporate decisions to trade with a particular foreign country—all of these may have a direct impact on national security. They all add to the plethora of United States foreign *policies*.

The factors which lead to fragmentation of authority and lack of coherence in foreign policy and the resources which the contestants in the battle have at their disposal will be examined in Chapters 5 through 8. Here, it is enough to emphasize that the public conception of policy tends to focus on the unity and coherence which characterizes the concept, rather than the fragmentation which characterizes the reality. This conception is encouraged by responsible officials; the Department of State, for example, puts out a series of "Foreign Policy Briefs" designed to answer the question of American citizens, "What is our policy toward X?" Even the highest public officials, though they would explicitly recognize the fragmentation of policy and policy-making, offer evidence of preferring unity and coherence. W. W. Rostow, then Chairman of the Department of State's Policy Planning Council, is said to have asked during the Kennedy administration for a compilation of a series of papers which would provide a handy reference to American policy toward the various countries of the world.[10] This "snapshot" approach imposes an artificial unity. The "moving picture" of foreign policy as a continuous process of more or less subtle changes punctuated at infrequent intervals by dramatic decisions is nearer the mark.

The plethora of individuals, groups, and institutions which influence foreign policy-making and the fragmentation their involvement generates raises another question perennially debated by political philosophers: is it possible to have a foreign policy in a democratic political system? Alexis de Tocqueville put the negative case so persuasively that his views influenced successive generations of analysts:

> *Foreign policy does not require the use of any of the good qualities peculiar to democracy but does demand the cultivation of almost all those which it lacks. Democracy favors the growth of the state's internal resources; it extends comfort and develops public spirit, strengthens respect for law in the various classes of society, all of which things have no more than an indirect influence on the standing of one nation in respect to another. But a democracy finds it difficult to coordinate the details of a great undertaking and to fix on some plan and carry it through with determination in spite of obstacles. It has little capacity for combining measures in secret and waiting patiently for the result. Such qualities are more likely to belong to a single man or to an aristocracy. But these are just the qualities which, in the long run, make a nation, and a man too, prevail.*[11]

Other scholars and statesmen have disputed these views, arguing that the strength of pluralism and the competition of ideas characteristic of democratic political systems more than offset the weaknesses to which de Tocqueville points. For example, after an extensive survey of American and British experience in foreign policy, Kenneth Waltz concludes:

> *In a world where military technology places a premium upon speed and opponents at times appear to be implacable, the flexibility, dispatch, coherence, and ruthlessness of authoritarian states have been thought to be decisive advantages. But the characteristics which, it is said, democratic governments cannot display are, despite the*

assertion, in part within their capacities and in part absent also in other forms of government. Disagreement about ends openly expressed in democratic states may cause some opportunities for gaining national advantage to be missed. But the running of risks foolishly is then also impeded. Democracies less often enjoy the brilliant success that bold acts secretly prepared and ruthlessly executed may bring. With the ground of action more thoroughly prepared and the content of policy more widely debated, they may, however, suffer fewer resounding failures. Coherent policy, executed with a nice combination of caution and verve, is difficult to achieve in any political system, but no more so for democratic states than for others. [12]

THE LEVEL OF ANALYSIS PROBLEM

The tendency to view policy as a coherent whole is also encouraged by the nature of the international system and much of the writing about it. The international system is populated by nation-states, the "actors," historically defined and perceived as independent and sovereign. International politics is made up of the interactions of these "actors." From this perspective, the relevant data for understanding international politics are the actions and interactions of states, normally the official policies of the decision-makers empowered to act on behalf of states. Writers who view foreign policy from the international perspective tend to treat the policies of states as if they were coherent, unitary wholes. Internal opposition or the pursuit of alternative policies takes on importance only if and when it commands the support of those in a position to make the authoritative decisions on behalf of the state.

Although most people are well aware of the oversimplification of this conception when it is focused on their own national policy process, they frequently succumb to it when thinking of other countries. Thus, Americans, who are well aware of the existence of "hawks" and "doves" in their own society and, indeed, within their own administration, are apt to assume that no such categories exist in other powerful states such as the Soviet Union. Many observers still see the Soviet Union as the archetypical example of a monolithic decision-making agency, speaking with one voice, singlemindedly pursuing a given course of action, invulnerable to internal shifts of power and opinion. The authoritarian nature of the Soviet political system increases the tendency of foreigners, including Americans, to see its actions as unified and coherent. Moreover, Soviet authorities possess monopoly control over communications within their country, and secrecy is more characteristic of their decision-making style than it is in the more open societies of the West. Internal divisions on policy are more difficult to discover and, hence, more frequently assumed not to exist.

The tendency to assume coherent unitary policy is not confined to the analysis of authoritarian regimes though it is perhaps more exaggerated in such cases. The logic of international systems theory fosters such assumptions in all cases. For writers on international politics, it is France or Britain or India which acted in any given situation or took a given position. The internal political process by which such decisions are reached is subordinated in the analysis.

Of course, political systems differ in the degree of cohesion in their foreign policy-making processes. In some states, notably open democratic systems, more varied institutions such as press and public opinion will be intimately involved in the policy-making process. In others, notably authoritarian systems, fewer institutions will be directly involved; policy will not only appear more unified and coherent, it will actually be so because fewer loci of decision-making are involved in its formulation. Nevertheless, in all systems, it is necessary to look within the system to understand its foreign policy.

For some scholars, foreign policy is the product of internal political struggle and is described and analyzed in terms which often exclude or de-emphasize the international aspects which condition policy choice. Approached from this level of analysis the international arena is seen as a blank slate on which the decision-maker can write with a free hand circumscribed only by the ebb and flow of domestic power and circumstance.

Americans seem most often to view their own government in this light. They assume that their leaders possess much greater control over events abroad than they, in fact, possess. For example, in the days of implacable hostility to the Communist government in China, critics often charged that the Truman administration "lost China." The assumption was that President Truman and his advisors had a wide measure of freedom to determine the course of events in China subject only to the constraints of internal politics in the United States. This was never the case. China was never "ours" to lose. Most of the factors which contributed to the displacement of the Nationalist Government by a Communist one were completely beyond the control of American policy-makers; they were part of the external environment in which those policy-makers worked. F. S. Northedge has observed that "effective freedom in foreign affairs . . .is [the] capacity to choose between relatively few options."[13] American policy-makers had very little choice in the rise of a Communist government to power in China in 1948.[14]

The tendency on the part of Americans to view their own foreign policy process from the domestic perspective increases the political significance of the assumption, referred to earlier, that foreign policy is not a legitimate subject for partisan political dispute. Such an assumption strengthens the belief that decision-makers have almost complete freedom in foreign affairs. A recent study has shown, for example, that a "rather large body of [public] opinion" is inclined to follow the President's lead on such things as war policy.[15]

We have now come full circle. We started this chapter by contrasting those who see foreign policy essentially as an outgrowth of domestic politics with those who see it in an essentially international frame. Actually, both international and domestic levels of analysis are crucial to understanding foreign policy.[16] Despite the assumption of freedom of action, the reality is a milieu of international *and* domestic political forces which limit the range of choice and condition the decision-making process in ways which serve to underline the importance of "relatively few options" described in Professor Northedge's remark. It is precisely these limiting factors which give foreign policy decision-making the appearance of a disorderly character. Unity and coherence in the face of such a substantial set of limitations are only exceptionally achieved.

CONCLUSION: THE MAKING OF FOREIGN POLICY

To stress the chaos and confusion, the fragmentation and pluralism of policy, as we have done, is not to argue that policy is purposeless. On the contrary, the very act of policy-making, in which many intelligent and determined individuals are consciously engaged, accurately suggests the deliberate pursuit of goals. Sometimes these goals are explicitly stated; sometimes they are only dimly perceived or even subconsciously assumed. The fact that policy-makers have diverse and divergent interests and levels of involvement and influence in the policy process does not mean that no order can be found in that process. The fact that they sometimes perceive only dimly what they are doing does not mean that they are acting at random. It does mean that a thorough examination of the entire policy process is essential to an understanding of America's foreign policies.

In order to establish priorities and regularities within an inclusive foreign policy process, many scholars have turned to systems analysis.[17] Use of various types of systems analysis in the study of all aspects of politics, including foreign policy, is prevalent today and certainly has influenced much of the presentation of American foreign policy in later chapters. The terminology of systems analysis is not emphasized in these chapters, however, because of the prior and extended explanation of terms that would be required. Instead, an effort is made to address directly some of the basic questions that systems analysis helps to generate: What are the sources of foreign policy in the American setting? Stated somewhat differently: what are the determining inputs in the policy-making process and how do they affect policy outputs? What are the principal interactions within the policy system and how do they affect outputs? And, what are the results or outputs of the foreign policy process and how do they, in turn, affect the nature of the foreign policy milieu and system? Figure 1 presents diagrammatically an elementary conception of the American foreign policy process. In succeeding chapters, this skeletal conception will be expanded and many of the relationships suggested in the diagram will be described.

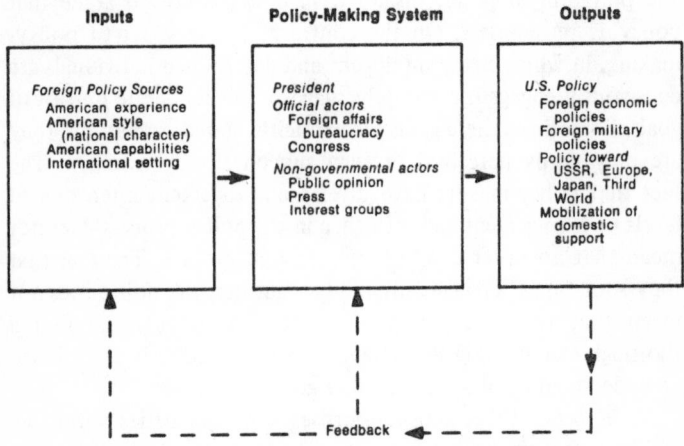

FIGURE 1. *THE FOREIGN POLICY PROCESS*

Foreign policy sources will occupy the next two chapters. The machinery of the policy system and the non-governmental foreign policy establishment will be treated in Chapters 5 through 8. Chapters 5 and 6 will focus on the primacy of the President in the American setting and the forces which contribute to his position. Chapters 7 and 8 will examine the limitations under which the President must operate. Finally, in Chapter 9, we will examine the performance or outputs of the system.

To assert that policy-making is a purposeful activity in no way diminishes the importance of the American experience and national style which provide the foundation on which policy is built. These factors help to establish the framework, define the possible, and set the limits within which the policy-maker works. They are the sometimes only dimly perceived intellectual and cultural accoutrements which he and his colleagues bring to their responsibilities. Seldom are the American experience and national style formally invoked to justify policy decisions. When they are, they usually play a relatively minor role in explanations of policy. However, they undergird and surround every policy decision. The errors of policy learned from American diplomatic history are often results of policies formulated by people who misread the American experience and character. The American experience will be treated in the next chapter and the related concept of national character in Chapter 4.

3.   The Legacy of Experience

*"The United States' long experience
in self-reliance has been followed
by global entanglements which,
while often brilliantly managed,
have brought enormous disappointments
and frustration."*
              —Stanley Hoffmann, 1968

National experience is an important ingredient in understanding a country's foreign policy. It reveals patterns of thought and action which influence decision-makers. An understanding—more or less accurate—of the lessons of the American experience in foreign policy is part of the intellectual orientation any decision-maker brings to his job and also a part of the prism through which international events are filtered and take on meaning for him. A few examples will illustrate how interpretations of experience condition future choices. The legacy of the Monroe Doctrine and the belief that the United States has a special responsibility for Latin America clearly conditioned the policy choices of the Eisenhower administration concerning Guatemala in 1954, the Kennedy administration concerning Cuba in 1961 and 1962, and the Johnson administration concerning the Dominican Republic in 1965. The isolationist heritage was an important factor in the rejection of the League of Nations after World War I and in the neutrality acts passed by the Congress on the eve of World War II. The conviction that "private" enterprise "explains" American prosperity has played an important part in creating an American preference for loans over grants as instruments of foreign aid.

This does not mean that Americans—more than other peoples—are the prisoners of history. In a limited sense they are; some decisions predetermine future decisions. But this is not always true; the perceptions of history are only some of the important factors determining how a foreign policy problem is defined, how alternatives are seen, and what choices are made. We can profitably recall that Franklin Roosevelt and Harry Truman defied over 150 years of "isolation" to take the United States into the United Nations even if their policy was conditioned by the lessons they read into the League of Nations experience of two and one-half decades earlier.

Americans, more than others, are apt to discount the constraints of history for they are a supremely ahistorical people, characterized by what Stanley Hoffmann has called "a perpetually renewed historical virginity."[1] The influence of history is not directly perceived. Instead, perceptions of historically conditioned principles, possibilities, and constraints tend to be implicit and assumed. Moreover, each policy-maker will see the lessons of experience in a different light and will perceive different aspects of that experience as relevant to the immediate problem he confronts. As Arthur Schlesinger, Jr., has reminded us, "History offers the lawyer or scholar (or policy-maker) almost any precedent he needs to sustain what he may consider, in a concrete setting, to be wise policy."[2] Nevertheless, the influence of history remains extensive, especially historically shaped themes which run through much of the interpretation of American experience in foreign affairs.

Until World War II, American foreign policy was dominated by isolationism, a policy of separation and aloofness from and often disinterest in the affairs of the world, especially European affairs. The popular understanding of the American national experience holds that the wise and prudent policy of isolationism dominated the nation's foreign policy with few, short-lived, and usually unfortunate exceptions until the changes of the World War II era thrust the United States unwillingly onto the world stage.

As a description of experience, isolationism contains some important elements of fact and some characteristics of myth. It is fact that after the Monroe administration, most Americans—officials and private citizens alike—gave only sporadic attention to foreign affairs. They formed few views about the nature of the world and America's place in it except to assert that world affairs were of little import to America and Americans. They were psychologically and emotionally isolated from the world.

Nonetheless, those who managed American foreign policy were establishing other habits of mind, other methods of acting in the world, other rationales for policy which were to carry over in important ways to the post-World War II era of American involvement when all Americans were forced to abandon the comfort of isolationism. A detailed summary of pre-World War II American foreign policy is beyond the scope of this book[3] but it is important to examine the principles which evolved in the "isolationist" period, for we will see them intruding in significant ways into postwar policy.

THE PRINCIPLES OF THE ISOLATIONIST ERA

The notion of isolation from world affairs is usually traced to the sage advice of America's first President, George Washington, who, in his famous farewell address, outlined the principles which were to be accepted as the framework for American foreign policy for one hundred and fifty years.

"It is our true policy," he said, "to steer clear of permanent alliances with any portion of the foreign world." Recognizing that "extraordinary emergencies" might require American involvement, he advised that, in such circumstances, "we may safely trust to temporary alliances." These sweeping policy recommendations were not to interfere with the fullest possible exploitation of commercial opportunities. Between commercial and political involvement, Washington drew a sharp distinction: "The great rule of conduct for us in regard to foreign nations is, in extending our commercial relations to have with them as little *political* connection as possible." Similarly, he made clear that his recommendations were not universal but directed primarily at Europe: "Europe has a set of primary interests which to us have none or a very remote relation. . . . It must be unwise in us to implicate ourselves by artificial ties in the ordinary vicissitudes of her politics or the ordinary combinations and collusions of her friendships or enmities."

Washington's remarks were made in the context of the internal disputes between the Republican followers of Thomas Jefferson who wanted to continue the Revolutionary alliance with France and the more pro-British Federalist followers of Alexander Hamilton. It was an occasion when a presidential statement motivated by immediate and essentially domestic political considerations so well captured the later public mood and national situation that it became an enduring policy prescription.

At the time the isolationist policy was forged, the fledgling republic of the United States had little alternative. Circumstances compelled such a policy. The United States was a weak power facing strong European states. Involvement in European quarrels could only result in the kind of dismemberment which was so often the fate of the weak states in Europe. The existence of common boundaries with British, French, and Spanish colonies in the new world emphasized the wisdom of a cautious approach. But these boundaries also served to make at least limited involvement with the European powers inevitable. If the United States had little or no interest in the power struggles of Europe per se, it had an enormous interest in the effects of those struggles on the fortunes of Britain, France, and Spain in the new world.

The United States was the only major indigenous power on the continent and was more interested in continental expansion than in the quarrels of Europe. It had a continent to win and develop and this, too, dictated isolation from the quarrels of Europe. Furthermore, the moral principles which Jefferson,

Paine, and others had mobilized to justify the American Revolution, were taking root. They generated a suspicion of European power politics which was to characterize American foreign policy for the duration of the isolationist period and even into the post-World War II era. Americans believed they were engaged in a unique political experiment in republican self-government; they did not want it contaminated by the base power struggles of Europe.

Throughout the nineteenth century, President Washington's farewell speech provided the principal guideline for American foreign policy. It was a century of isolationism. But isolationism did not mean an inactive foreign policy. American effort was engaged in the geographic expansion by which the country was spreading across the continent. Settlers were following what a New York newspaperman called America's "manifest destiny to overspread and to possess the whole of this continent which Providence has given us. . . ."[4] In the eyes of most Americans, this had little or nothing to do with foreign policy. Yet, since most of the lands into which the United States expanded were claimed by other peoples—the British, the French, the Spanish, the Mexicans, and the Indians—foreign entanglements inevitably developed. The means of expansion varied in the cases of Britain, France, or Spain, from negotiation, arbitration, and purchase to limited war, and, in the case of Mexico and the Indian tribes, to the forceful methods familiarly used in conquering the West.

There were complex reasons for American expansionism. Americans genuinely believed that this large territory belonged together. As the Indian tribes were not nations in the European sense, their territory was considered unoccupied and unsettled. It was customary to believe the Indian lands were destined to belong to an indigenous power, the United States, rather than to an alien one. Security considerations were also important. As European powers strengthened or extended their territorial base in the New World, the eventual conflict seemed more likely to be between them and the United States. If strong powers could be excluded from the New World, the more secure the United States would be. The United States also expanded for economic reasons. The effort to gain and protect commercial access to the mouth of the Mississippi River caused conflicts with Spain and France and led to the Louisiana Purchase in 1804. Efforts to protect the lives and property of American citizens, usually traders and business-men, were responsible for the acquisition of Florida in the 1800s, war with Mexico in 1849, and many of the Indian wars throughout the century.

During the early expansionist period, American foreign policy-makers played an active and, on the whole, skillful role. They negotiated favorable settlements to the wars, favorable purchase terms, and favorable arbitration treaties. In part, this success was due to an ability to keep their eye on the narrow self-interest of the United States while understanding the needs of the European powers. They did not seek to alter the European balance of power but to use it as an asset in expanding the territorial boundaries of the United States. They kept out of the quarrels of Europe, as Washington had urged, and instead exploited those quarrels for American self-interest in much the same way that modern small powers are often able to exploit the rivalry of the superpowers for their interests.

For most Americans, isolationism meant a psychological and emotional separation from external affairs; for policy-makers, it meant staying out of the European balance-of-power politics. To accept the aid of a European state in achieving a foreign policy goal would drag the United States into the European quarrels of that state. Yet such aid could often be very useful to the still relatively weak American nation, especially when European quarrels spilled over into the Western Hemisphere. The clearest example of this dilemma came in the second decade of the century when the Spanish empire in Latin America began to break up. American sympathies were with the Latin Americans who followed their northern neighbor in declaring independence from the mother country, but the United States feared the possibility that some strong European power might try to intervene while the Spanish were being forced to withdraw. The British, mindful of the importance of the new world in the balance of power in the old, harbored similar fears.

When English diplomats approached the United States for a joint warning to European powers to stay out of Latin America, the dilemma was clearly posed: to ally with Britain for this mutually desirable purpose and thereby become involved in British interests in Europe, or to refuse and risk the reestablishment of European power in the Western Hemisphere. President Monroe and his Secretary of State, James Madison, found a way to escape between the horns of this dilemma. They refused the British proposal for a joint declaration. Instead, they unilaterally declared that European powers should establish no new territorial control in the Western Hemisphere. The implicit alliance with the British, dependent on their willingness to use the Navy to insure compliance, made the Monroe Doctrine of 1823 a success. The United States achieved its foreign policy objective and avoided the entangling alliances Washington had cautioned against. Moreover, the United States successfully established itself as the paramount power in the hemisphere and assumed a special responsibility for political developments in Latin America

Although the domestic upheavals of the Civil War forced the United States to acquiesce temporarily in the establishment of a French client state in Mexico, the notion of a special American role in Latin America and the exclusion of European powers from the area has remained fixed United States policy from the enunciation of the Monroe Doctrine to the present day. At the beginning of the twentieth century, President Theodore Roosevelt gave a much more activist cast to the Monroe Doctrine. Concerned about the inclination of European powers to involve themselves in Latin American affairs (ostensibly to secure compensation for default on financial obligations by various Latin governments), Roosevelt announced a new United States policy which was to become known as the Roosevelt Corollary to the Monroe Doctrine. Under this new policy, the United States would unilaterally intervene in Latin American countries when, in American judgment, such intervention was required to insure "responsible" financial management by the country concerned. As Roosevelt put it in his annual message to Congress in 1904, "... in the Western Hemisphere, the adherence of the United States to the Monroe Doctrine may force the United States, however reluctantly, in flagrant cases of such wrongdoing or importance, to the exercise of an international police power."[5]

The United States sent expeditionary forces to eight Latin American countries between 1904 and 1934, took over customs collection duties in two countries and militarily occupied five countries for periods ranging from a few months to 19 years. In the judgment of one authority:

> *United States policy in the Caribbean clearly worked for the advancement of its own interests there, and in the long run for the protection of the Latin Americans. Few could deny, however, that it was an arrogant policy, insensitive to the rights of the Latin Americans. The United States in the beginning of the twentieth century was young as a great power and overused its strength.*[6]

The United States had established its own exclusive sphere of influence in Latin America. Its policy was to maintain and foster exclusive or at least predominant influence in Latin America. Involvement was primarily economic, but military and political intervention were not barred whenever the predominant role of the United States was threatened.

American economic expansion also brought considerable involvement in East Asia during the early twentieth century. With less overwhelming power, the United States contended with the European powers for economic advantages. Policy reflected the difference in the two situations. In the Far East, the United States advocated an "open door" policy, no preferential treatment for any foreign power in opportunities for trade and investment. For the United States, the Far Eastern experience fixed the notion of "open door" or "no preference" in commercial matters as a cornerstone of foreign policy outside the Western Hemisphere—one which under different labels was to continue to influence American foreign policy significantly well into the post-World War II era. It also marked the spreading of American involvement to another area of the globe, limiting isolationism even more firmly to noninvolvement in strictly European power politics.

By the end of the nineteenth century, emphasis shifted more and more to economic expansion. American companies became heavily involved in the exploitation of natural resources in Latin America and in opening East Asia to lucrative trading activities. Most Americans still thought of this as having little to do with foreign policy. Economic expansion was the business of private citizens, not governments. Although they were more and more involved in foreign countries, Americans were still isolationists. Policy-makers, however, understood it to be the legitimate role of government to protect and facilitate economic activity. American diplomatic and consular officials devoted a great deal of time to encouraging American economic expansion. Businessmen were often given consular appointments and fulfilled their economic and political roles simultaneously.

Like the physical expansion across the continent, economic expansion into Latin America and East Asia took place within the framework of isolationism. Through most of the nineteenth century, Americans—the general public and policy-makers alike—had followed Washington's advice, seeking commercial advantage and avoiding political involvement. The United States pursued its interests carefully and judiciously. Despite some deplorable, even brutal actions, notably in the approach to the Indian tribes, the young democracy had defined its interests narrowly and generally pursued them with wisdom and restraint born of relative weakness in confronting the European great powers.

The Moral Dimension

At the turn of the century, however, a competing notion of America's role in world affairs began to challenge the guidelines set down by Washington. Usually associated with another President, Woodrow Wilson, this notion of a special moral mission for the United States has roots which go back considerably farther. Washington's farewell address was a political polemic as well as a policy guideline in which he attacked those who favored American assistance to the revolutionary government in France. Supporters of the French Revolution believed in the essential rightness of the American experiment in self-government and urged the government to accept an obligation to actively encourage similar developments in other countries. The American people and their leaders instead followed Washington's advice and rejected the notion of an American mission to bring freedom and democracy to the world; they accepted a narrower and less moralistic definition of American interests. John Quincy Adams clarified the issue in an oft-quoted passage:

> *Where ever the standard of freedom and independence has been or shall be unfurled, there will be America's heart, her benedictions, and her prayers. But she goes not abroad in search of monsters to destroy. She is the well-wisher to the freedom and independence of all. She is the champion and vindicator of her own. She will recommend the general cause by the countenance of her voice, and by the benignant sympathy of her example.... [Otherwise] she*

*might become the dictatress of the world. She would no
longer be the ruler of her own spirit.*[7]

Adams' view was accepted for nearly a hundred years.

The Spanish-American War of 1898, however, raised the issue once again. That "Splendid Little War," as it was called, was motivated in part by the desire to liberate Cuba from the weakened but still oppressive yoke of Spanish rule. It ended with the United States in control of Cuba and the Philippines. It also set off one of the most heated and fundamental debates that dot the landscape of American diplomatic history. The imperialists, who showed little reluctance to apply that label to themselves, urged the United States to accept the obligation to expand both American economic opportunities and the American political message. The anti-imperialists pleaded for the restricted view of the national interest which had characterized the first century of national existence. Although the United States became a colonial power as a result of the war, intense debate soon faded. The controversy over the American mission in the world was to erupt again in the aftermath of World War I and, in its major outlines, during recent years.

President Wilson did not set out to revolutionize American foreign policy. He did not espouse the cause of the imperialists of 1898 despite ordering American marines to intervene in the affairs of several Latin American countries under the Roosevelt Corollary. In fact, he continued Washington's policy of aloofness from the quarrels of Europe throughout his first and much of his second term in the White House and well into the Great European War of 1914-1918. Finally, unrestricted German submarine warfare which threatened the American principles of commercial freedom and citizen safety compelled, in Wilson's view, American entry into the war. Wilson still claimed to be following an isolationist policy. The United States, he argued, could send an expeditionary force to fight in the Great War without becoming involved in the politics of that war. His view was accepted by most Americans. The United States was not fighting for the petty power advantages which motivated the European powers; instead, it was fighting for higher, more moral, more universal goals to end war and to make the world safe for democracy. Unlike the European powers, for the United States self-interest played only a marginal role in the expression of war aims. The United States could stay out of European quarrels even while becoming involved in European wars.

In the aftermath of World War I, however, Wilson abandoned the isolationism of his predecessors completely. He preached a moral mission which he urged the United States to accept—a mission to foster the right of self-determination among subject peoples; to establish and operate machinery to put an end to war; to revolutionize the diplomatic methods by which the Europeans had played the games of power politics. Basically he envisioned the United States accepting the role of world power, using its benevolent influence to encourage and strengthen freedom and welfare around the world. Wilson redefined the national interest to lead the United States to abandon the isolationism of the previous hundred years and to bring moral and political virtue to bear on world problems.[8] The moral commitment which had earlier supported non-involvement—the commitment to a uniquely moral policy uncontaminated by the baser motives of European power politics—was turned outward by Wilson. No longer was the American mission simply to "insure the blessings of liberty to ourselves and our posterity" but, where possible, to others as well.

The new Wilsonian "idealism" was embodied in his statement of American war aims, the famous Fourteen Points delivered before Congress in January, 1918, and in the Treaty of Versailles ending World War I. The Fourteen Points portrayed a vision of a virtuous international order in which secret treaties would have no place, national groups would be free to determine their political status, war would be unnecessary, and an organization of states would insure peace by collective resistance to aggression. It was a powerful vision and it won the hearts of many Americans and Europeans. But it failed to convert many European statesmen schooled in the balance-of-power tradition of European diplomacy and many American politicians devoted to the isolationist principles of the past.

President Wilson went to Paris to participate personally in the drafting of the peace settlement and the League of Nations Covenant. The complications of the principle of self-determination were at once brought home to him as more and more national minorities in Europe looked to him to insure their right of self-determination in the face of determined opposition from the Great Powers of Europe. Unable to do much about their cause, Wilson resolved his dilemma by accepting Great Power determination of most of the vexing European boundary questions. This acceptance did not modify his sermons—delivered to both Europeans and Americans—on the virtue of self-determination. From Wilson down to the present, a moral commitment to self-determination, democracy and freedom has been used to justify American involvement—including military intervention—in the affairs of other nations, including Vietnam.

The League Covenant was a peculiar blend of American idealism and pragmatism which appeared naive and a little mysterious to some Europeans. Wilson attached a higher priority to the development of machinery for avoiding future wars than to the self-determination he preached so eloquently. European statesmen saw less danger—and even some advantages—in international organization than they had seen in the doctrine of self-determination. Wilson was more successful in gaining their acceptance of the League machinery. The League embodied the cherished principle of national sovereignty by requiring unanimity for decisions. At the same time, it established the idea of collective security whereby an aggressor, identified as an international law-breaker, was to be met by the collective resistance of the law-abiding states of the international community. Though the procedural protections for national sovereignty and American freedom of action were iron-clad, the implications of collective security contributed to rejection of the treaty by the United States Senate.

Debate over the League was heated. Many Americans supported their President's desire to join. If his health had permitted him to complete his public campaign for the League, he might have been able to bring popular pressure on the Senate to accept the Treaty; if he had been more sensitive in handling prickly and petulant Senate leaders from the start, he might himself have persuaded the Senate to accept the Treaty. But such "ifs" only make interesting speculation. The Senate *did* reject the Treaty. Following its lead, most of the American people conceived of themselves as retiring behind the comfortable isolationist screen. Defeat of the League really represented an unwillingness on the part of Americans to accept an institution which even by implication might involve a permanent commitment or some marginal restriction on unilateral freedom of action. The defeat of the League was a triumph for the unilateralist theme which has always been strong in United States foreign policy.[9]

AMERICA ON THE EVE OF WORLD WAR II

The domestic defeat of Wilsonian idealism was temporary and incomplete. The apparent victory of isolationism in the battle over the League coupled with the domestic trauma of the Great Depression of the 1930s gave a rather low profile to American foreign policy during the interwar period. Nevertheless, some features of Wilsonian idealism began to influence American policy. Despite its absence from the League of Nations proper, the United States took a leading role in attempts to establish a more stable international order and give moral principles greater standing in the international system. It played a significant role in the disarmament conferences of the period, in postwar relief activities and in attempts to codify and strengthen international law. Two American initiatives in particular revealed the extent to which idealism had become an important theme in American foreign policy. In 1928, the American Secretary of State, Frank Kellogg, joined French Foreign Minister Aristide Briand to sponsor the Kellogg-Briand Pact in which the signatory powers renounced war as an instrument of national policy. Kellogg's successor, Henry L. Stimson, announced in 1932 in response to Japanese aggression in Manchuria that it would be the policy of the United States not to recognize any territorial changes which violated the Kellogg-Briand Pact or the Covenant of the League of Nations. Moral censure in the form of nonrecognition, he implied, should deter aggression. It did not!

The older isolationist themes were very much alive in the interwar period as well. They were most often exhibited by the congressional majority which, following the defeat of the League, played an important role in formulating foreign policy. The continuing reluctance to become involved in European affairs could be seen in the isolationists' public and congressional attacks on President Franklin Roosevelt's speech in 1937 urging that the United States play a role in quarantining the European nations contributing to international lawlessness, a thinly veiled attempt to move the United States toward the anti-German coalition then forming in Europe. Isolationist influence was even clearer in the series of acts passed by Congress on the eve of World War II proclaiming American neutrality in the emerging European conflict.

These competing themes gave a kind of schizophrenic cast to American policy in the interwar years. On the one hand, the semblance of isolation, the emphasis on commercial opportunity, the tendency to go it alone, and a narrow definition of the national interest reflected the continuing importance of the isolationist heritage. At the same time, the acceptance of significant roles in efforts to stabilize the international system; the tendency, often naive, to urge the acceptance of American moral principles as guidelines for international politics; and the adoption of broader definitions of the national interest heralded the emerging importance of idealism in foreign policy. All of these themes would continue to influence foreign policy into the post-World War II period.

In spite of the domestic troubles of the 1930s which temporarily muted the expression of these themes in American foreign policy, the United States was, by 1939, already one of the most powerful nations in the world. Its overseas commerce, although relatively unimportant to the national economy, had worldwide importance. Its foreign investment was large and growing. Its military power was weak but potentially—as was soon proven—the greatest in the world. In pure and applied research, the basis of modern economic and military power, it was among the world's ranking powers. Even the League system—as distinct from the League itself—relied heavily on American involvement in such specialized agencies as the International Labor Organization, the Permanent Court of International Justice, and innumerable ad hoc international conferences on diverse subjects.

The United States was a great power, though its preoccupation with domestic problems caused Americans to be somewhat tardy in realizing this fact, and American absence from the day-to-day quarrels of Europe made statesmen from other countries slow to perceive its power. Great powers and small powers alike pursue policies which are designed to create and preserve an international situation most congenial to their respective goals. Great powers are able to use their power—economic, political, and military—in more widely separated areas of the globe. Thus it was predictable that the United

States, as it grew in power, would use its power on behalf of goals it held dear. It should not be surprising that, finding itself first among the great powers in the aftermath of World War II, it should pursue its goals on a global scale.

THE EMERGENCE OF THE POSTWAR WORLD

The seeds of postwar policy were planted by the Roosevelt administration in the light of prewar and wartime experience. The administration of Harry Truman set the broad outlines and developed the rationale for the policies, and forged the consensus to support them. Eisenhower broadened the consensus and extended the policies, and the Kennedy-Johnson administrations pressed them to their fullest implementation. Future historians will bear the responsibility for assessing the extent to which the Nixon administration's cautious rhetoric and policy mark a genuine shift in American foreign policy from the postwar consensus.

The United States emerged from World War II with one major assumption clearly in view: neither its power—now overwhelmingly preponderant economically as well as militarily— nor interests would permit it to remain aloof from the political maneuverings of other nations, as it attempted to do after World War I. Roosevelt had the political skill Wilson lacked to insure American participation—indeed, leadership—in the United Nations. This leadership was also present in the establishment of the UNRRA (United Nations Relief and Rehabilitation Administration) and the Bretton Woods conference, devoted to insuring postwar economic reconstruction and the restoration of a viable international monetary system. In fact, much of the planning for postwar institutions was conditioned by Roosevelt's determination to avoid what he thought were the political mistakes of Wilson. Thus, he involved large numbers of Republicans, including Republican Senators, in the development of the

United Nations from the beginning. He and Truman, who succeeded him on the eve of the United Nations Conference in 1945, rushed that conference into session in order that a United Nations framework might be created while wartime cooperation continued among the allies. Learning from Wilson's mistake, they also divorced the United Nations agreement from the postwar peace treaties—a valuable tactic since the German peace treaty has not yet been concluded.

The United Nations embodied the principle of collective security characteristic of the League of Nations. This time, however, the principle of national sovereignty was modified by removing the unanimity requirement which had hamstrung the League. The Great Powers, of which the United States was one, continued to protect their unilateral freedom of action by claiming a veto power for themselves in the Security Council, the only major organ of the United Nations empowered to take binding decisions. As the Cold War developed, the United States acquired a nearly automatic majority in both the General Assembly and the Security Council, which precluded its resort to the veto for the first twenty-five years of the UN's existence. The United States was originally as insistent on the veto as was any other major power. It was a clear reflection of the premium any great power places on unilateral freedom of action when joining a permanent collective security alliance.

THE COMING OF THE COLD WAR

There were some who thought and still more who hoped that the alliance forged in war could be carried over into times of peace. The United Nations Charter was based, to some extent, on the assumption that a measure of cooperation could be maintained between the Great Powers (France, China, Britain, the United States, and the Soviet Union).[10] Such hopes were soon dashed when the wartime allies fell to bickering about postwar arrangements even before the armistice.

The formal arrangements for the postwar settlement were made in a series of conferences involving principally British, Americans, and Russians. The most significant of these was the Yalta Conference which was held in early 1945 shortly before the death of President Roosevelt and the Potsdam Conference which occurred soon after President Truman took office and dealt with issues unresolved at Yalta. Though general agreement was reached at these conferences on a wide range of issues, it soon became clear that the interpretations of these agreements by the British and Americans on the one hand and the Russians on the other were sharply at odds. The first major question over which disagreement arose was the creation of a postwar government for Poland. In that unhappy country on the border of the Soviet Union and thus often in the path of invasion to or from Russia, the British, with American support, sought to install the pro-British government which had been in exile in London during the war. The Russians, on the other hand, supported the so-called Lublin Government, dominated by Communists and friendly to Moscow. The conflict over which government should be established, and how it should be legitimized, deeply divided the wartime allies. The military situation at the end of the war prevailed rather than diplomatic arrangements as was the case in many other aspects of the postwar settlement. At the close of the war, the Red Army occupied Poland and proceeded to establish the Lublin Government.

A second major contention was the German settlement. Questions about the division of Germany, the extent of reparations, and the status of Berlin were to be major stumbling blocks in the perpetuation of the wartime alliance. Britain and the United States, having escaped German occupation and the worst of Hitler's horrors, and also remembering the role of the harsh World War I settlement in the rise of Hitler, were inclined to be less harsh toward the defeated Germany than the Soviet Union, which had been partly occupied and had suffered more extensive casualties and destruction during the war. During and immediately after the war, strong motives of revenge were mixed with security concerns in conditioning Soviet policy. As the Cold War developed, the Western allies became less and less willing to deal harshly with the defeated nation. France, which also experienced occupation, entered the postliberation period determined to insist on penalties so harsh as to guarantee against the possibility of a resurgence of German power. As the Cold War developed, France, convinced that its future lay with the Western allies rather than with the Russians, reluctantly moderated its position and shifted to cooperation with Great Britain and the United States.

A third major issue which divided the wartime allies was the interpretation of the Yalta and Potsdam agreements for the establishment of freely elected democratic governments in the countries of Eastern and Western Europe which had formerly been occupied by the Nazi armies. The Russians interpreted these agreements as supporting their policies of installing governments of the left, usually dominated by Communists, responsive to the Soviet Union. The Russians justified their exclusion of right and centrist pro-Western elements on the grounds that "democratic" included only those elements which favored a proletarian revolution. Capitalist elements were reactionary and, therefore, "undemocratic." Obviously, the Americans and British did not share this interpretation and saw the Russian action as a flagrant violation of the agreements made at Yalta and Potsdam. As with Poland, the issue was settled by the military situation at the close of the war. The Russians established regimes friendly to them in the East and conducted what they defined as free elections. The British and Americans supported and encouraged governments friendly to them in the West.

Winston Churchill, with a wisdom born of long experience and the study of European politics, realized that the postwar settlements would be determined largely by the position of the respective military forces at the time of the armistice and on occasion sought to formalize this essentially into a spheres-of-influence arrangement. He was overruled by American officials who tended to divorce the military conduct of the war from the political planning for the postwar settlement. It was typical of the American approach to foreign policy that military matters were left to the generals and that political matters were considered separately. The military position at the close of the war developed with little thought by the United States of its political consequences.[11] Furthermore, Roosevelt, and Truman after him, explicitly rejected the notion of spheres of influence either as a model for the United Nations as Churchill once advocated or as a basis for the postwar arrangements in Europe. In this respect, Roosevelt was in the tradition of Wilson and foreshadowed the globalism later given new content by Presidents Truman and Johnson. What the United States never accepted in principle, however, it was compelled to accept in fact and it finally acceded to the de facto division of postwar Europe with a Soviet sphere of influence in the East.

The division was not hard and fixed from the outset. Certain areas on the dividing line were troublesome and gradually became catalysts for the development of principles which guided America's postwar policy. Russian reluctance to withdraw its armies from Iran after the war provided one example of the tensions emerging between the wartime allies. American pressure, principally through the United Nations, finally induced the Russians to withdraw in 1946. The gradual breakdown of the agreements governing the control of Berlin further exacerbated relations. Greece and Turkey were also significant border areas. In early 1947 Greece was embroiled in an increasingly hard-fought civil war in which the conservative royalist government was receiving money, material, and political support from the British. The leftist, primarily Communist, rebels were receiving similar support from nearby countries, especially Yugoslavia. The prognosis for the survival of the government (a royalist regime with pronounced autocratic tendencies) was guarded at best. In Turkey at the same time, new expression of an ancient confrontation between the Turks and the Russians over access to the Mediterranean through the Dardenelles was continuing in increasingly bitter fashion. The Soviet Union was pressing for a predominant role in the control of access routes through the Dardenelles while Turkey, supported by Great Britain and the United States, insisted on its right to exclusive control of these areas or, failing that, broader international control.

The Truman Doctrine

On February 21, 1947, the British Chargé d'Affaires in Washington called at the Department of State with a note from the British Government announcing that it was necessary to relinquish the responsibilities it had been carrying in Greece and Turkey. For the United States, this note was not a complete surprise, but it made explicit what was still disputed by many American decision-makers: the British would be unable to carry a major share of the Western responsibility in the postwar world. Thus, the question was posed: would the United States pick up the burden which the British had been forced to lay down and assume the major responsibility for resisting Soviet and other Communist expansion? For Harry Truman, there was no doubt; on March 12, 1947, he appeared before a joint session of the Congress to announce what came to be known as the Truman Doctrine.[12] He described the Greek and Turkish situations and asked the Congress to appropriate $400 million in assistance to those regimes, but Truman did not restrict his rhetoric to the situation in the eastern Mediterranean. "At the present moment in world history," he said,

> *nearly every nation must choose between alternative ways of life. The choice is too often not a free one.*

One way of life is based upon the will of the majority, and is distinguished by free institutions, representative govern- ment, free elections, guarantees of individual liberty, freedom of speech and religion, and freedom from political oppression.

The second way of life is based upon the will of a minority forcibly imposed upon the majority. It relies upon terror and oppression, a controlled press and radio, fixed elec- tions, and the suppression of personal freedom.

In a world so divided, Truman prescribed United States policy:

I believe that it must be the policy of the United States to support free peoples who are resisting attempted subjuga- tion by armed minorities or by outside pressures. I believe that we must assist free peoples to work out their own destinies in their own way. [13]

This enunciation of policy was to remain the justification for American intervention at widely scattered points around the globe for at least the next two decades.[14]

A fuller explanation of the rationale behind Truman's broadly conceived policy is usually attributed to George F. Kennan, a distinguished historian and long-time Department of State official who had served in Moscow and was soon to serve as head of the Department's Policy Planning Staff, and later as Ambassador to Russia and to Yugoslavia. In the July, 1947, issue of the influential journal, *Foreign Affairs,* his article—a slightly revised version of a long cable he had sent to the Department of State while still attached to the embassy in Moscow—on "The Sources of Soviet Conduct" appeared. The byline "X" was used because of his official position, but anonymity could not be maintained for long. Soon, excerpts from the article, now attributed directly to Kennan, appeared in other publications and were cited as the official rationale for what was coming to be called the "Containment Doctrine."

In his analysis, Kennan found the sources of Soviet conduct in traditional Russian national interests and in Communist ideology, both of which impelled the Soviet Union toward a policy of expansionism in Europe. To Kennan, the policy implications for the United States were clear:

> *The main element of any United States policy toward the Soviet Union must be that of a long-term, patient but firm and vigilant containment of Russian expansive tendencies. . . . Soviet pressure against the free institutions of the western world is something that can be contained by the adroit and vigilant application of counter force at a series of constantly shifting geographical and political points, corresponding to the shifts and maneuvers of Soviet policy. . . .*[15]

The Marshall Plan

Truman and his advisors considered Europe the first and most important sphere for the application of the new doctrine. Battered by war and nature (the severe winter of 1946-47) and insufficiently supported by the recovery arrangements which were a part of the postwar plans, some European countries were, by 1947, on the verge of political chaos and economic collapse. The United States government sought to meet this challenge by a major program of economic assistance known as the Marshall Plan (named for Secretary of State George C. Marshall) in which $17 billion in American aid was programmed for Europe over a five-year period. Explicitly designed to insure the economic recovery of Europe and encourage cooperative efforts among European nations, the Marshall Plan was also related to the

Containment Doctrine since it was based on the assumption that economic collapse and political chaos provide a fruitful breeding ground for Communist expansion. Only a little over $13 billion of the planned $17 billion was ultimately expended, but the Marshall Plan was an enormous success.[16]

NATO

When Soviet policy took a military cast with the Berlin blockade of 1948 and the Communist coup in Czechoslovakia in the same year, the Containment Doctrine was implemented by military means. In 1949, the United States and eleven other West European and North American countries[17] signed the North Atlantic Treaty, by which they agreed that "an attack against one or more of them in Europe or North America shall be considered an attack against them all." From the outset, the negotiations leading to the treaty clearly implied substantial American military assistance to its European allies. By 1950, with the heightening of concern brought on by the start of the Korean War, American officials had decided that military assistance was not enough and would have to be supplemented by standing NATO forces and a joint cooperative NATO command structure. Such a structure was created under the command of General Dwight D. Eisenhower. The permanent stationing of American troops in Europe resulted.

The Meaning of Containment

The policy enunciated by Truman in 1947 and the rationale provided by Kennan suggested little in the way of limits. It appeared to be an open-ended commitment which the United States was adopting. However, it soon became clear that Truman did not interpret his own doctrine as an unlimited commitment. While committed to containment in Western Europe, he decided against a full commitment to the nationalist government of Chiang Kai-shek in China, increasingly threatened by the

Communist forces of Mao Tse-tung in the Chinese Civil War. Though the American government sent some assistance in the form of money and material to Chiang, and though there was congressional pressure for more, Truman and his advisors concluded that Chiang's government could not be sustained by American intervention at an acceptable cost. When Mao's forces succeeded in establishing the People's Republic of China and putting it in control of the mainland in 1949, the Truman administration was much criticized.

A different assessment of costs was made less than a year later when the North Koreans invaded South Korea. In this case, Truman decided the Containment Doctrine was applicable and, with minimal support of the United Nations (made possible because the Soviet Union had absented itself from the Security Council over the Council's refusal to seat Mao's government and, therefore, could not veto the American-sponsored resolution), American troops prevented the success of the North Korean effort.

A Revolution in American Foreign Policy?

The policies of the Truman era—the Truman Doctrine, the Containment Doctrine, the Marshall plan, NATO, and the Korean War—are often characterized as the elements of a "revolutionary" change in American foreign policy.[18] To some extent, they were, but the threads of continuity with earlier patterns of American policy were at least as apparent as the ways in which Truman's policies differed from the past. American goals had actually changed very little. The United States still sought commercial freedom, a broadly interpreted "open door", and the safety of citizens: a liberal capitalist world. As the major threat to these values was believed to come from an expansionist Soviet Communist power, American foreign policy became increasingly geared to the containment of Russia's sphere of influence. If limitations of power had earlier prevented active pursuit of such goals on a global basis, restricting them first to Latin America and gradually to Asia, the preeminence of American power now permitted a global scope to foreign policy. Furthermore, policy remained heavily dependent on military and economic means.

There were ways in which Truman's approach to foreign policy was a significant departure from that of his predecessors. These differences can be seen primarily in his redefinition of the isolationist approach which had characterized American policy in an earlier era. Truman redefined isolationism but did not abandon some of its important features. Henceforth, it was not to be construed as barring long-term commitments abroad nor long-term alliances in the pursuit of American goals. This is a significant change, especially when one considers that it strikes at the heart of the isolationist prescription. The North Atlantic Treaty is a remarkable document in the context of American history for it involves a twenty-year renewable commitment by the United States to go to war in defense of an ally if that ally is attacked. The Truman Doctrine, though not so precise in its commitment, is an even more remarkable document because of the comparatively unlimited nature of the commitment contained therein. It is also remarkable for having been the policy adopted by a President who had never been elected, was not expected to be elected in 1948—or even renominated—and who needed approval from a Congress controlled by the opposition and pledged to balance the budget and reduce taxes.

Still, it was hardly a revolutionary reinterpretation as it came to be implemented, for much of the unilateralism of traditional isolationism remained. The American government was to decide when and where its commitments became operative. The Marshall Plan, despite statements that the Europeans should devise their own plans and statement of needs, was essentially prescribed by the Americans at every step. Secretary Acheson insisted that NATO in no way obligated the United States to act in any way other than it would act without the treaty, i.e., through the war powers of the Congress. Furthermore, the Americans insisted on the appointment of an American general as NATO commander. Korea was essentially an American operation with fortuitous token support from the United Nations. General MacArthur, the United Nations commander in Korea, reported later, "The entire control of my command and everything I did came from our own Chiefs of Staff. Even the reports which were normally made by me to the United Nations were subject to censorship by our own Departments of State and Defense. I had no direct connection with the United Nations whatsoever."[19]

In short, many features of an insistence on unilateral freedom of action could be seen behind the facade of multi-lateralism. Multilateralism could work in the context of American unilateral impulses because American power was so overwhelming in the aftermath of World War II that multilateralism and American hegemony were virtually synonymous. Our argument, briefly put, is that the Truman era in foreign policy is best seen, not as a revolution—a turning around—in foreign policy, but as a logical extension of the historical legacy with which the United States entered the postwar world, coupled with the overwhelming predominance in power which the United States found she held at the end of the war. As Walter LaFeber concludes, "The mood emerging in late 1949 was not founded upon reform but upon conservation and consensus."[20]

We have emphasized the importance of the Truman era because of our conviction that it established the framework for American policy for at least the next two decades. It established a consensus—an agreement on policy goals—which precluded serious debate over American policy for the same period. With few exceptions, the "great debates" of the 1950s and early 1960s were debates over the means of foreign policy within the framework of essential agreement about the ends. The role of the United States as a global power, to stem the tide of Soviet expansion that was thought to threaten all non-Communist nations, was rarely questioned. How America could best perform such a role was often the subject of bitter and partisan dispute, but the dispute remained essentially within the context of the postwar consensus.

The United States, by the end of the Truman administration, had adopted a policy of global support of the nations of the non-Communist world. Succeeding administrations added their own particular stamp to the implementation of policy without changing its fundamental character.

THE EISENHOWER ADMINISTRATION

The Eisenhower administration responded vigorously, often with rhetorical "overkill," to Communist maneuvers. Eisenhower and his Secretary of State, John Foster Dulles, occasionally seemed to be engaged in a holy war against Communism. They promised to do more than "contain" Communism; in line with substantial congressional pressure, they promised to "roll back" Communism and "liberate" the Communist-controlled areas of Eastern Europe. When the Soviet invasion of Hungary came in 1956, however, the Eisenhower administration showed the same restraint which had characterized the Truman administration. The United States protested while the Soviet Union crushed the rebellion in Hungary. Clearly, "roll back" and "liberation" were not to be undertaken without consideration of costs. In Hungary in 1956, cost calculations dictated discretion.

Dulles went beyond the Truman approach in more than the use of language. Whereas Truman and his advisors had aimed formal American commitments at the European and North Atlantic arena and the traditional American sphere of Latin America, Dulles sought to ring the Soviet Union with NATO-type organizations. In the early years of his tenure in the State Department, much of his effort went into the creation of SEATO

(Southeast Asia Treaty Organization) in 1954; the Bagdad Pact, subsequently rechristened CENTO (Central Treaty Organization) after an Iraqi revolutionary government withdrew from the Pact; and, supplementing Truman's bilateral arrangements with Japan and the Philippines, bilateral security treaties with South Korea and Taiwan.

Historic American reluctance to enter long-term treaty commitments was ignored although each of these treaties contained protection for unilateral American freedom of action.

In spite of the commitments implied by this series of treaties, Eisenhower demonstrated clearly the limitations he placed on the interpretation of American interests. He rejected Dulles' advice that the United States provide substantial men and material—especially in the form of air power—to assist the French attempt to sustain their rule in Indo-China in the face of a determined effort by Communist forces under the leadership of Ho Chi-Minh in 1954. Ironically, Eisenhower's restraint was partly the result of reluctance on the part of congressional leaders including Lyndon Johnson.[21] In America's traditional sphere of influence, Eisenhower showed no hesitation in mounting a clandestine American effort to overthrow the leftist Arbenz government in Guatemala. Nor did he show much hesitation in sending American troops to Lebanon in 1958 to help stabilize tottering but friendly governments in the area. This was done under the Eisenhower Doctrine which, with the approval of the Congress, authorized the President to send American troops to the Middle East for almost any purpose if he thought it would help prevent the expansion of Communism.

National Security Policy

The Truman administration had demobilized rapidly in the aftermath of World War II. With the coming of the Korean war, in which atomic weapons seemed almost irrelevant, Truman accepted the need for a balanced national security establishment capable of meeting a variety of Communist challenges. The land component of the American military arsenal was hastily rebuilt and the principle of substantial investment in a varied and balanced force was enshrined in the now famous though still classified NSC 68, an official statement of policy endorsed by the National Security Council.[22]

Eisenhower came into office committed to ending the stalemated Korean War and to reducing the budget, including the military component. Throughout the early years of his administration, Eisenhower reduced the emphasis on expensive ground forces and came to rely more and more heavily on relatively cheaper strategic air power and American nuclear superiority. Dulles gave the impression that reliance on nuclear weaponry was a strategic doctrine, which he labelled "massive retaliation." The phrase implied that if the Communists embarked on the road of aggression anywhere in the world, they risked instant massive retaliation on their homeland. By the end of the Eisenhower administration, as the Soviets developed an increasingly sophisticated nuclear capability of their own, and as the more flexible Soviet leadership which succeeded Stalin developed new and more subtle ways of expanding their influence, overwhelming reliance on strategic air power seemed less adequate. Though no dramatic decisions were taken, budgets toward the end of the Eisenhower administration began to reveal a gradual return to the more balanced conception of national security which had characterized the latter years of the Truman administration.

The Third World

The Eisenhower administration was the first American administration confronted with the necessity of formulating a comprehensive policy toward the large number of countries emerging from colonial rule. The great postwar tide of anti-colonial revolutions had begun during the Truman administration and Truman and his advisors had taken some steps toward formulating policies to govern America's relations with countries engaged in revolution. For example, as early as his 1949 inaugural address, Truman had enunciated the Point IV program designed to provide American technical assistance in the struggle many of the newly independent countries were waging to reduce poverty and develop their industrial capacities. Truman followed Roosevelt and Wilson in his sympathy for these movements and his suspicion of the European allies who seemed reluctant to relinquish their colonial empires.

When the Eisenhower administration came to power, the anticolonial tide was in full sway. The new administration found it essential to develop a more comprehensive policy than the Truman administration. Furthermore, the Soviet Union, especially after the death of Stalin in 1953, had become more active in wooing these newly emergent nations. Partly for this reason, Secretary Dulles did not view the so-called Third World in the context of colonialism and imperialism but in the context of the Cold War. His attitude toward newly independent countries was substantially determined by their stand on the issues of the Soviet-American rivalry. To him, those who were not for us were against us; there was room but no desire in this world view for neutralism. He took literally the passage from Truman's 1947 congressional message that "nearly every nation must choose between alternative ways of life." Those who refused to choose could no more expect American help than those which chose the other side. Such a position gave a global complexion to the Soviet-American rivalry; it was the most far-reaching expression of American anti-Communism.

THE KENNEDY-JOHNSON ADMINISTRATIONS

By the time the Kennedy administration came to power in 1961, the postwar world was entering a period of decisive change. The notion of a monolithic Communist bloc in unified opposition to the West had no validity after the Sino-Soviet split began to widen in the late 1950s. Moreover, both Soviet and American governments found it increasingly difficult to sustain the level of commitment to the Cold War which had characterized the first decade and a half of the postwar era. Domestic problems, pushed into the background by the rigors of Cold War preparedness, were taking on new urgency in both countries.

The response of the Kennedy and Johnson administrations to these changes was to adapt and modify the policies supported by the Cold War consensus. The rhetoric of the day, especially the articulate and often inspiring speeches of President Kennedy, suggested new departures in the American approach to world affairs,[23] but the policies adopted by these administrations did not fundamentally change the pattern of postwar policy.

The most far-reaching modification affected relations between the United States and the Third World and relations between the United States and the Soviet Union. An early casualty of the Sino-Soviet split was Dulles' notion of a world divided into two, and only two, mutually exclusive and all-encompassing blocs. Moreover, in spite of Dulles' posture, several states—most notably India, Egypt, and Yugoslavia—had managed to play an active role in international affairs without systematically supporting either side in the Cold War. Kennedy and his advisors accepted the existence and even the desirability of nonalignment in world affairs. He offered American friendship as well as assistance to some of these nations. American foreign economic aid began to flow in significant amounts to nonaligned states as well as to American allies.

Kennedy's policy of greater friendship with nonaligned countries proved a somewhat qualified success though it was clearly a more even-handed approach than that of Dulles. The nonaligned countries retained many of their suspicions of American motives and their sensitivity to congressional strings. Moreover, America's allies in the Third World were irritated to see nonaligned countries, often countries they considered adversaries, receiving aid and support without making the political commitment which had been required of them. This problem was particularly troublesome for American policy toward India and Pakistan and in the Middle East. The net effect of the Kennedy approach to nonalignment was an appearance of backing away from the global features of the Cold War anti-Communism of the Eisenhower-Dulles era, though critics charged it was a more subtle and sophisticated version of the Dulles policy. No longer were relations with the Third World to be governed exclusively or even primarily by Cold War considerations.

The more open approach to neutralism can also be seen in the Kennedy policy toward Laos, the problem Eisenhower thought the most serious bequeathed to Kennedy. There a three-cornered war had been in progress for some time between the pro-Western government of Phoumi Nosavan supported by the United States, the neutralist Prince Souvana Phouma who commanded a substantial amount of whatever popular support existed in that country, and the Pathet Lao, an indigenous Communist group which received varying degrees of support and assistance from North Vietnam, Communist China and the Soviet Union. Throughout the 1950s, Laos had been the scene of intermittent fighting among these groups. Efforts to reach a settlement had floundered at least partly because of the intransigence of Phoumi Nosavan, who was backed by the United States. As the situation deteriorated in the early months of his administration, President Kennedy decided that a stable neutralist government was preferable to an unstable pro-Western one which evidently could be maintained only by increasing American support. The cost of maintaining a pro-Western government had become too great and neutralism had become less of an ogre. At the Geneva Conference of 1962, arrangements were made for the withdrawal of American support from Phoumi Nosavan and the acceptance of a neutralist government under Souvana Phouma was ratified. While the situation in Laos remained shaky, partly because of internal weakness and partly because of the spillover from the Vietnam War, the 1962 agreements seemed to establish a reasonably satisfactory short-run situation. The Laotian settlement was widely viewed as reflecting the Kennedy administration's shift on neutralism. Kennedy recognized significant limits on the ability of the United States to fully control developments in the Third World.[24]

Unfortunately, a similar solution in South Vietnam was not available. Among several reasons for this predicament was the absence of a strong neutralist leader.

Relations with the Soviet Union were even more complex. The confrontation in 1962 over the stationing of Soviet missiles in Cuba indicated that the Kennedy administration was prepared to go even closer to the brink of nuclear war to maintain the strategic status quo of the Cold War than its predecessors.[25] The same point was made in the periodic crises over Berlin. But the missile crisis also indicated that Kennedy and his advisors accepted the tradition of unilateral American responsibility for Latin America. The public pledge by the United States not to invade Cuba may have seemed to Americans a small price to pay for the removal of Soviet missiles; such an invasion seemed unlikely to them. But in light of earlier American military interventions in Cuba (the most recent of which only predated the missile crisis by some 18 months) and in other Latin American countries, it may have seemed no small achievement to the Soviets and the Cubans. Indeed, the Johnson administration was to intervene militarily in the Dominican Republic less than three years later to help prevent a popularly elected government from taking power. Worldwide obligations and speedy communication may have made American intervention in Latin America less frequent and freewheeling than in an earlier era, but the United States was obviously still prepared to intervene on occasion in what it considered its own special sphere of influence.

On other fronts, however, the United States and the Soviet Union found themselves pressed by similar problems. Both were troubled by serious domestic situations which demanded the reallocation of scarce resources and both were confronted by increasingly restive and powerful challenges to their leadership from within their respective blocs. In spite of the Cold War confrontations in Cuba and Berlin and on less crucial issues, they began to make cautious moves toward normalizing their bilateral relations or, as some critics put it, establishing duopolistic control over international affairs.

These moves were embodied in two major Soviet-American treaties of the Kennedy-Johnson years, the Nuclear Test Ban Treaty of 1963 and the subsequent Nuclear Non-Proliferation Treaty (NPT). The first of these treaties was designed to meet the growing condemnation of atmospheric pollution from testing and as a first step to ease the financial burden of weapons development. Experts considered nuclear weapons technology to be at rough parity between the superpowers. Each was prepared, indeed wanted, to divert scarce resources to other needs, both military and nonmilitary, if it could be sure the other side would accept similar limits on further nuclear development. The Test Ban Treaty provided that assurance in the limited area of nuclear tests above ground.

The NPT was designed to limit the possession of nuclear weapons to a small number of powers. In the NPT, the Soviet Union and the United States agreed to refrain from giving nuclear weapons to non-nuclear powers or assisting them in the development of such weapons.

At Soviet and American urging, many other countries adhered to these treaties. Two notable exceptions were China and France. Both charged that the ulterior motive of these Soviet-American agreements was to freeze the hegemonic position of each within its own bloc. There was more than a germ of truth in the charge. Both superpowers were plagued by increasingly restive allies of which China and France were but the most troublesome. These treaties provided a neat way to encourage détente between the superpowers while fostering hegemony in their respective spheres of influence. Though there was some modification of independent American action in relations with the Soviet Union, the tendency of the United States to go it alone within its alliances seemed as strong as ever.

This is even more clearly demonstrated by President Kennedy's attempt to resolve the crisis in the Atlantic alliance by the so-called MLF (Multi-Lateral Force), a scheme which was also pursued with a noticeable lack of enthusiasm by the Johnson administration. The long-lasting "crisis" of NATO, stripped of its personal and political jealousies, is over American leadership of the alliance. That leadership—a manifestation of American unilateralism—was acceptable enough to the weakened states of Western Europe in the aftermath of World War II. But as they regained strength and independence, they began to chafe under the American yoke, the more so as the United States became increasingly protective of its nuclear superiority within the alliance and increasingly insistent on a significant conventional contribution by the European allies. The prescribed American solution was a mixed-man force of nuclear-armed ships which would be used only if all participating countries, including the United States, agreed. At the same time, the United States would retain its own independent nuclear striking force subject to exclusive American control. It is not surprising that the Europeans saw in this proposal no alteration in the traditional American unilateralism which was less and less convincingly masked by the facade of multilateralism within the alliance. The basic problem remains to this day.

On the national security front, the Kennedy administration stepped up the movement toward balanced military forces already cautiously begun in the closing years of the Eisenhower administration. Special emphasis was given to the capabilities for unconventional warfare. The Defense budget grew in spite of increased efficiency. Increasing costs of national security played an important part in stimulating the challenge to consensus in the latter years of the Johnson administration.

The need for forces especially trained for guerrilla warfare was based on Kennedy's reading of events in Southeast Asia, particularly in Laos and Vietnam. With the more or less satisfactory resolution of the Laotian crisis in 1962, attention was focused on Vietnam, which was to become the Achilles heel of the Johnson administration. All the unhealthy features of the American foreign-policy tradition came together in a constellation which very nearly destroyed that unhappy country and contributed to the greatest crisis of self-confidence in American history.

Isolationist tendencies, in part, led American policy-makers to disregard the well-intentioned advice of allies that the United States extricate itself from Vietnam and to misinterpret the restraint of the major adversaries, the Soviet Union and China, in that war. The American moral commitment, which generated sincere popular sympathy for freedom and well-being around the world and supported significant American involvement in relief and development operations, spurred the United States to an excessive commitment in Vietnam and simultaneously blinded it to the nature of the war and the regimes on both sides. The conjunction of these detrimental aspects of the American foreign policy tradition, permitted and fostered by the Cold War consensus described in Chapter 1, contributed to the most extensive unilateral American military intervention in the country's history. During the Kennedy-Johnson administrations, direct American military intervention had an enormous impact on the domestic and international politics of Southeast Asia, Europe, and Latin America, and American military assistance policies significantly influenced the domestic and international politics of additional countries in these areas and in Africa, the Middle East, and South Asia. Sometimes those effects were stabilizing and contributed to values espoused by the United States; more often they were destabilizing; always they were massive and sometimes overwhelming. The limits on American intervention receded farther and farther into the background. Limits were still present, as in President Kennedy's refusal to provide the air support necessary to give a chance of success to the Bay of Pigs invasion in Cuba in 1961. But the Kennedy-Johnson administrations represented the culmination of earlier trends discernible in postwar American foreign policy, the most extensive application of American power on a global basis.

THE NIXON ADMINISTRATION

The Vietnam War shattered the Cold War consensus. For the first time since World War II, there was no foreign policy to hand over to the new administration in 1968. One thing was clear, however: the highest priority was to clarify the limits under which American policy could operate. In the Nixon Doctrine, enunciated first at Guam in 1969[26] and expounded more fully in a series of "State of the World" messages,[27] President Nixon outlined the limits his administration intended to set on the course of American foreign policy. The Nixon Doctrine represented no change in the broad goals of American policy nor in the global sweep of those goals. In this respect, Nixon adhered to the tradition of his postwar predecessors. The change from past policies was his clearer and more limited definition of acceptable means for achieving these goals. Thus, he stated that he had no intention of using presidential powers to send American troops to support tottering governments around the world. American support of governments would be limited to financial and material measures and, in rare cases, assistance in advising and training military forces. The United States would not fight other countries' battles for them. In the battle then being waged,

"Vietnamization" would be the means for fulfillment of American commitments.

In the realization of the Nixon Doctrine, there was some ambiguity. In Indochina, moves toward Vietnamization, though steady, were slow, uneven in success, and marked by a sharp increase in the role of American air combat forces. Presidential initiatives in relations with the Peoples Republic of China and with the Soviet Union suggested an awareness that the more limited means available under the terms of the Nixon Doctrine would require more "normal" relations with the two Communist giants. The continuation of the Kennedy-Johnson administrations' cautious moves toward détente with the Soviet Union marked a further erosion of the unilateralist tradition. The agreement in the first round of the Strategic Arms Limitations Talks (SALT) to limit the deployment of defensive missiles gave further evidence of the willingness of the two superpowers to shift resources from the arms race, given adequate mutual guarantees.

On the other hand, the American (and, to a lesser extent, the Soviet) approach to the multilateral Conference on European Security offered signs of an unwillingness to surrender hegemony within the respective spheres of influence. Similarly, American opposition in some quarters to West German Chancellor Willy Brandt's *Ostpolitik* (the establishment of ties between West Germany and the East European countries, including East Germany) indicated a continuing preference for maintaining American control of political initiatives. The unilateral moves in the area of international monetary affairs and thinly veiled attacks by the Nixon administration on the European Common Market reinforced this predisposition. The Nixon proclamation of 1973 as the "Year of Europe" implied some willingness in the administration to take a fresh look at relations in the Atlantic area. At this writing it seems doubtful whether modifications in the traditionally hegemonic approach toward the European allies will become characteristic of American policy.

President Nixon's policy toward the Third World was a policy of "benign neglect." In part this was forced upon him by a Congress ever more hostile to foreign aid; in part, it reflected his own view that the highest priority in American foreign policy is Soviet- and Sino-American relations. Where policy toward the Third World became entangled with policy toward the Soviet Union or China, as in the Bangladesh Crisis of 1971, Nixon made his priorities very clear: nothing must be allowed to obstruct moves toward the normalization of relations with the two major Communist powers. That normalization was essential to making the Nixon Doctrine work. American power is no longer pre-eminent in the way it was throughout most of the postwar era[28] nor does the Cold War consensus support an unlimited global role. The Nixon Doctrine requires at least implicit cooperation with the Soviet Union and China in some areas, as the Monroe Doctrine required implicit cooperation with Great Britain.

CONCLUSION: THE LEGACY OF EXPERIENCE

What does our experience as a nation tell us about our approach to foreign policy?

Contrary to much conventional opinion, we are not immune from the tendency of all great powers to intervene in the affairs of smaller and weaker states in order to achieve our aims in foreign policy. Stated differently, we share the tendency of great powers to expand their "sphere of influence," though the term does not come easily to American lips, at the expense of both small and great powers. This tendency toward intervention and expansion is strengthened by long experience, beginning with settlement of the continent and gradually expanding, as American power grew, to Latin America, Asia, Europe, and the entire globe.

Until the last decade or so, the general interpretation of our national experience places little emphasis on interventionism or expansionism. Americans do not generally see their country's foreign policy experience in this light, largely because the isolationist theme is too deeply rooted. Americans often define the policies pursued in quest of "manifest destiny" and the acquisition of the Indian lands as being outside the realm of foreign policy. To fight the Indians, Mexicans, and Spaniards was not interventionist or expansionist but merely filled out the American union as Providence had ordained. Even when the United States involved itself in European affairs in two World Wars, isolationism maintained its hold over the American people. Accordingly, American intervention was not of its own making; it was thrust upon the United States against its will. Americans tended to ignore the evidence of interventionism in Latin America where the United States had behaved most clearly in the pattern of a big power.

For most Americans, involvement in world affairs, even after World War II, was never seen in the same light as intervention by other great powers; it was unrelated to the kinds of power considerations prevalent in the international system. It might be seen in terms of power politics by other states, but never by Americans, who were convinced that the acceptance of the postwar challenge had nothing to do with their own power interests but involved the altruistic acceptance of responsibilities unsought and unwanted.

Thus, the legacy of American experience is one of interventionism—very often military in character—coupled with an interpretation that discredited power factors, self-interest, and often, the facts. In one sense, the mythical aspects of isolationism are more important than the reality. Americans absorbed little understanding of great-power politics because their expansionist tendencies were pushed out of their consciousness. With a self image of uninvolvement they learned little from their experience in world affairs. They entered the post-World War II period with a naiveté which belied past experience. In this sense, American experience is unique.

Two other themes appear prominent in American experience in the area of foreign policy: an extreme form of self-centeredness or unilateralism, and the tendency to define American policy in terms of a moral crusade. American unilateralism, a propensity to act differently from other states, is the essence of Washington's farewell address and is embodied in the Monroe Doctrine. The theme has been muted under a facade of multilateralism embodied in the postwar alliances constructed so painstakingly by successive American Presidents and Secretaries of State. Beneath the surface of multilateralism is the insistence on American preeminence as in NATO, SEATO, OAS, and the American tendency to go it alone as in arms limitations talks, foreign assistance programs, international monetary adjustments, Soviet-American and Sino-American relations.

The tendency of Americans to think of their foreign policy as a moral crusade received its fullest expression in the Wilsonianism of the two World Wars and the anti-Communism of the Cold War. By now equally firmly rooted in experience, this dimension of the American approach to foreign policy is reinforced by facets of the national character we shall examine in Chapter 4.

We have described these legacies of experience as tendencies. They are strongly influenced but not determined by the American experience. In fact, throughout our history, they have operated within strict, though changing, limits determined by the actions of others as well as foreign policy choices. An unfortunate by-product of the great debate which has reasserted limits in the consideration of foreign policy has been a wholesale reaction against the concepts of unilateralism and interventionism. Both of these concepts have become epithets to be hurled at those who devise American policy, as if both contain inherent evil. The reality of international politics is quite different.

The highest goal of foreign policy in any country is the maintenance of national political independence and territorial integrity. In pursuit of this goal each country must finally determine unilaterally the requirements of foreign policy. No state, if it is to continue to be a state, can abdicate these crucial decisions to any other state or international body. This is what is meant by sovereignty in international politics. It is one of the central attributes of statehood. The exercise of sovereignty implies unilateral decision and action. In this sense, unilateralism is a core feature of the foreign policy of all states, especially all great powers. The critical question is under what circumstances a great power will modify and restrain its predispositions to act alone in the interest of multilateral understanding and international stability and comity. The United States, not alone among great powers, has often lacked a clear conception of the appropriate occasions for unilateral action and for restraint.

Similarly, all great powers, by their very nature, intervene in world affairs of other states. Indeed, it would be impossible for them not to do so. Their trading capacity, military capacity, investment resources, and the range of their political interests preclude nonintervention. The moral dimension of the American tradition has stimulated intervention by the United States. At its best, the United States has intervened to help create a stable, orderly, and progressive international system through its leading role in disarmament negotiations, arbitration treaties, international organizations; its genuine if sometimes blunted sympathy for anticolonialism; its support for economic and political development through its foreign aid and technical assistance programs; and its usually speedy dispatch of humanitarian assistance in the event of natural disaster. But, especially in the postwar era, American intervention has all too often been excessive, self-righteous, disdainful of the wishes and interests of other states, and designed to fulfill the objectives of some self-defined moral (generally anti-Communist) crusade. The question for the future is not whether the United States should intervene but, "How can American intervention be guided by appropriate, sensitive, and realistic guidelines?"

4. *The National Style and the International Setting*

"We are willing to help people who believe the way we do, to continue to live the way they want to live."
–Dean G. Acheson

The historical experience of a nation is one major influence in the making of foreign policy. Other major influences are the national character of a people and the international setting in which a nation is situated. These influences have received much attention from social scientists in recent years. In this chapter, we will examine some of their findings which relate to United States foreign policy.

NATIONAL CHARACTER

The concept of national character—psychological characteristics shared by a national population—is among the most used and abused concepts in the social sciences. Few deny its importance. Yet few students of foreign policy attempt to deal with it in a systematic way, perhaps because of exaggerated claims that is has the power to explain national behavior, which have been made by some social scientists.

The Role of Stereotypes

At its most elementary and simplistic level, national character analysis is an exercise in stereotypical thinking. Certain character traits pop into the minds of most Americans, indeed, most people, when they hear mention of a nation other than their own.[1] Thus, widespread images of Latin peoples—Italians,

Spaniards, and Latin Americans—as indolent, romantic, and emotional; of Germans as authoritarian; of the English as staid and pragmatic, strike a responsive chord in most Americans. Americans who have had extensive contact with these national groups will recognize that such stereotypes are simplistic at best and often misleading.

The fact that such stereotypes are superficial does not prevent them from being of crucial importance in international affairs. Napoleon's characterization of the British as a nation of shop-keepers provides an early example of superficial national character analysis which affected his strategic judgment. Hitler's judgment of the American, British, and Russian national characters led to well-documented and serious misjudgments in his conduct of World War II. More recently, General de Gaulle's image of the British as an "insular" people who could never become full participants in the "construction of Europe" contributed to his decision to veto the British application for membership in the Common Market in 1963. In another part of the world, the widespread image of the Bengalis as emotional, literary, and hopelessly impractical—"the Italians of Asia"—contributed to their underrepresentation in political, military and civil service cadres of Pakistan, an important element in the crisis that led to the breakup of Pakistan and the creation of Bangladesh in 1971.

While influential, stereotypical thinking in international affairs is generally inadequate for serious and sophisticated analysis of national behavior in the international arena. Nevertheless, observers have shared with practitioners a tendency to employ this type of analysis.[2] During and after World War II, for example, social scientists often explained German agression by citing theories of national character and authoritarian attitudes. After the war, some anthropologists suggested that Russian expansionism could be explained by the fact that Russians swaddled their babies. This type of controversial analysis must be set alongside the intuitive analyses of perceptive observers such as

Alexis de Tocqueville.[3] His comments on American national character in the 1830s remain a stimulating guide to understanding America today and demonstrate the possibility of usefully explaining national attitudes, perceptions, and behavior.

What is National Character?

Any concept so widely and confusingly discussed needs precise definition. Kenneth W. Terhune defines national character this way: "any internal psychological qualities of a nation which are relatively enduring and which may serve to distinguish that nation from others."[4] This definition suggests many questions to the student of foreign policy. Chief among these are: Are there psychological characteristics shared within a nation which can be significantly differentiated from those of other nations? How can these characteristics be discovered? and, Does national character affect national behavior in foreign policy?

After examining available social science findings on the concept, Terhune concludes that "there is evidence of (a) differences in central tendencies [values and value-orientations, especially] among national samples, and (b) cross-regional similarity of central tendencies within nations."[5] In other words, there is such a thing as national character which can be used to differentiate one nation from another.

Terhune also provides a survey of the methods by which national character can be discovered, including survey research, widely administered personality tests, both systematic and intuitive observation, analysis of rituals and customs, and analyses of cultural thought systems and institutions.[6] These methods have varied in the degree to which they have yielded reliable insights into the psychological attributes of nations. Few of them have proven notably successful in discovering the linkage between national character and national behavior.

There are several reasons for this lack of success. First, few of these methods are able to get at the range of individual variation in personality traits within a nation. Variation is enormously important in setting permissible limits on foreign policy decision-makers. What proportion of the population must possess a certain personality trait for it to constitute a part of the national character in the sense of being important in decision-making? Does the necessary proportion vary from trait to trait? Does the socio-economic status of the proportion possessing a given trait matter and, if so, in what way? In influencing national behavior, to what extent do elites differ from informed publics and from mass publics?[7] Are the personality characteristics of elites more important than those of nonelites and, if so, to what degree?

The enormity of the problems and the inadequacy of the tools for investigation have led serious students of foreign policy to develop less ambitious concepts. Stanley Hoffmann, for example, prefers to talk about "national style," by which he means the unique way Americans perceive the world and their place in it.[8] The notion of national style may narrow our focus somewhat and simplify some of the difficult methodological problems but it, too, contains a set of questions which pose serious problems of analysis, as Hoffmann recognizes. Who embodies the national style? Who expresses it? Whose concept of it determines policy? How far do decision-makers and general populace share a national style? How does one cope with inconsistencies in the national style? What determines which elements of the national style will be deemed relevant to a given policy issue? How are national style and individual foreign-policy decisions linked? Is there really any continuity of national style from generation to generation, from administration to administration? How can we discover the substantive features of America's style?

These important questions cannot force us to suspend consideration of national style; to do so would be to exclude a whole range of information which plays a crucial role in the making and understanding of foreign policy. They do alert us to be cautious in our approach; we must not claim too much for national style. We would do well to affirm at the outset that the national style in no sense fully determines all, or any, foreign-policy decisions. It is only part of the framework (as the national experience is part of the framework), a part of the milieu, in which the policy-maker works and in which the informed and interested public judges his work. It sets limits because it involves perceptions of what action is possible, but it does not control policy. Often, it conditions the way in which policy is articulated and explained and, as such, it becomes self-reinforcing.

The national style is always changing. Like all cultural characteristics, the national style is learned, and learning is a continuous process stimulated and changed by the perception of events. One might be even more tempted to expect fundamental change in the national style after an intense period of national self-examination such as the one brought on by the Vietnam War. Nonetheless, one remarkable feature of the literature on American character and style is the extent of agreement among diverse observers. From Alexis de Tocqueville in the 1830s through Civil War, recession, Depression, two World Wars, and even Prohibition, observers discern the same basic characteristics in the American policy. Therefore, predictions of change in the fundamental values and predispositions of Americans should be carefully examined. On the other hand, in view of the trauma of the 1960s, at least as it relates to foreign policy, one cannot be complacent about predicting continuity of national values and attitudes. Ultimately, it must be left to the scholars of the 1980s and 1990s to discern whether patterns of change or continuity in values best characterize recent developments in the national style.

Hoffmann finds the key to America's style in her past, her principles, and her pragmatism. He discovers the content of these factors from analysis of America's experience and the perceptions of astute observers of American behavior.[9] Gabriel Almond, whose analysis of the subject first appeared more than twenty years ago, also makes use of available survey research data.[10] But Almond, like Hoffmann and others, relies most heavily on materials from history and informed commentaries on American behavior. In spite of the unscientific and sometimes impressionistic character of this approach, it has provided useful insights into the complex phenomenon of American style.

American National Style

What are Americans like when they approach foreign policy?

1. *Material success and the dominance of private over public values.* "The business of America is business," President Calvin Coolidge is reported to have said. Charles E. Wilson, President Eisenhower's Secretary of Defense, and former head of General Motors, allegedly uttered the classic statement, "What's good for General Motors is good for the country."[11] Such statements reflect both the materialism and the dominance of private over public values which characterize American culture. No single feature of American culture is more widely discussed—both by those who applaud and those who condemn—than its materialism.[12] Success is judged in material terms and the achievement of material success becomes a widely shared individual and social goal. That quest generates a fierce competitiveness among Americans both in their individual and collective capacities. Americans seem driven to "succeed" at whatever they are doing. Most evident in the American approach to sports, it is also reflected in other facets of American life, not least in the oft-articulated goal of Americans to have their nation become and remain the "first" in the world: first in military power, first in economic prosperity, first in space exploration, and so on. There is an almost pathological fear of becoming a "second rank" power.

The value placed on material success generates an openness about American society not usually found in other societies.

Since success is judged primarily in material terms rather than in terms of social background or education, American society permits—indeed, encourages—a great deal more mobility, both social and geographical, than other societies. However imperfect the egalitarianism of the American dream—and some groups such as blacks and Indians have never been allowed full participation in it—it is nevertheless true that the opportunities for achieving success have been more equally shared than in most other societies. The individual has had opportunities to achieve which were unknown elsewhere, and these opportunities in turn have given rise to an individualism unknown abroad.[13]

Egalitarianism, social and geographical mobility, and individualism are mutually reinforcing but not without costs. If the individual enjoys mobility and opportunity, he faces society alone, without the support of family, or a close-knit community. Individualism and mobility, especially when combined with increasing urbanization, bring a sense of rootlessness, of separation from supportive institutions like family and community. The society has taken on an atomized quality. Americans are lonely and self-reliant compared to other peoples. Various observers have attributed the relatively high suicide rate, the high rates of mental illness, of violent crime, and of drug abuse to the absence of a supportive local society. In any event, the atomization of society does seem to generate a need in Americans to feel that material success brings not only the respect, but the affection of their fellows as well.

This contributes to another characteristic more pronounced in Americans than in most other nationalities: the dominance of private over public values. The American ideology has always posted material success, the economic orientation on which it is based, and the egalitarianism and individualism which are its corollaries, as appropriately private concerns. The role of the public sector is to create and maintain a climate in which these private values can operate unimpeded by public restrictions or foreign interference. The reality has often strayed far from the ideal. Government has frequently been called on to do far more than create an appropriate climate. It has developed ties—both supportive and regulative—and has become at times almost mercantilistic in its relations to business. Nevertheless, dominant private values retain their hold on the ideal culture to which Americans aspire. The reality of intimate ties between business and government, which has seriously blurred the distinction between "public" and "private," has been largely suppressed from the American mind. Such ties continue to be considered inappropriate by most Americans to a degree which would be startling in most other countries.

These aspects of the American style have been the target of increasingly vocal critics of American culture in recent years. The critics have condemned a materialism that makes it difficult to focus on other aspects of the quality of life. They have challenged a set of values which tolerates public want in the midst of private wealth. But, however true their challenge rings, private material values continue to dominate the American scene.

In foreign policy, the public orientation toward material values has an enormous impact. It strengthens the tendency to view material factors as predominant in international politics. Thus, Americans have tended to assume, in spite of abundant evidence that this view is vastly oversimplified, that poverty—the lack of material well-being— is the primary cause of revolution and political instability and provides a fertile breeding ground for Communism. Such thinking was behind many of the plans for economic reconstruction after World War II and the Marshall Plan for rebuilding Europe, and provides one of the key rationales for America's foreign aid programs in the 1970s. Materialism inclines Americans to an analysis based on economic determinism.

Similarly, the material success of the United States tends to confirm for Americans the validity of their own values. They see these values as an appropriate model for economic and political development in other societies. It was fashionable in American academic and governmental circles a few years ago to treat the "battle" between Communism and "freedom" as if it would be won by the success or failure of India or China in the area of economic development. Whatever the merits or demerits of this thesis, it reflected the American emphasis on the self-justifying character of material success as the sole or, at least, the primary determinant of winning.

The dominance of private over public values has a further impact on foreign policy. We have already suggested that it contributes to the American preference for loans over grants in foreign aid programs and to the standards by which Americans judge potential aid projects, usually finding public-sector projects less worthy than private-sector ones. But, in another area, American values foster a tendency to see the activities of private American corporations as outside the realm of foreign policy and beyond the legitimate arm of governmental regulation, however much they may affect American interests abroad. Protection without regulation is the "proper" role of government at home and abroad. It is, of course, a fact that "private" enterprise has developed enormous and intricate relations with government and that a great deal of governmental activity is devoted to the regulation and support of business and industry, but the emphasis on private values makes it easy for Americans to push these connections into the background. By and large, this value structure has inhibited governmental interference in the foreign operations of American corporations more than it has in their domestic operations. Similarly, governmental efforts to protect overseas operations, though enormously significant in terms of American foreign policy, have not been notably successful from the corporate point of view.

The separation of public and private values leads decision-makers to underestimate the economic tools of foreign policy and the level of American economic intervention overseas. In the military sphere, by contrast, the tools of power are possessed by government and must inevitably be used in accordance with government policy. In the economic sphere, these tools are divided between the government and the private sector. Since government possesses only a fraction of American economic power, and since the separation of public and private sectors is assumed in American society, decision-makers tend to underestimate the level of American economic influence overseas. They find it difficult to think comprehensively about using economic tools in pursuit of specific policy aims or about accepting public responsibility for doing so. Moreover, since control over economic tools is divided, it is far more difficult to develop and implement a consistent foreign economic policy. The intimate connection between domestic and foreign economic policy further complicates the picture. Control over the *government's* economic tools is fragmented within the government, with much of it lodged with departments such as Treasury or Commerce whose interests and expertise lie primarily in the domestic sphere. None of this diminishes the impact abroad of preponderant economic power which is in many ways more pronounced than the impact of American military power.

The predisposition of the policy-maker to subordinate or underestimate American economic influence—the product of unique features of the American style—is largely unperceived by foreigners who see the impact of the United States' economy, whether public or private, as looming large in their countries. Americans were aware that the decisions of TWA and Pan Am to cancel their options to buy the Anglo-French supersonic airliner, Concorde—decisions which had serious financial implications for the taxpayers of both countries—were private and nongovernmental. This distinction was implausible to many Englishmen and many Frenchmen.

2. *Sense of political virtue.* The second major theme which runs through analyses of the American national style is a belief in the unique political virtue of the United States. In part, of course,

this sense of political virtue stems from the success ethic and the enormous material achievements of Americans. The fact that the United States has the highest per capita income and the highest standard of living in the world is seen as evidence of the unique virtue of the American political and economic system. Such rewards are the result of the American discovery of the "best" political and economic system, one believed to have universal applicability.

The special sense of political virtue generates a paradoxical approach to nationalism by Americans. In one sense, they transcend nationalism for they see little special about America which cannot and should not be spread throughout the world. It is not American control that they want to spread around the world, but the American way of life. In another sense, this is the most pervasive nationalism of all for it gives Americans a certain missionary zeal in their approach to other nations, a mission of bringing to an unenlightened world the blessings of democracy and free enterprise which have been revealed to them as superior forms of economic and political organization. Thus, as Stanley Hoffmann points out, Americans do not see themselves as imperialists—in the classic sense that they identify with Europe—but rather as involving themselves in the affairs of other nations the way missionaries involve themselves in the lives of other people: to bring to them the "good news" of an economic and political system which has been "revealed" to be good and right for all people.[14]

The origins of this sense of political virtue go back to the beginning of the Republic. The Founding Fathers, long in advance of the material success of the union, had the sense that they were creating a political system uniquely virtuous, uniquely in harmony with Divine Will. In the Declaration of Independence, Jefferson argued the revolutionary case on the grounds that it was in harmony with natural law: "Man is endowed by his Creator with certain inalienable rights . . ." and Americans, alone among the peoples of the world, had the unique opportunity of creating a political system which would be in harmony with these divinely ordained rights.

Americans have subsequently believed that the framing of the Constitution was a uniquely virtuous political act. Charles Beard was viciously attacked and his book banned from some American libraries when he suggested that the framers had been motivated at least partly by economic self-interest. Nor is it surprising that James Bryce, that distinguished 19th-century English commentator on the American character, claimed that Americans not only believed that majority decisions should prevail, but that such decisions were always "right."[15] Nor is it surprising that when Grenville Clark and Louis Sohn, distinguished American students of international law, came to draft a constitution for a proposed world government, it bore an uncanny resemblance to the American constitution.[16]

Years ago, Alexis de Tocqueville commented on the moral dualism which characterized the American culture.[17] By this, he meant the unbridled quest for material gain and the dominance of private over public values, coupled with periodic outbursts of evangelism devoted to individual and social regeneration. In the early nineteenth century, when he wrote, he observed this moral dualism in the history of periodic outbursts of religious revivalism, such as the 18th-century Puritan revival movements of Jonathan Edwards which swept the land. In these movements, Americans put aside—but not very far aside—the quest for material success to turn their attention temporarily to other virtues.

In more recent times, a secular and political evangelism has replaced the religious variety, but the dualism noted by de Tocqueville remains. A political system characterized by self-interest has seen periodic outbursts of moral crusades. The Wilsonianism of World War I is the most clear-cut example; there are many others such as the crusade to "free" Cuba from the onerous Spanish yoke in 1898, the defense of the Atlantic Charter principles in World War II, and the "holy crusade" against "atheistic" Communism in the postwar world. Wilson was really the American political evangelist par excellence. He acted in America's self-interest but he preached the gospel of disinterested self-sacrifice for freedom and democracy. And for the generations of Americans who came after him the notion of self-interest and disinterested self-sacrifice became ever more confusingly linked. He set the tone for the later evangelists who would strive to win the world to the American sense of political virtue. Here are the words of John F. Kennedy:

> *We dare not forget today that we are the heirs of that first revolution. Let the word go forth from this time and place, to friend and foe alike, that the torch has been passed to a new generation of Americans—born in this century, tempered by war, disciplined by a hard and bitter peace, proud of our ancient heritage—and unwilling to witness or permit the slow undoing of those human rights to which this nation has always been committed, and to which we are committed today at home and around the world. With a good conscience our only reward, with history the final judge of our deeds, let us go forth to lead the land we love, asking His blessing and His help, but knowing that here on earth God's work must truly be our own.* [18]

There is an important corollary to this unique sense of political virtue. The periodic national outbursts of evangelism demand of the United States a kind of total commitment not required of a state which is less often convinced it is involved in a moral crusade. After all, if the United States "stands at Armageddon and battles for the Lord," how can it do so with less than total commitment to the cause and how can it accept less than total victory over the foe? One reason the old European balance of power system is so uncongenial to Americans is that wars in that system were fought for limited objectives. Adjustments in power and territory were made in the peace settlements and defeated and victorious powers alike rejoined the international system. Americans have found *total* commitment to *total* victory more congenial to their character. The insistence upon "unconditional surrender" is a typically American approach to war. Though revolution in the technology of weapons has made such an approach unfeasible in the postwar world, and Americans have had to adjust to the notion of limited war for limited objectives, the adjustment has been difficult and incomplete, as the Truman-MacArthur controversy over Korea and the frustrations of Korea and Vietnam so clearly illustrate.

The combination of America's unique sense of political virtue and her outbursts of evangelism leads to a sequence of periods of total commitment and international evangelism alternating with periods of withdrawal. Again, World War I is the classic example, but the rapid demobilization after World War II provides another case in point, and there are those who interpret the current American mood as one of withdrawal following the evangelical exertions of the Cold War.[19]

The American sense of moral superiority fosters a predisposition to accept the use of whatever means are necessary, since the end for which they are employed is, by definition, good. Since Americans assume their goals to be morally superior, they find it relatively easy to justify actions taken by their own nation which they would condemn if performed by another nation. The sense of moral superiority and political virtue also reinforces the American tendency to intervene in the affairs of other nations: intervention by another state is self-interested imperialism, but American intervention is based only on disinterested, virtuous motives. It also reinforces the tendency toward unilateralism. An America, suspicious of the motives of others but confident of the virtue of its own, finds it difficult to work in harness with other states in the international arena.

3. *Ambivalence toward power and violence.* Growing out of materialism and a sense of political virtue is a third major aspect of the American national character which affects its approach to foreign policy—an ambivalent attitude toward power, authority, and violence. There are two dimensions to this ambivalence. First, Americans have a healthy respect, even admiration, for power and authority. They take an enormous pride in their ability, individually and collectively, to acquire the tools of power and are invigorated and excited by the exercise of power. At the same time, however, a deep suspicion of those in positions of authority and a distrust of those who wield power runs through the American culture. Second, Americans tend to judge their own exercise of power by standards which are very different from those they apply to the exercise of power by others.

The positive aspect is related to the materialism of American culture. Competition generates a respect for those who acquire the power which goes with material success in American society. They have "made it" in terms of socially defined standards of success and, as we have seen, this success confirms that they are worthy of respect and admiration. Similarly, the power of a nation, including the United States, confirms the degree to which that nation is worthy of respect. At the same time, there lurks deep in the American mind a suspicion that those who have acquired power may not have done so in ways which would bare close scrutiny. The ambivalence is reflected in the American mother's ambition to have her son grow up to be President, coupled with her reluctance to have him become a politician. The same dualism is found in the definition of a statesman which former Vice President Alben Barkley was fond of citing: "A statesman is a dead politician." Though it was an Englishman, Lord Acton, who said, "Power tends to corrupt;

absolute power corrupts absolutely," his statement seems more often quoted in the United States than in his native land. Indeed, the whole basis of the American political system—its Constitution, with checks and balances and separation of powers, its undisciplined party system, its federal structure—rests on an attempt to prevent the concentration of power and reflects the suspicion of power and power-holders. In the words of Andrew Hacker, an astute observer of the American scene:

> *Far from being deferential to their betters, Americans are loath to admit that they have any betters at all. Men and women are elected to public office not to be given a chance to govern but to be kept under constant surveillance lest they exercise their own judgment or discretion. The American tradition, going back to Jefferson, is that all opinions are equally expert and all perceptions of reality are equally acute. . . .*

> *And the lesson of the Constitution itself is that government is not to be trusted, that the men we elect to lead us must be checked lest they exceed their mandate.* [20]

The anthropologist, Margaret Mead, has related this distrust of power to the immigrant origins of Americans, arguing that most of them rejected first the authority of the old country and then the authority of their immigrant parents. This rejection of authority spills over into a rejection of all authority, combined with a somewhat ambivalent conformity to transitory norms and fads, and reflected in politics by a dogmatic belief in majoritarianism. [21] Whatever its source, distrust of power and power-holders has characterized Americans since the days of the Founding Fathers.

In the international arena, suspicion of power and the powerful has been reflected in the attitude of Americans toward the "power politics" of Europe. There is a dualism in the American analysis of power which reflects psychological and emotional separation from the machinations of the European powers. European references to power balances make Americans suspicious. Their own power calculations are seen in a quite different light. Stanley Hoffmann perceptively notes:

> . . *Americans seem to ask for special treatment. Thus, when we speak the language of force, we do not quite avoid implying that although we recognize power as a universal commodity and the necessary, amoral means for all nations, our power is somehow morally superior and deserves a privileged position; that we can trust ourselves but not others; and that others can trust us, but nobody else.* [22]

The dualism in the American approach to power can be seen in various efforts by the United States to insure the perpetuation of the American nuclear quasi-monopoly within the Atlantic alliance. America's assumption was that she could be trusted to manage nuclear weapons wisely and prudently, and the British could also be trusted because of their original contributions and "special relationship" with the United States. Leaders of other states could not be trusted to have a "finger on the nuclear trigger." French and other "Gaullists" claimed that American power should be judged by the same standards as the power of other nations. This attack on America's conception of her own special political virtue in the use of power made the American dispute with General de Gaulle particularly bitter.

A related aspect of the double standard Americans apply to national power is the ambivalence of Americans toward violence. Americans dislike—even abhor—violence. They claim with all sincerity to be a peace-loving people. Yet, like the crusaders of old, Americans, with full faith in the righteousness of their cause, readily resort to excessive violence to compel conversion to that cause; Americans resort to the violent use of power with genuine reluctance, but once the decision to resort to the use of force is made, all sense of proportion seems to disappear. The revolution in weapons technology has imposed some limits on the unrestrained use of force but, as Stanley Hoffmann notes, they are externally imposed and do not come spontaneously from within the American approach to war.[23]

Examples of excessive violence resorted to by the United States are found in domestic as well as in foreign affairs. In foreign affairs, the clearest example is, of course, Vietnam and, later, Cambodia. The unrestrained bombing of North Vietnam, which was President Nixon's response to the suspension of the Paris peace talks in December, 1972, is a particularly striking example of a lack of proportion. One of the major criticisms most frequently leveled at American policy in the Vietnam War by observers, who otherwise supported American aims, was the flagrant violation by the United States of the principle of proportionality.

4. *Pragmatism.* Another feature of the American style noted by many astute observers is pragmatism.[24] American pragmatism is of a special kind. It does not assume that ideological ends are unimportant, as pragmatism in the British tradition does. It is far more ideological and it grows out of the special American sense of political virtue. It assumes that ideological ends, however important, are inappropriate subjects of debate because they will be readily agreed upon by men of good will. American pragmatism assumes a consensus upon ends. It focuses policy debates on means rather than ends. As Kenneth Kenniston has put it, "Ours is a how-to-do-it society, and not a what-to-do society."[25] Again, it is Stanley Hoffmann who summarizes the connection of this attitude with the realm of foreign affairs when he says, "this type of pragmatism works satisfactorily in domestic affairs where the belief in agreed goals is an accurate reflection of reality, but it is inappropriate in foreign

affairs for there is no consensus on goals among nations—even allied nations."[26]

American pragmatism leads to an engineering approach to problem-solving or what Hoffmann calls "skill-thinking." This approach is characterized by the search for mechanical solutions, the substitution of organization and reorganization for political analysis, and the quest for efficiency and quick and visible solutions.[27] The old saw about the college faculty which, when told the second coming of Christ was imminent, decided to establish a committee to study the matter, is humorous precisely because it is an extreme reflection of a more general tendency of Americans. The efforts of successive American Presidents since the war to "solve" the "problem" of the Department of State by sweeping reorganization[28] or the many reorganizations of the American foreign aid program are more realistic, if less humorous, reflections of the same tendency.

No single aspect of policy better illustrates the effects of pragmatism and the engineering approach than America's activities in the field of international organization. After World War I, when Americans rejected membership in the League of Nations, they shared Wilson's conviction that the "problem" of war had been "solved" by the creation of the League machinery. They watched with a dismay that only strengthened their suspicion of European power politics as that machinery fell into disuse and finally into uselessness. After World War II, Roosevelt and Truman were determined not to suffer the same fate as Wilson. With haste, they devised makeshift solutions to the genuine problems of the United Nations Charter while the wartime coalition was still intact under the pressure of war. Once again, Americans placed their hopes for postwar reconstruction and for the avoidance of future war on the machinery of international organization. When it became apparent that the postwar world was one in which the United Nations would play only a peripheral role in the maintenance of international peace and security, Americans lost interest in the machinery which had "failed" them. Though they continued to support the United Nations financially and rhetorically, it ceased to be a central factor in the development or implementation of American foreign policy. Instead, American policy-makers turned to other mechanistic solutions such as the creation of formal alliance organizations like NATO, SEATO, and the OAS. None of this is said to condemn international machinery per se; it is necessary to the transaction of the business of international politics. Rather, it is noted to point out the tendency of Americans to hold an exaggerated faith in the ability of political machinery to resolve difficult national and international problems and to search for solutions first through mechanistic engineering. Since such faith is exaggerated and often misplaced, it frequently goes unrewarded. The resulting frustration contributes to the often-observed gyrations in the popular mood and in that of policy-makers.

These are examples of what Hoffmann calls "skill-thinking." He finds it most pronounced in the tendency of American policy-makers to think strategically. The heavy focus on strategic considerations leads to policy-making which ignores crucial political factors because they are not easily subjected to the engineering approach. Strategic and technical thinking become substitutes for political judgment.

In policy-making, pragmatism and the faith in the engineering approach leads to improvisation, the tendency toward artificial separation of policy areas, and the absence of long-term planning. The anti-planning bias of American pragmatism is illustrated by a conception of foreign policy which is primarily concerned with crisis management. A conception of policy as moving from crisis to crisis emphasizes the impromptu nature of policy-making and implies a separation of policy areas.

Students of the Department of State as well as students of other policy-making agencies have long commented on this tendency toward improvisation in policy-making. The fate of the

Department's effort toward long-term planning in the postwar period dramatically illustrates the pervasiveness of the pragmatic mind in America. With much fanfare, the Department created the Policy Planning Staff during Secretary Marshall's tenure in the late 1940s. Some of the best and most experienced individuals in and out of the Department have served on its staff. Its avowed purpose was to do the long-term planning which had previously been neglected. However, almost all who have been connected with the Policy Planning Staff testify to its failure to achieve that goal, except briefly during the Acheson tenure as Secretary. When it was devoting itself to long-term planning, it discovered it was divorced from, and considered irrelevant by, the rest of the Department. More often, however, members of the Planning Staff found themselves being pulled away from planning by the more immediate demands of crisis diplomacy. During the Kennedy administration the Department gave up the effort to establish a separate policy planning organization in a central role. Even in the Bureau of Intelligence and Research (INR), whose purpose is not policy planning and where the perspective on events is broader than in the more pressured operational bureaus, many officials feel that they are ignored by the rest of the Department. A recent decision of the Department to let INR bear the lion's share of the personnel cuts imposed on the Department by the Nixon administration suggests that their impression is shared by the higher echelons of the Department. Experience with the Policy Planning Staff approach is a key indicator of the consequences of American pragmatism.

If pragmatism makes planning difficult, it also generates an impatience to see positive results of policy. Impatience is, of course, directly related to the preference of Americans for the creation of machinery; machinery is at least visible and gives one the sense that something has been done about the problem. There is, however, another side to this coin. If results are not achieved at once, impatience contributes to the demand that some other policy be improvised which will "solve" the problem quickly. The reaction to American foreign-aid policy is an excellent case in point. The enormous and speedy success of the Marshall Plan for assistance in the economic reconstruction of Western Europe after World War II created expectations of equally speedy results from the application of American aid to other parts of the world. When such results were not forthcoming, frustrated critical voices were raised within the foreign policy establishment as well as within Congress and among the informed public.

Another implication of American pragmatism is the tendency to oversimplify complex problems. Impatience, improvisation, and the emphasis on the speedy search for solutions imply that problems must be reduced to their simplest form if they are to admit of such solutions. Their simplest form is often over-simplified. The tendency—especially pronounced during the Truman and Eisenhower administrations—to see the world in terms of free versus Communist is perhaps the clearest example of such oversimplification. To let the Communist or non-Communist character of any revolutionary movement dominate the search for policy is to oversimplify the enormously complex forces at work in any revolution; yet that very oversimplification has led American policy-makers down many a garden path to disaster, including the disaster in Vietnam. But this is only the broadest of the oversimplifications which have influenced policy-makers in the American government. A similar one is the assertion—widely articulated during the Truman administration—that poverty is the breeding-ground of Communism and that a measure of economic well-being is the best deterrent to indigenous Communist success.

Finally, pragmatism and the preference for mechanical solutions leads to a kind of anti-intellectualism and an ambivalent attitude toward expertise which has characterized American policy-making through the years. If common sense is the preferred method in the search for solutions to problems, then years of study and specialized knowledge contribute nothing to an ability to find appropriate solutions. It is a short, but unfortunate, step from the belief of democratic egalitarianism that all men are equal before the law to the notion that all men's ideas have equal merit, and that all men are equally qualified to formulate foreign policy or any other policy. Thus, the intellectual and the expert are suspect if they have too large a role in policy-making. Reactions in many parts of the country to the "intellectuals" who surrounded Roosevelt and Kennedy demonstrate the strength of the anti-intellectual bias in the American character. This predisposition is not necessarily blameworthy. On the contrary, anyone who has served on a college faculty is likely to feel that William F. Buckley's assertion that he would rather be governed by the first two thousand names in the Boston telephone book than by the Harvard faculty contains a germ of wisdom. We simply point to the tendency of Americans to be suspicious of intellectuals and experts who are important in the formulation of foreign policy.

Coupled with suspicion, there is a grudging respect for the expert who, in an increasingly complex society, can sometimes make things work and always provide an explanation. There is a long-standing tendency to defer to the judgment of generals in time of war even when the decisions are of overwhelming political importance, as was the case with so many decisions during World War II. Still, Americans, including Presidents, find themselves ill at ease with intellectuals and experts and unable, since there are no agreed-upon guidelines, to know how and when to use their expertise.

5. *Optimism.* Americans are an optimistic people. Optimism is, of course, intimately related to the other characteristics of Americans which we have already discussed, especially the sense of moral superiority and the pragmatism which characterize the American approach to the world. If America is unique in its political virtue, presumably it is bound to prevail.

Americans expect success in whatever they are doing. They are fond of the expression, "The difficult we will do tomorrow, the impossible may take a little longer."

Stanley Hoffmann has captured this predisposition vividly:

> *Problems other nations' leaders would consider insoluble, issues they would leave to the mysterious resources of time, foreign upheavals which they would want to stay away from—these are seen as America's business. The buoyant optimism that worked miracles at home propels Americans abroad, yet the failures of these well-tested tools to do abroad the job they performed at home exposes Americans once again to frustration, especially since their pragmatic approach often excludes the long-range vision that either would give them greater finesse in the use of the tools or would tell them that they need not and cannot be used.*[29]

As a corollary, nothing frustrates Americans more than failure because it contravenes their expectations. American reaction to the United Nations is a case in point. Americans entered the postwar world with excessively optimistic expectations about the role the United Nations could play in resolving the serious problems of adjustment to and maintenance of peace. When those optimistic expectations were unfulfilled, they found themselves frustrated to the point of indifference by the role which the United Nations could play. A similar frustration marked the gradual awareness that the war in Vietnam, contrary to the optimistic expectations which were continually voiced and believed during the early part of that war, could not be won at an acceptable cost. In their frustration, Americans often turn inward in search of a villain-of-the-piece. We noted in Chapter 1 that this was the case with American reaction to Vietnam. Frustration attendant upon optimistic but unfulfilled expectations can result in wild gyrations of policy.

THE INTERNATIONAL SETTING OF AMERICAN FOREIGN POLICY

American foreign policy is limited and conditioned by facts of international politics partly beyond the control of American policy-makers. The international setting, in which the decision-maker must work, informs his deliberations, shapes his decisions, defines his options, and often determines the success or failure of the policy adopted. When Americans assumed the center of the international arena in the aftermath of World War II, they found an international environment very different from that which had characterized the preceding three centuries.

The world we live in and the world in which American policy-makers function is a revolutionary world. There are almost as many formulations of the revolutionary characteristics of our age as there are commentators on them.[30] For our purposes, three basic changes or revolutions, occurring simultaneously, are crucial: the anti-colonial revolution, the technological revolution, and the revolution in the power relations of international politics.

The pre-1940 world was one of relatively few nation-states and was largely confined to the European continent. Most of the rest of the world was, from a political point of view, an appendage of Europe. Much of it was ruled directly by the European powers and, with the exception of the United States and Japan, those areas which were not were so small, so poor, or so lacking in power as to be all but meaningless in the international arena. There were indications of change. The Japanese shocked the world by defeating a great European state, Russia, in the Russo-Japanese war of 1905, an accomplishment that had previously been inconceivable. In some of the colonies of the European states, there were the beginnings of independence movements. The United States, as we noted in Chapter 3, was commercially active throughout the world. None of these facts altered the essential Europe-centered nature of international politics.

World War II changed the situation. It destroyed the former ascendancy of Europe and the possibility of European resistance to a great wave of anti-colonial revolutions which swept country after country in Asia and Africa to independence. Twenty-five years after the end of the war, the number of nation-states in the international system had more than doubled. By 1973, there were 135 purportedly sovereign nation-states which held membership in the United Nations and several others—Bangladesh, the two Koreas and Vietnams —played important roles in the international system. Most of these new states were poor, self-conscious, and nationalistic. They had acquired independence after sometimes violent and protracted, sometimes relatively easy and quick, struggles for freedom from colonial rule by European powers. They assumed independence with a determination to play a significant role in international politics. Furthermore, their new leaders largely believed that their states' absolute or relative poverty was attributable to the fact that former colonial masters had systematically exploited them for the economic benefit of the metropole.[31]

By and large, the leaders of these new states entered the international system determined to disregard the priority of the Cold War in international politics and to dispute the influence of the former colonial powers whom they held responsible for the exploitation which their states had suffered as colonies. They were determined also to secure their fair share of the world's wealth and power. However, they found that they had few resources with which to press their claims. One of the few resources they did have was a vote in the United Nations equal to that of any other state and many of them focused their attention on gaining influence in that organization. Beyond this effort, it was apparent their strength lay in numbers, but the exercise of that strength required organization and unity. Attempts have been and are being made by these states (variously called "emerging" or "developing" or "underdeveloped") to establish the unity and organizations necessary to make their voice heard effectively. By the mid-1970s several of these efforts had foundered, though the successful example of the Organization of Petroleum Exporting Countries (OPEC) illustrates the importance of these states and their potential for organization. The existence of these new states and their potential effectiveness in organizing are significant factors in the international environment in which American policy-makers work.

The anti-colonial revolutions have often captured the imagination of Americans, both at the citizen level and at the policy-making level. Understandably so, since several were partly inspired by the successful anti-colonial revolution of the Thirteen Colonies against the British Crown and by the prophetic sermons on self-determination preached in Europe and America by President Woodrow Wilson.

Though the anti-colonial revolutions and the related revolution of rising expectations may have considerable long-range importance in the international system, the technological revolution and the revolution in power relations, mentioned earlier, have had far greater immediate impact.

An important part of the technological revolution is in the area of communications and transportation. It is now possible to deliver a nuclear warhead on a target half-way round the globe in a matter of minutes. Twenty years ago it required hours and often days to deliver a comparatively small-yield bomb across oceans and continents. Whole armies can now be transported from the United States to Europe with less difficulty then it took to transfer the allied armies from England to the Continent for the Normandy invasion in June, 1944. Furthermore, the techno-logical revolution has made it possible to activate weapons from afar, to direct them with precision from great distances, and to detect enemy weapons with ever-increasing speed and accuracy.

As a result, the nature of weaponry itself has also changed dramatically. One 20-megaton nuclear bomb, exploded on the ground of Columbus Circle in New York, would destroy nearly all of Manhattan with its severe blast damage. Blast damage would be felt through most of New York City and fires would be raging over a circular area with a diameter of 36 miles, reaching to Connecticut, New Jersey, and far out on Long Island. The weapons of war have become too powerful to help achieve reasonable goals. Moreover, the development of defensive weapons capabilities has lagged far behind the development of offensive weapons. Thus, not even the superpowers have developed defensive systems which will insure the survival of their nations in the face of an all-out strike by the other side. All nations are fully vulnerable and this fact has altered the calculations of warfare. Despite their powerful and awesome weapons, the superpowers are deterred from attacking by the realization that they cannot destroy the second-strike capability of their adversary and are vulnerable to damaging retaliation for their initial attack.

The third revolution, in the power relations of international politics, ensues from the dominance of offensive over defensive weapons in the contemporary period, which has substantially reduced the capacity to make effective use of powerful weapons in the pursuit of international political goals. It follows that the very possession of nuclear weapons by both superpowers has had the opposite effect on their capacity to act from what would have been expected. Their power may be great but it is far less "super" than the power of their weapons would indicate. The gap between the superpowers and the middle powers and even the small powers is far less significant than would appear to be the case on superficial analysis. For the United States—and for the Soviet Union as well—this revolution in the power equation serves to limit freedom of action in the international sphere. The paradox of modern weaponry is that the enormous capabilities of each superpower are essential for nuclear deterrence in the modern world. But these enormous strategic capabilities are nearly irrelevant to the numerous relationships of each superpower with other countries. Thus a staggering investment of resources is required by each superpower; the pay-off is to be found only in a narrow—albeit crucial—area of their relations. In the broader and more immediate issues of international politics, their possession of enormous military power becomes less and less relevant, though it remains the central background factor without which the fragile stability of the international system might be even more in jeopardy.

These revolutions have contributed mightily to the development of an international system with characteristics enormously different from those of the pre-World War II international system. This transformed system is the milieu in which American decision-makers work. Among its chief characteristics are: (1) a tenuous balance between conflict and cooperation in which there is neither war nor peace; (2) a bipolar overlay to the international system; (3) the slow transformation of the traditional nation-state; (4) the accelerated democratization of international politics; and (5) an enormous increase in the pressures of time and complexity in decision-making.

The postwar revolutions have blurred the once-sharp dividing line between war and peace. American decision-makers find themselves operating in a world where there is neither all-out war nor stable peace. In relations between the superpowers, the absence of both war and peace led to the development of the Cold War. It is important to note that with the Cold War came the notion of implacable hostility between the superpowers and the military preparations impelled by that notion. Both societies organized and mobilized themselves for a war that has not yet directly occurred and the danger of which seems to be receding, at least moderately. The implications of such a mobilization for these societies and for their patterns of decision-making are still with us in the form of increased governmental authority, procedures for the allocation of resources, and tolerance levels for diversity of opinion.[32]

Moreover, in the aftermath of World War II, and the destruction wrought by it, the Cold War inevitably took on a bipolar character in which the events of international politics and the policies of states were defined and evaluated in terms of their impact on the power positions of the two giants of the international arena. Little else mattered. As the destruction of the war was repaired and as the revolution in weapons technology led the superpowers to restrain one another, the international system began to take on the more multipolar character which is familiar today. Much of the earlier bipolar character of the international system remains and this concept of the world still carries considerable weight in the analyses conducted in the foreign offices of nations. It still leads statesmen—and perhaps American statesmen more than many others—to judge international events and plan international strategy in light of Soviet-American relations. But the more multipolar character of the contemporary era has complicated the considerations of international policy. Policy-makers must now give greater weight to the impact of policy on other states, especially the potential superpowers of China, Japan, and Europe, which, in turn, have developed the strength and the will to act with greater independence of the wishes of the superpowers.

If the line between war and peace is blurred in relations between the superpowers and the potential superpowers, it is perhaps even more blurred at other levels. The absence of war in the last three decades has in no way signified the absence of fighting. On the contrary, the period has been extremely violent, but violent in a way that does not fit the traditional and legal categories of war.

Chief among these new forms of international violence are guerilla or partisan warfare and international terrorism. Guerilla warfare was waged prior to the end of World War II, but it became increasingly important in the aftermath of war. It is to some extent a product of the anti-colonial revolution. It is practiced frequently, though not exclusively, in nationalist struggles for independence from foreign or foreign-dominated rule. Its practitioners do not respect the classic rules of warfare. They live off the countryside thereby making lines of supply less important than in conventional war. They are not respectful of international boundaries; thus fighting fronts in the conventional sense have no meaning to them.[33] Those who battle guerillas using conventional approaches to war place themselves at a serious disadvantage. It has proven difficult for established nation-states, including the United States, to succeed against guerillas.

A novel and specialized form of guerilla warfare is international terrorism, a product of the technological and anti-colonial revolutions. The terrorist, able to travel easily and often to gain access to supposedly secure places, unconcerned for his own safety, and committed to the ideal for which he is fighting, brings havoc, destruction, and death to his enemy and to the innocent alike in order to seize the spotlight which the mass media automatically places at his disposal. Terrorism has not been confined to the post-World War II era; one has only to recall the assassination of Archduke Francis Ferdinand of Austria in Sarajevo which triggered World War I to realize its importance in an earlier era. But the revolutions previously discussed have moved it from the level of isolated event to part of the international environment which confronts decision-makers all over the world. The international violence which has typified the last three decades is new—unknown on this scale before—and fostered by recent revolutionary movements. As a new phenomenon, it is more troublesome to statesmen who are unable to activate relatively standardized responses to it.

Another characteristic of the international system is the slow but decisive change in the scope and functions of the nation-state. The boundaries of the nation-state were a casualty of the technological revolution. Basic changes in weaponry, communications, and transportation wiped away the military, ideological, and informational boundaries which had formerly enclosed the nation-state. The revolution in technology, and the industrial revolution which preceded it, destroyed the self-sufficiency of the nation-state. The concepts of sovereignty and territorial inviolability have lost much of their meaning.[34] Such concepts are still characteristic of the thinking processes of policy-makers but their significance has been transformed. The argument is not that nation-states are obsolescent as the critical units of foreign policy analysis. With apologies to Mark Twain, the news of their death has been greatly exaggerated. Instead, the claim is that the nation-state, the basic element of the international political system, has been transformed by the revolutions of our time; it is not the same phenomenon that dominates the documents and texts of diplomatic history. In the international system, changes within the nation-state have enormously increased the interdependence of states. This interdependence is singularly incompatible with the classic notion of the sovereignty of the nation-state, yet it is the reality with which every student of the international political environment must live and work.

Another dramatic change in the foreign policy environment is the accelerated democratization of foreign policy. In an earlier era, foreign policy was the preserve of foreign offices and they, in turn, were in the hands of a national elite. The public was insulated from foreign policy decisions and largely from the effects of those decisions. Foreign affairs was considered by many public figures to be too complicated and too sensitive to allow public involvement. Even in Britain, where the evolution to democratic government was more gradual and sustained than in almost any other country, the extension of democratic control to the foreign policy sphere came late.[35] Today, in both Britain and the United States, "elitists" argue that the sensitivity of foreign policy calculations make them less suitable for the usual methods of the democratic process than other areas of government policy.[36] Regardless of the arguments for or against popular participation in the making of foreign policy, the fact is that the revolutions we have described have made the public more intimately concerned with, affected by, and desirous of control over foreign policy than was true in an earlier age. Foreign policy and international politics have become increasingly subject to popular participation.

The technological revolution and the substantial resources required for the execution of a vigorous foreign policy have made publics more inclined to, and desirous of, playing a role in foreign policy formulation than ever before. This, in turn, has provided spokesmen for alternative foreign policies with the incentive to appeal to the public over the heads of their leaders, regardless of whether such spokesmen are part of the domestic political opposition or are foreign political leaders. Similarly, decision-makers now feel compelled to take their case to the people in ways which were not formerly thought necessary, and to accept some of the limitations placed on their actions by public opinion. The effects of world public opinion are usually exaggerated, but, significant of the change in times, the mere mention of such a phenomenon as a "public" opinion forty years ago would have appeared ludicrous. Now, though it is still of minimal importance, it has at least become a factor which must be considered in policy-making.

Finally, all of these changes and the revolutions which undergird them have combined exponentially to overwhelm policy-makers, intensifying the press of time and complexity of their tasks. The problem of juggling the myriad factors that go into policy-making and effects that come out of it has, as we remarked in Chapter 2, become much more vexing.

CONCLUSION

Both American national character and the international setting in which American policy-makers act condition the options open to them and create predispositions for certain types of action and for certain choices.

The emphasis Americans put on material success and the dominance of private over public values, their sense of political virtue, their ambivalence toward power and violence, their pragmatism and optimism—all of these traits of the American national character combine to set Americans apart from the nationals of other countries. They condition the perceptions of policy-makers and citizens alike about policies and events in other countries. They are a barrier to understanding the motives and actions of others and yet are vital to a full understanding by foreigners of the actions of the United States. These traits are the wellspring, the impetus for much of American policy—for its humanitarianism, its generosity, its concern, but also for its arrogance, its lack of proportion, and much of its tendency to intervene in the affairs of other states. They are among the natural inclinations which policy-makers consciously or sub-consciously feed into their deliberations on foreign policy. As such, they are essential to an understanding of the end product—the foreign policies of the United States.

The international setting is the stage on which American policy-makers work. It is a revolutionary setting in which historical precedent offers little guidance. Revolutions in the nation-state system and in technology have created a new situation—a situation of neither war nor peace, of bipolarity in the face of increasing assertiveness by middle-ranking powers and even small powers, of accelerated democratization of foreign policies, and of unprecedented complexity in the task confronting decision-makers.

5. The President Makes Foreign Policy

"I make foreign policy."
                    —Harry S. Truman

At this juncture, the question arises as to whether anybody "makes" foreign policy in the United States when so much seems determined by national experience, culture, power, and the international setting. These factors, and institutional and political factors to be discussed in later chapters, are powerful restraints on decision-makers and narrow the range of choice in foreign policy-making substantially. But they should not be seen only as restraints. They are also the basis a skillful policy-maker uses to gain his objectives. They not only limit; they provide opportunities. A policy-maker may consider these factors limiting and accept what he perceives as pre-determined, or he may view these factors as resources by which he can seek to alter existing foreign policy. The policy-maker whose response to these factors is most important is the President of the United States. Whether he sees them as limitations or opportunities; uses them effectively or flails ineffectually against them; controls them or is controlled by them, will largely determine whether historians judge him a strong or weak President. Legally and historically, the making of foreign policy is centered in the hands of the President.

Of course, the limits to presidential power are important. Theodore Sorenson, an intimate aid to President Kennedy, listed some of these limits. The President, he said, is constrained by the limits of permissibility, prior commitments, and the availability of resources, time, and information.[1] These limits are sufficiently imposing that Richard Neustadt, a distinguished academic student of the Presidency has pictured the occupant of that office to be a beleaguered man, buffeted on all sides by pressures over which he does not have full control.[2] Many Presidents have reinforced this view, bemoaning their inability to control foreign policy and its implementation,[3] a subject about which we will have more to say in Chapters 6, 7, and 8.

On the other hand, many Presidents have expressed exactly the opposite view. To the question of who is responsible for foreign policy, President Truman, with whom Neustadt worked for a time, had a ready answer for a visiting group of Jewish War Veterans while discussing the office of Chief Executive, "I make foreign policy."[4] The same conviction was colorfully if indiscreetly registered by Theodore Roosevelt when he told a university audience, "I took the canal zone and let Congress debate, and while the debate goes on the canal does also."[5] It was Truman, once again, who provided the most memorable explanation for why the President's position is generally considered paramount in the making of foreign policy, this time in the form of a small, hand-lettered sign on his desk which informed visitors, "The buck stops here."

Truman was right: *The President makes foreign policy.* But to that dictum, we must add an important qualifier, *when he wants to.* Time, of course, does not permit him to take a personal interest in every foreign policy question. Furthermore, his power and prestige are not inexhaustible resources. If he chooses to use them to achieve one foreign policy goal, he will find them altered and possibly less serviceable for gaining another foreign policy goal. Nonetheless, it is clear that the resources of the Presidency provide the President with a nearly free hand to make foreign policy on that range of issues to which he attaches high priority and on which he is willing to expend his resources.

Though he can, with few exceptions, impose his will on the foreign policy machinery in the United States and make American foreign policy, it does not follow that a President has similar freedom to work his will around the globe. The international setting and the actions of other states set limits within which the objectives of foreign policy can be realized. To venture outside these limits, through choice or inadvertence, is to court disaster. But, within the United States, it is primarily the President who has defined what is possible and made the choices.

With power goes responsibility. All Presidents since Washington have assumed that their office carries the ultimate responsibility for conducting American foreign relations, a position repeatedly dramatized in moments of crisis. A familiar and fully documented instance of ultimate presidential responsibility in the making of foreign policy was President Kennedy's role during the Cuban missile crisis when, according to Arthur Schlesinger, Jr., the President "never had a more sober sense of his responsibility." This attitude was ironically conveyed by his remark to a friend, "If it weren't for those people that haven't lived yet, it would be easy to make decisions of this sort."[6]

The Cuban missile crisis is only the best known among numerous examples, dotting the memoirs of Presidents and their advisors, of the exceptional authority assumed by the Chief Executive in moments of crisis, periods when momentous issues of war and peace are involved and in which the President is rarely challenged by the general public. The phenomenon of ultimate presidential responsibility is scarcely a post-World War II phenomenon. President McKinley, sleepless, haggard, and susceptible to tears on the eve of his intervention message to Congress in 1898 leading to the Spanish-American War, later claimed that he had had "responsibilities enough to kill any man."[7] Lincoln and Wilson and others, excluding Teddy Roosevelt who relished his responsibilities, would have voiced similar sentiments. But it is true that the frequency of decisions involving war and peace has increased significantly since World War II. Decisions a President makes in these circumstances, with a few rare and relatively recent exceptions, contribute to the strengthening of his public support and, at the same time, the reinforcement of his primacy in the handling of American foreign relations.

In this chapter, our first purpose will be to describe the factors which give the Presidency a privileged and dominant position in the conduct of United States foreign policy. Secondly, we will examine the political resources Presidents have customarily used to maintain a position of primacy in the domain of foreign affairs.

Certainly, as a former presidential advisor reminds us, "the President is only one man."[8] He does not enjoy complete authority in making foreign policy but is buffeted by circumstance, oppressed by time, and beleaguered by foreign and domestic enemies, critics, and competitors for influence. According the President ultimate responsibility and the primary position in the conduct of foreign policy, as we do in this book, implies a judgment about his relationship with his "family of advisors," his Cabinet and the bureaucracy, Congress, the press, interest groups, and public opinion. In succeeding chapters, we will turn our attention to these relationships. In this chapter, however, we will confine our discussion to the basis for the President's position as "ultimate decider," "ultimate coordinator," and "ultimate persuader."[9]

It is a widely accepted description of the reality of foreign policy-making that there has been a strong concentration of authority within the Executive during the course of American history, especially during the past three decades. The desirability of this authority, however, has been seriously challenged, primarily since the mid-sixties and the initial escalation of the Vietnam War. This challenge is among the most prominent and potentially far-reaching consequences of the breakdown in the consensus on the purposes of American foreign policy. In the final chapter, we will undertake a less descriptive and more critical reassessment of the Chief Executive's role.

THE CONSTITUTIONAL TRADITION OF PRESIDENTIAL PRIMACY

The tendency for the power of the President to increase in the conduct of American foreign relations, often but not always at the expense of other political institutions, is a long and continuing one, not totally dependent on the behavior of any particular office-holder. The original concept of the "foreign affairs Presidency" within the Constitution is stated concisely; however, in context, it demonstrates the intent of the Founding Fathers to apply the principle of a separation of powers to the realm of foreign policy as to every other function of government, but with significant variation. The President was explicitly assigned in Section 2 of Article II the position of "Commander in Chief of the Army and Navy of the United States, and of the Militia of the several States, when called into the actual service of the United States . . . ." Using their constitutional authority as commanders-in-chief, Presidents have regularly justified their assignment and use of troops "to provide for the common defense." Under the authority of these few words President Lincoln fought the War Between the States, President Wilson intervened in Latin American countries with U.S. troops, President Truman fought the Korean War, and Presidents Kennedy, Johnson, and Nixon sent American combat troops and bombers to fight in Vietnam.

Another major responsibility of Presidents also contained in Section 2, is the treaty-making power, a power assigned solely to the Chief Executive "by and with the Advice and Consent of the Senate . . . provided two-thirds of the Senators present concur." In addition, the President "shall nominate, and by and with the Advice and Consent of the Senate, shall appoint Ambassadors, other public Ministers and Consuls." Furthermore, according to Section 3, "he shall receive Ambassadors and other public Ministers." But applying the principle of separation of powers to foreign policy, the Founding Fathers assigned to the Congress the fundamental responsibility for declaring war—the legal basis for much heated congressional opposition to the Vietnam War—as well as major functions such as "to raise and support armies" and "to regulate Commerce with Foreign Nations . . . to establish an uniform Rule of Naturalization," and sundry other functions indirectly related to the conduct of foreign relations.

If the Constitution and events in successive periods of American history have revealed serious ambiguities in the division of powers between the Executive and Legislative Branches of government, those ambiguities have been expressed differently in debates on control of foreign policy as compared to domestic policy. When Alexander Hamilton argued in support of George Washington's Neutrality Proclamation that the Executive clause of the Constitution was a general grant of power, he was able to support the argument in terms of power politics and national interest. James Madison's response, written at Thomas Jefferson's prodding, claimed that Hamilton's interpretation seemed to "strike at the vitals of the Constitution" and argued for a strict construction of the Executive clause.[10] Yet both Jefferson and Madison, in their own actions, were zealous guardians of Executive power and proved effective in extending presidential control over foreign policy; this was particularly evident in Jefferson's willingness to dispatch special missions, enter into purchase negotiations for Louisiana, and lead the nation to the strengthening of its militia, army, and armaments factories.

Not all Presidents followed Jefferson's example. During the 19th century and the early part of this century, presidential supervision of foreign policy varied considerably according to the temperament of individual office-holders and the presence of crisis situations. The isolationist tradition, often associated with passivity in dealing with other states and the tenure of "weak" Presidents, was at least partially balanced by increasing foreign economic activity especially in Latin America and the Far East, and largely confined to the private sector.[11]

The unmistakable trend, however, accelerating during this century, has been toward strengthening the President's constitutional position as chief diplomat and Commander-in-Chief. This trend has been marked by a series of Supreme Court decisions listed in Table 2.

Besides the historical glimpse provided by Table 2, it is helpful to see the concentration of authority in the Executive Branch as a two-staged process in which the national government first gains at the expense of the states and in the second stage, the Executive gains at the expense of Congress and the Courts. In the first stage, the Court's position was unequivocally stated in *Missouri* v. *Holland,* 1920. In this case dealing with a treaty between the United States and Canada governing the protection of birds migrating from Canada, Justice Holmes firmly argued the supremacy of a treaty and a national implementing statute over a state-sponsored measure to prevent the national statute from being enforced. This position has remained unchanged. One of its most vigorous defenses is in the *Sabbatino Case,* 1964, where the Court asserts that it is "constrained to make it clear that an issue concerned with a basic choice regarding the competence and function of the Judiciary and the National Executive in ordering our relationships with other members of the international community must be treated exclusively as an aspect of federal law." [12]

In the second stage, the Supreme Court established the Executive's ascendancy in its relations with other branches of the federal government, although the congressional challenge, which we describe in Chapter 7, has not thereby been laid to rest.

The Court's position in support of presidential primacy in foreign affairs is most strongly asserted in *United States* v. *Curtiss-Wright Export Corporation*, 1936. In this case, Congress sought to limit a war that was breaking out between Bolivia and Paraguay by granting the President power to prohibit the sale of arms and munitions. The defendant corporation, charged only with conspiring to sell fifteen machine guns to Bolivia, claimed

TABLE 2
CHRONOLOGY OF MAJOR SUPREME COURT DECISIONS ON PRESIDENT'S CONSTITUTIONAL POSITION IN FOREIGN AFFAIRS

Case	Date	Summary of Relevant Ruling
The Prize Cases	1862	President can accord belligerency status to those who attack U.S. and is "bound to resist force by force"
Missouri v. Holland	1920	The treaty power is delegated to the federal government and not reserved to states by the 10th Amendment
U.S. v. Curtiss-Wright Export Corp.	1936	In the international field, Congress may "accord to the President a degree of discretion and freedom from statutory restriction which would not be admissible were domestic affairs alone involved"
U.S. v. Belmont	1937	Executive agreements have the status of law of the land; Executive agreements do not need Senate consent
U.S. v. Pink	1942	Executive's position strengthened in concluding Executive agreements

TABLE 2—Continued
CHRONOLOGY OF MAJOR SUPREME COURT DECISIONS ON PRESIDENT'S CONSTITUTIONAL POSITION IN FOREIGN AFFAIRS

Case	Date	Summary of Relevant Ruling
Banco Nacional de Cuba v. Sabbatino	1964	Courts should defer to Executive discretion only when there are significant implications to the outcome
Zschernig v. Miller	1968	Executive's advice not binding on courts in matters of foreign policy
New York Times Co. v. U.S. (Pentagon Papers)	1971	Various views against the Executive's claim to be justified in seeking a "prior restraint of expression," i.e., to gain an injunction against publication of *The Pentagon Papers*

that congressional delegation of powers to the President was invalid. In the Court's opinion, a sharp distinction is drawn between the powers of the federal government in foreign and domestic affairs. In its extended dicta, it declared, "The President alone has the power to speak or listen as a representative of the nation. He *makes* treaties with the advice and consent of the Senate; but he alone negotiates. Into the field of negotiation the Senate cannot intrude; and Congress itself is powerless to invade it." The delegation of authority by the Congress to the President was duly noted as well as the need to accord wide discretion to the President in the exercise of that authority.[13] Reaffirming this view as late as 1963, the Court upheld the right of the Congress to delegate extensive and only vaguely defined powers to the Executive noting that, where the delegation of powers to the Executive was concerned, Congress had always been permitted to "paint with a brush broader than that it customarily wields in domestic areas."[14]

The liberal construction of the Executive's role in foreign affairs in relation to Congress is not so explicitly stated in the case of the Executive's relation to the courts themselves. Nonetheless, the accumulated jurisprudence suggests that the same considerations apply. *The Sabbatino Case* again merits attention. In this complex litigation dealing with claims based on Cuban decrees expropriating American-owned sugar plantations, the Court says: "the less important the implications of an issue are for our foreign relations, the weaker the justification for exclusivity in the political branches."[15] Careful reading leads to the conclusion that courts should voluntarily defer to Executive discretion in issues with significant implications, a conclusion that is borne out by the Court's behavior. Especially in time of war, the Court has been loath to interfere with the President's prerogatives in foreign policy. It has generally exercised restraint by deferring consideration of a case until the war is over and the point becomes moot. When this is not possible or during peacetime, the Court has taken refuge in the argument that it cannot decide a political question; such questions seem mysteriously to appear more often in foreign affairs than in the domestic arena.

While the concentration of authority in the Presidency is undisputed in relation to other branches of government, its power vis-à-vis the individuals, groups, and corporations of the private sector is not so firmly established. During the Korean War, the authorization granted to the Secretary of Commerce by President Truman to seize and operate the steel mills because an impending strike would impair national security, was overruled by the Supreme Court (*Youngstown Sheet and Tube Co.* v. *Sawyer*, 1952). Again, in the *Pentagon Papers Case*, 1971, the Court refused to sustain the prerogative argued by the Executive Branch whereby the *New York Times* and *Washington Post* would be ‹njoined from further publication of the "History of U.S. Decision-Making Process on Viet Nam Policy." These decisions, however, are limited in their reach and do not settle the larger question of the role of the Executive Branch in relation to private sector overseas activities, an area in which the guidelines of the Court are either lacking or in need of review. Particularly as American business extends its foreign operations, this issue will become increasingly urgent.

RECENT SOURCES FOR THE STRONG FOREIGN AFFAIRS PRESIDENCY

The buttressing of presidential authority by the Supreme Court faithfully reflects a wide range of attitudes and circumstances conducive to the centralization of power in the making of United States foreign policy. Four of these factors deserve special emphasis: (1) the perception of the Communist threat; (2) extension of foreign policy to new areas; (3) the marriage of diplomacy and force in the adoption of a "national security" perspective; and (4) presidential purpose.

1. *The perception of the Communist threat.* From the late 1940s, an operative consensus on the urgency and gravity of the Communist threat existed. The only comparable national obsession was directed against the Axis during World War II and, in that case, did not persist so long nor represent the same degree of concern with an internal enemy expressed during the early witch-hunting days of the Cold War. Different levels of

sophistication about Communism were naturally apparent in different sectors of society. Significantly, much of the strongest anti-Communism was voiced among those most closely involved in the direction of United States foreign policy. Dean Acheson, looking back to the origins of the Cold War, compares the task of those responsible for American foreign policy after World War II to Genesis. "That [task] was to create a world out of chaos; ours, to create half a world, a free half, out of the same material without blowing the whole to pieces in the process." [16]

The analysis of the Soviet threat by Acheson and the entire top level of officials responsible for foreign policy was contained in the still-classified document known as NSC-68, the basic rationale for more than a decade of American foreign policy. According to Acheson, "our analysis of the threat combined the ideology of Communist doctrine and the power of the Russian state into an agressive expansionist drive, which found its chief opponent and, therefore, target in the antithetic ideas and power of our own country." [17] NSC-68, which became policy in April, 1950, was both the basis for educating public opinion about the nature of international Communism and the concrete expression of those attitudes that allowed an unprecedented growth of administrative machinery and Executive discretion in "meeting the threat." As earlier described, the entire system of defense alliances created by Truman and Acheson and extended by Eisenhower and Dulles met only scant opposition in the Congress and throughout the informed sectors of public opinion, as well as from the general public.

The belief that Communism was a real and present danger to national security, once embedded in the national consciousness, was employed to justify virtually every foreign policy action and the immense growth of a semi-autonomous defense establishment. In each instance where appropriations were required, guidelines set by Congress were only general directions given to the Executive; specific implementation of policies was placed within the discretionary boundaries of the Executive. It is instructive to read, almost at random, Administration justification for national security or mutual security (foreign aid) appropriation requests during the 1950s.[18]

Furthermore, the Congress seemed even more eager to grant broad discretion to the President where appropriations were not at issue. One notable example was the Eisenhower Doctrine of 1957 in which the Congress authorized the President to take such action—including military action—as he deemed necessary under the most generally stated guidelines. The Eisenhower Doctrine authorized the President, among other things, to employ the armed forces of the United States "as he deems necessary" to aid any nation in the Middle East requesting assistance against overt Communist aggression.[19] Interestingly, when President Eisenhower got around to using the military intervention clause of his Doctrine in Lebanon in 1958, even these loose guidelines were too strict since there was no apparent communist aggression involved. Undeterred, Eisenhower dispatched the U.S. Marines and claimed the authority of the Eisenhower Doctrine. The Congress, confirming presidential primacy even more than the passage of the Eisenhower Doctrine itself, did nothing.[20]

2. *The extension of foreign policy to new areas.* A second source of Executive primacy originating during the period of the Cold War has been an extension of foreign policy from traditional patterns—exchange of diplomatic missions, visits by foreign dignitaries, regulation of trade—to activities hitherto confined to the private sphere of international affairs or nonexistent. By the end of World War II, basic changes in diplomacy had already evolved from earlier periods.[21] Tweeds and shirtsleeves had displaced powdered wigs, striped trousers, and homburgs. More important, communications and transportation technology had made possible Summit and multilateral, or conference diplomacy. But it is the Cold War which has had most impact on the language and subject matter of foreign policy. The understatement of

traditional diplomacy—"your Excellency," "as an interested Power,"—has given way to overstatement—"aggressors," "imperialists," "capitalists," "Communists"—used in the most deprecatory sense. Diametrically opposed ideological rivalry replaced the shared values of the European-centered world of a half-century earlier and the discourse and gentility of diplomacy suffered accordingly.

Furthermore, the democratization of foreign policy[22] relegated traditional diplomacy, even in its more droll forms, to the sidelines, largely replaced by the more varied strategies of the "battle for the hearts and minds of men." Foreign policy now comprises economic assistance, probably the most important of the new techniques of foreign policy. An information agency was created by the Smith-Mundt Act in 1948; a peacetime intelligence organization, the Central Intelligence Agency, was created by the National Security Act of 1947; scientific and cultural exchanges acquired a political coloration as did performances at the Olympic Games. The Department of Agriculture acquired a substantial role in the conduct of foreign policy with the passage of P.L. 480, The Agricultural Surplus Commodities Act. There were, of course, precedents for each of these new undertakings but they did not presage in scope the size and intent of the Cold War panoply of new foreign policy organizational "weapons." Pulling together all of these disparate and often competing strands of foreign policy could only be done in one place—the office of the President. The Congress lacked the resources and, in any case, was often controlled by the opposition party. Other Executive agencies were in the thick of the fray. Only the President could provide the necessary coherence, though he did not always do so. However, the fact that, despite competing interests, the buck was often passed to the President reinforced his primacy in the field of foreign affairs.

Credit for expanding the scope of foreign policy owes much to Lenin and his followers who eagerly and consciously sought to circumvent existing regimes in states of the capitalist world by fostering strong opposition parties. The techniques and success of these Soviet efforts are described in detail by several scholars who have closely observed Russian foreign policy since the Bolshevik Revolution of 1917.[23] Our concern here is to recognize that presidential primacy in the making of foreign policy has been reinforced by reactions to the policies of other states, notably the Soviet Union. But developing a capability to react also provides a capability to initiate action, one of the compelling reasons for reassessing present-day conduct of United States foreign policy.

3. *The national security perspective.* A third reason for concentration of power in the Presidency is that diplomatic and military perspectives had combined into a single "national security" outlook on the position of the United States in world affairs. The organizational expression of this outlook was the passage of the National Security Act of 1947 and the subsequent elevation of the National Security Council under President Eisenhower to the supreme policy-making body in the government. Associated with this outlook is the national acceptance of a huge permanent military establishment—maintained by the draft or, recently, volunteers—directly contrary to the strong tradition opposing "standing armies," an opposition described by Hamilton as being virtually a national hereditary trait.[24] Adoption of a national security outlook has had the practical consequence of involving the President (and his White House advisors) in the minutia of his role as Commander-in-Chief to an unprecedented degree.

Civilian supremacy in dealings with military leaders has always been a central feature of modern democracies and a strongly supported tradition within the United States. But in the past, Presidents have willingly consigned to the military a wide latitude of responsibility in strategic planning and military preparedness. This was the usual practice of Roosevelt during World War II except for the crucial decision of opening the

Second Front in Western Europe and, in this case, he repeatedly deferred to Churchill. In other instances when Roosevelt involved himself in strategy, he did so by adopting a completely military role and subordinating a guiding political perspective. Unlike Churchill or Stalin, he was rarely able to put military means in step with political objectives.[25]

In recent years, the practical division between the military and the President has drastically altered, a consequence primarily of the perceived need to exercise strict presidential control of nuclear weapons. How far this control should extend is one of those gray areas of national policy. In the 1964 presidential campaign, the Republican candidate, Barry Goldwater, suggested in a speech in Hartford, Connecticut, that NATO "commanders" should be able to use tactical nuclear weapons at their own initiative. The resulting public uproar and deft handling of the issue by Lyndon Johnson, the Democratic candidate, made it appear that only the President could and should be responsible for the use of even the "smallest" tactical nuclear weapons such as the DAVY CROCKETT, a recoilless rifle with an explosive power of "only" 40 tons of TNT.[26] In general, elaborate precautions insure that all nuclear weapons are maintained under rigorous presidential control. Push-button communications networks exist which can be activated to allow the President an opportunity to exercise his command prerogatives; the President's primacy has been extended in an area central to the nation's foreign policy but formerly subject to a greater division of responsibility between military and civilian leaders.

The intimate involvement of the President not only in determining the broad purposes for which military force is to be used but also in deciding tactical means by which those purposes are to be achieved appears to have had a cumulative effect. More extensive involvement by the President has further increased the political component of the use or contemplated use of military force. Nearly every characteristic of nuclear weaponry from the manufacture of nuclear warheads to the numbers of warheads produced, their deployment, their anticipated targets, and their deterrent effect has been subjected to close presidential scrutiny, thereby entering the domain of presidential politics. Moreover, in recent years the tendency of armed conflict to take the form of internal, guerilla wars—possibly a response to the effectiveness of the nuclear deterrent—has also been accompanied by a heightened politicization of these conflicts. In those wars involving the United States, notably Korea and Vietnam, the distinction between military and political decision-making—if it was ever valid—virtually disappeared.

Since the national security perspective has tended to strengthen the President at the expense of military leaders, it is a development that many observers applaud. The antagonism between President Truman and his field commander, General MacArthur, during the Korean War can be viewed from this vantage point as one of the last vestiges of an era in which military commanders enjoyed a comparatively high degree of autonomy. On the other hand, the President's hand is now strengthened in dealing with Congress and the public by the merger of diplomatic and military considerations in requests for appropriations and decisions involving the use of military resources. Critics of contemporary foreign policy often argue that collapse of the traditional American separation of military and political considerations has resulted not in the dominance of political considerations over military—which they would consider desirable—but just the reverse. They argue that the national security perspective has resulted in an increasing acceptance of the dominance of military considerations by civilian decision-makers including successive Presidents. Though this has meant a decline in the role of the professional military man in decision-making, it has brought an increasing militarization to American foreign policy.[27]

4. *Presidential purpose.* The sources of increased presidential authority in the field of foreign relations are not

customarily ascribed to the intent of the office-holder but, instead, to circumstances—the convergence of public attitudes, the challenges issuing from national adversaries such as Communist Russia, and the development of military technology. Presidents and their advisors cannot, however, be viewed as passive repositories of ever-increasing privilege and power. They could consciously resist a concentration of power in their office. Instead they have consistently abetted trends toward centralizing Executive power, the origin of which lies in circumstances they did not create.

One of the most revealing examples of the way Presidents and their advisors shape and use opportunity to increase their authority is the Gulf of Tonkin incident. In August, 1964, President Johnson ordered air strikes against North Vietnam in retaliation for alleged attacks first on the United States destroyer *Maddox* and a few hours later, the *Maddox* and another destroyer, the *C. Turner Joy*. These reprisals crossed an "important threshold in the war" and provided the backdrop for the Gulf of Tonkin Resolution passed by overwhelming majorities in Congress, leaving the President with virtually a blank check in conducting the subsequent escalation of the Vietnam War.[28] Another clear-cut case was President Eisenhower's dogged and successful opposition to the Bricker Amendment, designed, among other things, to limit the treaty-making power of the President by making Executive agreements subject to Senate approval. President Nixon went even further by refusing to discuss his Vietnam strategy even with members of the Congress, much less with the public. Refusal to outline his "peace" plan during the election campaign of 1968, the demurs of his spokesmen when pressed by the House Armed Services Committee in January 1973, and his invocation of "Executive privilege" to prevent so much as the appearance of some of his advisors before congressional committees are cases in point. Moreover, it is clear that President Nixon isolated himself and took little advice, even from within his own administration, before reaching his decision on bombing Hanoi and Haiphong in December, 1972. In addition to extra-presidential sources of increased authority, it is important to count the Presidency and its individual occupants among the reasons for presidential primacy in foreign affairs.

SAFEGUARDING THE PRIMACY OF THE PRESIDENT

Neither recent sources of presidential primacy in the conduct of United States foreign policy nor the judicial support given to the central position of the Executive Branch guarantees the stability of presidential authority. In succeeding chapters, we will survey the various political competitors to the President's position and the constraints from Congress, interest groups, and public opinion that limit the exercise of his powers. Simply to preserve his constitutional position, a President cannot remain entirely aloof or withdrawn but must, as in the case of all recent Presidents, be constantly alert and ready to act.

Depending on the setting, a President plays many roles which frequently involve acting very differently. The President who chairs a Cabinet meeting and relies on the power of persuasion is apt to deal very differently with a group of party leaders who respond more readily to such tangible political resources as promised votes or patronage. Nonetheless, there is some spillover from one role to another and, in the conduct of foreign policy, a President can often make use of the customary political resources of his office.

As so many Presidents have stressed, they are the leaders of "all the people." The popular mandate provides the President with a national constituency. President Truman put it succinctly at a dinner celebrating his birthday in 1954, "I used to say the only lobbyist the whole people had in Washington was the President of the United States ... It is the President's responsibility to look at all questions from the point of view of the whole people."[29]

Related to the President's popular mandate is the aura of the "highest office in the land," which itself is a formidable political resource nowhere better illustrated than in the deferential tone of Justice Felix Frankfurter's correspondence with Roosevelt. The appeal to public opinion, for support in opposing congressional restraints or against successive threats from abroad, is another traditional political resource of Presidents used with varying degrees of effectiveness. Finally, there is the wide but by no means absolute prerogative of the President to organize the Executive Branch according to his own estimation of the most effective means that can be developed to formulate and carry out his programs. We will turn our attention in the next chapter to the organization of the Executive Branch for the conduct of foreign policy and the liabilities, as well as opportunities, it presents to a Chief Executive.

Three political resources available to the President are uniquely part of making foreign policy: (1) secrecy; (2) personal diplomacy; (3) crisis management. While there are analogous methods for maintaining influence in the management of domestic affairs, they do not approach the importance of these three means of pursuing American interests abroad, either in frequency of usage or latitude accorded the President.

1. *Secrecy.* Defense of secrecy in the foreign policy-making process has its origins in Washington's first term of office. His vigorous justification for the privacy of negotiations of the Jay Treaty in a message to the House of Representatives in 1796 offers the same reasons often advanced today for classifying procedures in the foreign affairs agencies of the Executive Branch.

> *The nature of foreign negotiations requires caution, and*
> *their success must often depend on secrecy; and even when*

brought to a conclusion a full disclosure of the measures, demands, or eventual concessions which may have been proposed or contemplated would be extremely impolitic; for this might have a pernicious influence on future negotiations, or produce immediate inconveniences, perhaps danger and mischief, in relation to other powers.[30]

Washington's understanding that the "nature of foreign negotiation" requires secrecy which, in turn, must be guarded even in relations with other branches of government has reverberated throughout much of the diplomatic history of the United States. Washington's claim was approvingly cited by the Supreme Court in the *Curtiss-Wright* case and bolstered the key distinction made in that case between the President's responsibilities in domestic and foreign affairs.

Washington argued the case for secrecy in dealing with other nations and with other branches of government. A contradictory argument appeared after World War I when Woodrow Wilson's idealistic plea for "open covenants openly arrived at," the first of his Fourteen Points, challenged the usual practice of guarding negotiations with other countries in secret. Wilson did not intend negotiations, however, but only the fruit of negotiations to be open. The process of negotiation continues to be a highly secretive business, as President Nixon's handling of the Vietnam peace negotiations so well illustrated. There have been many examples, most notably the Molotov-Ribbentrop Pact of 1939, in which the fruits of negotiation remain secret for more or less extended periods of time.

The crucial question for students of American foreign policy today, as in the past, is the appropriate balance between the presidential need for secrecy in the development of foreign policy and the need of the public and the Congress to have adequate information on which to base a judgment of his performance. Obviously, the premature disclosure of information can be not only embarrassing but positively harmful to the orderly flow of foreign policy-making.

The issue was thrust into sharp relief by two series of events in the early 1970s, one which challenged presidential secrecy and one which extended it. In 1972, two Pulitzer prizes were awarded to journalists who publicly aired classified material: one to the *New York Times* and *Washington Post* for their publication and coverage of the Pentagon Papers and one to Jack Anderson, a syndicated columnist, for his reports on meetings of the Washington Special Action Group (WSAG), a top-level strategy panel assembled during the Indian-Pakistani crisis in late 1971.[31] Evidently, the President no longer has assurance that resorting to secrecy within the Executive Branch will be respected.

At the same time, a presidential confrontation with the Congress over the use of "Executive privilege" was increasingly in the headlines. The doctrine of Executive privilege is an old one by which Presidents have resisted the efforts of Congress to question them or their closest advisors on their actions. Congressional committees have long exercised the right to interrogate members of the Cabinet and their subordinates (they are, after all, statutory officials whose appointments are subject to Senate confirmation) but had been unable to interrogate the White House advisors of the President, for they served him alone and were not subject to Senate confirmation. With the shift of high policy-making toward the White House staff and away from the departments of government—a trend clear throughout the post-war era but most pronounced in the first Nixon administration—congressional desire to "get at" presidential aides became much more pronounced. President Nixon's successful resistance to these pressures—though not without its political costs—represents a defense of the importance of secrecy in foreign policy-making.

The arguments for presidential prerogative in carrying out negotiations in secret and maintaining the confidential atmosphere of the policy-making process are as vigorously advanced today as they were by Washington. Furthermore, the arguments, and the practice of secrecy they defend, provide support for the cumulative growth of presidential authority in the relations of the United States with the rest of the world.

2. *Personal diplomacy.* No stronger statement of a President's role as diplomat has been made than Woodrow Wilson's claim that "the initiative in foreign affairs, which the President possesses without any restriction whatever, is virtually the power to control them absolutely." Acknowledging that the Senate's consent is required to conclude a treaty with a foreign power, Wilson argued that nonetheless the President

> *may guide every step of diplomacy, and to guide diplomacy is to determine what treaties must be made, if the faith and prestige of the government are to be maintained. He need disclose no step of negotiation until it is complete, and when in any critical matter it is completed the government is committed. Whatever its disinclination, the Senate may feel itself committed also.* [32]

These words, written years before Wilson actually took office, were later used as a self-condemnation of Wilson's own failure to guide the Treaty of Versailles ending World War I through the Senate in 1918. Today, however, they stand as only a slight exaggeration of the actual power of the President as chief diplomatist. Even the limitation of Senate consent to treaties negotiated by the Chief Executive has been effectively skirted by increasing reliance on the negotiation of "Executive agreements." These arrangements, which do not require senate approval and, on occasion, are not even made public, are simply agreements between the President and the chief executive of a foreign country. Unlike a treaty, they bind only the executives concerned, not their successors, and may even be terminated by mutual agreement earlier. In addition to by-passing the Senate, they have the advantage, from the President's point of view of being more flexible and permitting the maintenance of greater discretion than is possible with formal treaties.

Most diplomacy conducted on behalf of the United States is carried out through officially designated representatives of the President. At the ambassadorial level, these representatives are subject to direct presidential appointment. Since some appointments are rewards for party loyalty and all require reporting to the President through the Secretary of State (occasionally circumvented as in John Galbraith's letters sent directly to President Kennedy from his post as Ambassador to India), responsiveness to presidential direction is not fully assured. At lower levels, these representatives are either career officers of the Foreign Service or officials of other agencies. As the number of intermediaries increases, the nature of the subject matter becomes more specialized, the link between policy pronouncement and substantive negotiation grows more tenuous, and the information flow becomes less susceptible to control, a President begins inexorably to sacrifice his position of primacy.[33] An obvious and favored method for reasserting it is to engage directly in the diplomatic process or to engage his closest associates in that process. Every President has adopted this method, some much more actively than others.

The most dramatic demonstration of the President's acting as chief diplomatist is the Summit Conference, a practice carried on by the sovereigns of Europe in past eras of aristocratic rule and continued to the present. Summitry restores the initiative in foreign affairs to a President and, despite admonitions that meetings at the Summit may unduly raise expectations, that they provide no alternative forum for resolving intractable issues, and that they needlessly invest foreign relations with superficial glamor, such meetings are certain to continue in the pattern of Roosevelt at Yalta, Eisenhower at Paris, Kennedy at Vienna, Johnson at Glassboro, and Nixon at Peking and Moscow.[34] Summit meetings permit personal evaluation and a "do-it-yourself" type of negotiation to substitute for the anonymity and careful hedging of assessments made within large organizations such as the CIA or the Department of State and the impersonal negotiation of traditional diplomatic machinery.

Each President since Franklin Roosevelt has met at least once at the Summit with his closest Russian counterpart and each President has also figured prominently in meetings with other heads of state or government on frequent occasions. Presidents since World War II have hosted more than 500 state visits from foreign presidents and prime ministers. Before World War I, there had only been 30 such visits.[35] When the President does not meet directly with a foreign leader, he still can seize the diplomatic initiative through the use of personal emissaries, a practice that also has precedents in a dim and distant past, but has no more dramatic illustration than that afforded by President Nixon's reliance upon Henry Kissinger.

Whether directly or through an emissary, a President, therefore, has the capability of seizing the diplomatic initiative in areas of his own choosing. Through press conferences, "background" interviews, foreign policy speeches, "State of the World" messages, personal correspondence, telephone or even "hot line" conferences, calculated "leaks" to the press and sundry other devices, a President seeks to retain the initiative in foreign affairs and to guide diplomacy in the directions he prefers. By means of these techniques, he does not control foreign affairs "absolutely" as Wilson incorrectly argued. Two instances of Anglo-American relations foundering toward crisis, the Suez Crisis of 1956 and the Skybolt Affair of 1962 have been analyzed in depth by Richard Neustadt and show the serious misunderstandings that can arise even with' direct presidential diplomacy operating in a milieu of mutual respect.[36] The techniques of personal diplomacy are, however, a significant added resource available to Presidents for maintaining their preeminent position in the making of foreign policy.

   3. *Crisis: a new testing of presidential primacy.* Crisis diplomacy and management dominate a major part of the record of American foreign relations during the Cold War period surveyed in Chapter 3. Taking into account the Russian challenge in Iran, the Berlin Airlift, the Civil War in Greece from which the Truman Doctrine ensued, the Czechoslovakian coup in 1948, Korea, Suez, Cuba, the Dominican Republic, Vietnam, and the numerous additional conflicts that have captured banner headlines over the past twenty-five years, it appears that crisis has become, paradoxically, endemic to foreign affairs.

   The Presidency has normally been enhanced in periods of crisis. Crisis has tended, at least until recently, to strengthen the President's position in the eyes of the electorate. It is to the President as well as the flag that the public traditionally rallies in the face of foreign threats. President Truman, for example, reversed his standing with the public after the start of the Korean War. Just before the North Korean attack 37 percent of those polled approved Truman's handling of his job and 45 percent did not. A month later, after the attack, 46 percent approved and 37 percent did not. After the disastrous and ill-conceived invasion of Cuba at the Bay of Pigs in 1961, President Kennedy's popular standing reached its highest point, 83 percent, and in 1962, after a steady decline in popularity, Kennedy's standing at the polls after the Cuban missile crisis soared from 61 to 74 percent.[37]

   As one long-time observer of national administrations has remarked, "Crisis is a crucible in which a President and his administration are tested as nowhere else. No other event tries so vigorously the physical endurance, self-confidence, and prudence of the President and his aides."[38] Crises are almost always characterized as unexpected situations thrust upon Presidents. The testing, therefore, depends on the President's accurate perception of the situation and ability to act calmly and reasonably. A president naturally gains respect and popularity by giving the impression of "managing" or keeping control of a crisis situation. The appearance of successful crisis management, however, is rarely conveyed by doing nothing. Expectations that the President will somehow manage a foreign or domestic crisis create a bias in favor of action, doing something to quell popular, and often congressional, concern.

In the best known foreign crisis of the postwar period, the Cuban missile crisis, every element in the situation militated in favor of the President's reacting with more than words to the Soviet dispatch of missiles to Cuba. The cumulative pressures to act, regardless of the customary restraints on a President, are the basis for the steady expansion of his position at the center of foreign policy-making. Similar pressures operate in domestic affairs. The influence of the Presidency leaped during the economic crisis of the early 1930s, particularly in the Hundred Days after Franklin Roosevelt's first inauguration. In domestic crisis, however, a balance of competing groups and political forces often exists, while international crisis usually involve competing national goals and a corresponding muting of domestic conflict.

Despite the propensity to view international crisis as a situation to which the President responds, there is considerable evidence that Presidents also can and do provoke crisis. The conduct of the Vietnam war furnishes repeated instances of presidential involvement on both sides of complex challenge-and-response crisis situations. A dramatic illustration of crisis generation was President Nixon's August 15, 1971, statement suspending the convertibility of the dollar.

There may be a point at which crisis becomes counterproductive for Presidents. Certainly there are indications, many directly related to the crisis atmosphere of the Vietnam War, that the expansion of the powers of the Presidency through crisis management had set in motion countervailing pressures. In recent years, Congress has become the locus of efforts to curb presidential powers, an important development we will examine in Chapter 7. Nonetheless, while expectations for presidential action in times of crisis remain strong, the surest way to curb increasing reliance on the President will likely be removal of the causes of crisis and changing the psychological predisposition to inject crisis considerations into every international situation that involves force.

CONCLUSION

In this chapter, we have emphasized the President's primacy in the conduct of United States foreign policy. Although the debates which preceded the drafting of the Constitution and the Constitution itself provided for foreign policy-making within the context of the separation-of-powers doctrine and created checks-and-balances to prevent the concentration of authority in any single branch of the national government, the Presidency has gradually, but with increased momentum during this century, gained an ascendant position in that area. In a series of decisions, the Supreme Court has lent legitimacy to the President's position.

Added to the Supreme Court's legitimizing imprimatur are a number of recent sources working to strengthen the President's position: the post-World War II concensus on a common enemy, Communism, which lasted until the later 1960s; new forms of diplomacy; adoption of a national security perspective that joins both diplomatic and military considerations in decision-making; and the President's own efforts to increase the reach of his influence. In maintaining his position, the President has relied not only on his customary political resources but also on those peculiar to the foreign policy process: secrecy, personal diplomacy, and crisis management.

The President's office, therefore, is the most formidable institution in deciding what American foreign policy should be, quite apart from its strengths and weaknesses on the domestic scene. There are important qualifications to be made on this assessment, which derive from the President's relations with other institutions and groups involved in foreign relations. Yet, even taking into account the various constraints operative on the President and the reciprocal nature of all influence that we will subsequently examine, it is not difficult to anticipate the issue we will return to in the final chapter: is the Presidency too powerful in foreign affairs?

6. Millstone or Stepping Stone: The Foreign Affairs Bureaucracy

"Because management of the bureaucracy takes so much energy and precisely because changing course is so difficult, many of the most important decisions are taken by extra-bureaucratic means."
—Henry Kissinger

In law and in practice, the President has the primary role in the conduct of United States foreign relations. According to the courts, presidential responsibility extends to all areas of foreign affairs: he appoints ambassadors, he is Commander-in-Chief; he is Chief Executive; he is Chief Diplomat; he takes charge in moments of crisis; he is the focus of congressional and public attention when policies go awry or when they succeed. Since the Constitutional Convention, the vast powers of the Presidency in the area of foreign policy have often been criticized, usually on the grounds that the President was too easily exempt from public accountability and thereby posed a threat to stable democracy.

Yet, as we stressed in Chapter 5, few incumbents have shared the view that too much influence is concentrated in the Presidency. Despite unparalleled political resources, they have often considered their powers too meager to deal with the problems of United States foreign policy. After his third-term electoral victory in 1940, Roosevelt was repeatedly frustrated in his attempts at persuading the country to face the threat of "foreign dictators." In a speech urging "speed and speed now" in boosting war production, he was confronted by a strike among coal miners, bureaucratic lethargy, and constant bottlenecks in reaching his ambitious production goals. Two months after his speech, the lend-lease program to Great Britain was in the midst of a crisis of nonperformance.[1] President Kennedy was regularly disgruntled by the failure of the Executive Branch, especially the Department of State, to respond to his direction. "Giving State an instruction," he remarked, snapping his fingers with impatience, "is like dropping it in the dead-letter box."[2] Presidents apparently do not see themselves as free to do whatever they please in conducting the nation's foreign relations. They feel constrained by tradition, the decisions being made in other countries and other areas of government, their own beliefs, and a vast array of political and social forces not entirely within their control.

When there is general acquiescence in the foreign policies of a President from the Congress, the courts, and the public, when a general consensus prevails in which dissenters are neither sufficiently numerous nor persuasive enough to provoke a serious response from leaders, the institution of the Presidency is the evident beneficiary. In such a situation (American entry into the United Nations, the Truman Doctrine, the Marshall Plan), the traditional system of checks and balances fundamental to the American Constitution has little bearing on foreign policy, unless it be a latent inhibition on the President's choice among various policies because of the anticipated reactions of others.

Nonetheless, even then the President is severely circumscribed in what he can actually do. President Truman, reflecting in 1952 on the possibility of being succeeded by Dwight Eisenhower, wryly described the predicament: "He'll sit here and he'll say, 'Do this! Do that!' *And nothing will happen.* Poor Ike—it won't be a bit like the Army. He'll find it very frustrating."[3] All Presidents have experienced similar frustrations. They are the product of a variety of forces, but, external limitations apart, they mainly reflect the fact that no one man can keep all of American foreign policy under his control. He must have aides to gather information, to think about problems he does not have the time to think about, to canvass alternatives, to carry out his decisions: in other words, he must have a bureaucracy to help him make foreign policy. And the American government provides its President with the most extensive and elaborate foreign affairs bureaucracy in the non-Communist world.

But any bureaucracy is a double-edged sword; it provides the essential assistance to an overworked chief executive, but it also creates and embodies a whole series of problems—management, discipline, loyalty, communication—which must be dealt with if it is to aid rather than hinder, to dispatch rather than delay, to process rather than impede. In reality, such problems are never wholly resolved and much of any President's time is spent in organizing and reorganizing—in managing—his foreign affairs bureaucracy. Every President has chafed under the limits and restraints imposed upon him by the machinery of foreign policy-making.

Several of these organizational restraints are common to all bureaucracies; some are peculiar to the impact of foreign affairs on bureaucratic structures. Paradoxically, organization also makes possible an expansion of the limits of presidential power. Eisenhower, the most organization-minded of modern Presidents, records in his memoirs that "to the young the word 'organization' has little meaning," and that for many adults " 'organization' seems to summon visions of rigidity and machine-like operation, with an inescapable deadly routine and stodginess in human affairs."[4] Eisenhower's own view was that organization is not the "enemy of imagination or of any other attractive human characteristic. Its purpose is to simplify, clarify, expedite, and coordinate; it is a bulwark against chaos, confusion, delay, and failure."[5] The paradox is partly accounted for by the failure of organization to regularly fulfill its purpose, and for the 'bulwark' to be either overwhelmed by or isolated from events and actions which constitute American foreign relations with other nations of the world.

In this chapter we will describe how the President uses his bureaucracy and how he is restrained by it. Our attention will be principally directed at the organization and functioning of the foreign affairs bureaucracy, the ways in which it aids the President in his task, the limits set on presidential action by this bureaucracy, and the various responses by Presidents to these limits.

THE FOREIGN POLICY EXECUTIVE BRANCH

Before understanding how organization can aid or limit a President in the conduct of American diplomacy, it is first necessary to know something about the principal institutional actors who participate in foreign policy-making within the Executive Branch. The next few pages, therefore, contain a brief introduction to the foreign affairs bureaucracy. We have abbreviated the description of Executive Branch institutions involved in foreign affairs because their influence and their structure are so variable, shifting with the issue under consideration and the perceived demands of international and domestic politics.

Institutional actors in foreign policy are numerically about equal to all the agencies of the federal government.[6] Even the Postmaster General has a share of the responsibility for the conduct of United States foreign relations; in fact, his agency is the only one which can negotiate treaties without the Department of State's supervision. One useful way of bringing some order into the extensive foreign affairs bureaucracy is to differentiate those institutions with general competence in all areas of foreign policy from those with competence in only certain areas of specialization. Breadth of competence and experience in foreign affairs does not guarantee preponderant influence in policy-making. In conflicts between specialists and generalists, it is the view of the former group which often prevails. A Department of the Treasury official who has expert knowledge of the intricacies of the Eurodollar market, for example, will probably carry greater weight in making decisions on investment controls over multinational firms in Europe than an official of the Department of State, despite his general familiarity with economic conditions in Western Europe. The distinction between departments with general and specialized competences nevertheless draws attention to the conflicts which frequently exist between expert and generalist knowledge on nearly every foreign policy question.[7]

Among institutional actors with a generalist orientation toward foreign policy, the Departments of State and Defense and the components of the Intelligence Establishment possess a range of competence which extends to every aspect of American foreign policy. A thumbnail sketch of each will acquaint the reader with the main governmental agencies involved in the policy-making process. The Executive office of the President is described in the concluding section of this chapter.

1. *The Department of State.* Originally State was the paramount institution within the Executive Branch of government which was concerned with foreign policy. Its head, the Secretary of State, was the chief foreign policy advisor to the President. Although its importance has declined, State still carries out the routine relations between the United States and other countries, provides staff work for Presidents on the whole range of foreign policy issues, and carries the primary responsibility for implementing decisions made by the President.

The Secretary of State must perform the twin functions of chief foreign policy advisor to the President and operating head of a large department. Often he plays another role as major negotiator with other countries. These functions can reinforce one another. A Secretary who is an influential advisor to the

President and has his confidence may be able to benefit from this relationship and to impose efficient operating procedures on his department and draw on its resources in ways that maintain a high sense of purpose and esprit de corps among its members. Dean Acheson, President Truman's Secretary of State, was the exceptional example of one who merged the advisory and management functions of his position. John Foster Dulles, on the other hand, carefully maintained an effective working relationship with President Eisenhower but sacrificed his administrative role by inadequately consulting his own department and thereby depriving its members of a sense of participation in policy deliberations.

The relationship between the Secretary of State and the President is a peculiarly personal one. Within the Department, however, there exists a highly structured bureaucracy. Below the Secretary are two Under Secretaries of State, one with broad responsibility for "political affairs" and one who serves as acting Secretary of State when the Secretary is unavailable; and two Deputy Under Secretaries of State, one of whom is responsible for economic affairs and the other, for the administration of the Department. A variety of staff aides support the policy work of these individuals who, together, constitute the top echelon of the Department. Below them, at the operational level, the Department is organized into both regional bureaus (European, Inter-American, East Asian and Pacific, African, Near Eastern and South Asian Affairs) and functional bureaus (Economic Affairs, Intelligence and Research, International Organization Affairs, Educational and Cultural Affairs, Congressional Relations, Public Affairs). Each is headed by an Assistant Secretary of State. In the regional bureaus, the Assistant Secretaries are supported by "country directors" who recently replaced the old country "desk" officers and whose job it is to maintain the necessary contact with the American mission in their respective countries and to keep abreast of developments which involve relations with the United States.

With the Rogers Act of 1924, the Department's nonclerical personnel in overseas missions below the Assistant Secretary and ambassadorial levels became members of a professional career Foreign Service recruited primarily by competitive examination. Since then, the Foreign Service has been amplified and extended by a variety of congressional acts.[8]

In 1969, there were about 15,000 U.S. citizen employees in the Department of State, of which roughly 3,500 were Foreign Service officers. Though budgetary problems forced some retrenchment in the early 1970s, especially in the size of overseas missions, the American foreign affairs establishment remains, with that of the Soviet Union, the largest in the world. The United States and the Russian embassies are the largest in most of the capitols of the world. Many observers argue that the foreign affairs machinery of the United States is vastly overstaffed. In an amusingly titled book, *The Foreign Affairs Fudge Factory,* the author asserts that "size is the first problem to attack, and bureaucractic surgery is the answer." He then argues that a "Five-Year Plan" might be adopted in order to trim Department of State personnel by 50 percent or more.[9] Whether this would improve the operation of the Department of State or contribute to a more "successful" American foreign policy is by no means certain, but it does represent a serious suggestion from a competent observer.

Recent Presidents, most notably Presidents Kennedy and Nixon, have tried to place the Department of State in a dominant position in the conduct of foreign policy and to strengthen the Ambassador's supervision of the overseas "country team." Involvement of a vast number of other departments and agencies has made it difficult for State and the Ambassador to fulfill this charge. In many overseas missions of the United States, Department of State personnel are actually in a competitive position with employees of other departments and agencies of the American government.

Whether size, multiplicity of departments and agencies, or commitment to a career service rather than to the President are responsible, it is clear that recent Presidents have found themselves frustrated in their attempts to get State to "take charge." Under President Truman, especially during the period when Dean Acheson was Secretary of State, the Department was the single most important institutional actor in shaping and implementing the transition from World War II to the challenges of the Cold War period. By the Kennedy administration, State had become the target of jibes and cynicism. President Kennedy himself noted that trying to get State to act was like "punching a bowl of jelly."[10] Nor have such frustrations been confined to Presidents. Secretary of State Dean Rusk bemoaned the unwarranted delay involved in State's elaborate clearance process, a process which insures that no answer, however simple, can be given to any question until everybody who thinks he has an interest in the issue has given his "clearance."[11] John Kenneth Galbraith's reflections on his years as Ambassador to India offer several examples of his inability to get so much as a response to his cables from State.[12] The announced intentions of Presidents Kennedy and Nixon upon taking office to restore the Department of State's formerly dominant position in making foreign policy have not yet been realized.

2. *The Department of Defense.* If the postwar years have witnessed the decline of State, they have simultaneously witnessed a sharp rise in the role of the Department of Defense (DOD) in foreign policy-making. Gone are the days of a relatively weak defense establishment sharply divided into departments for each branch of the services and loosely coordinated by a Department of War which was largely uninvolved in foreign policy until war broke out, and then only marginally involved in any decisions other than specifically military ones. The postwar blurring of the formerly sharp distinction between war and peace; the immense political stakes in varied military capabilities; the

increasingly long "lead time" required in military research, development, and procurement; the overwhelmingly military nature of the perceived Soviet threat; and the national security cast of foreign policy thinking contribute to the growing voice of DOD in foreign policy.

The Department of Defense has not been the passive recipient of these new demands. Under successive Secretaries of Defense, but, most notably, under Robert McNamara in the Kennedy-Johnson administrations, DOD has been reorganizing itself to exert a more comprehensive role in the determination of foreign policy. The traditional service rivalries which made the Joint Chiefs of Staff a bargaining committee and the Secretary of Defense little more than an arbiter have been muted by strong Secretaries, congressional legislation, and the creation of the post of Chairman of the Joint Chiefs of Staff, who is appointed by and responsible to the President and is no longer a spokesman for his service. Though much of the old inter-service rivalry remains, DOD today has acquired a single and effective voice in foreign policy-making.

Defense moved much earlier than State to develop expertise outside its own specialty. An Office of International Security Affairs at the Assistant Secretary level gave DOD the capability of developing well-supported foreign policy positions while State was still forced by lack of expertise to defer to Defense on military matters. In a world where the military and political issues are intimately intertwined, DOD gained a great advantage over State, only recently in the process of being redressed by personnel exchanges.

Defense, again under the leadership of Secretary McNamara, developed managerial and budgetary procedures which seemed to improve its efficiency and hence, its role in policy-making.[13] Perhaps defense decisions—so heavily involved with troop commitments, weapons procurement, and resource allocation—lend themselves more easily to the appearance of order, rationality, and cost-benefit analysis than do the less quantifiable and more subtle means of diplomatic discourse. Whatever the reason, DOD's managerial revolution has provided one more stepping stone to increase its importance in foreign policy.

Criticism of Defense, from both Presidents and outsiders, tends to be the exact opposite of the criticisms of State. DOD appears too well-organized, too precise and, to some, too powerful. There is no lack of civilian control here; that has, if anything, grown into an even more firmly fixed principle in the postwar era. But critics argue that the civilian chiefs of DOD are converted to a military perspective on foreign policy, and the growth of Defense's role in policy-making coupled with the decline of State has meant the increasing militarization of foreign policy decisions.

3. *The Intelligence Establishment.* Every government needs information. The quality of its information will often determine the effectiveness of its decisions. Accurate and full information does not guarantee wise decisions but lack of it almost certainly guarantees some foolish decisions. The American government has a multitude of information-gathering agencies of which the most widely known is the Central Intelligence Agency (CIA).[14] But State, Defense and each of the military services have their own intelligence branches. Coordination of these groups takes place under the United States Intelligence Board (U.S.I.B.).

The bulk of the work of these agencies consists of gathering and analyzing information from publicly available sources at home and abroad. The typical CIA employee is *not* in the James Bond image; he is much more akin to the research scholar delving into obscure Soviet and Chinese agricultural journals to glean information about harvests, crop failures, market conditions, and future prospects. Only a small portion of American intelligence is gathered by the "undercover agent," stealthfully creeping through the back alleys of Tangier (or, more likely, Berlin, or

Nicosia) with his coat lapels pulled up and his hat brim down. Even the undercover agent today is typically attached to an American embassy abroad and spends most of his time in routine activities.

The importance of intelligence to foreign policy formulation is only partly in its acquisition; of far greater importance is the sorting, sifting, analysis, and dissemination of the vast quantities of raw data that the intelligence machine gathers. It is at this point that intelligence becomes crucial to foreign policy-making. Every morning, the President receives reports that he can compare with current "National Intelligence Estimates." These reports are designed to keep him abreast of important current developments affecting American foreign policy and national security. The National Estimates are based on contributions from all of the intelligence agencies of the government under CIA chairmanship. They provide the best conjectures available within the government for the benefit of the President and the top officers of government.

Not all Presidents have the same appetite for information. President Eisenhower, it is said, wanted information concisely presented without extended background data unless requested. President Johnson, on the other hand, was eager to have minute details of foreign problems, which led some critics to charge that he lost sight of larger issues.

When things go wrong, no President thinks he has enough information of the right kind. When policy is successful, intelligence gaps don't matter much. This is the continuing dilemma of intelligence gathering and a major reason it is difficult to judge the effectiveness of intelligence agencies.

One aspect of intelligence activities, which usually receives the largest share of public attention despite being a relatively small part of intelligence activity, is covert operations. These operations, mounted by the CIA, include the successful coup in Guatemala in 1954 and the abortive Bay of Pigs operation in 1961.

A key problem in the United States has been one of insuring effective political control over such operations. The secrecy essential to their success vastly complicates the problem of control. In spite of abundant exposés of the CIA, there is little hard evidence that substantial operations have been undertaken without appropriate political control. Even the most spectacular failure—the Bay of Pigs—was approved by the President himself. On the other hand, the narrowness of political control has worried numerous observers. There are well-documented cases of American ambassadors being completely in the dark about CIA operations in the countries to which they were accredited. By their nature, covert operations raise vital issues of defining national security and insuring democratic control in the area of foreign policy, issues not yet resolved in the United States.

Most other governmental agencies have specialist roles in foreign policy. Thus, their participation is limited to specific policy areas. Usually, their domestic responsibilities far outnumber their foreign policy concerns. Among the more important of these agencies are:

The Department of the Treasury—Generally concerned with international monetary flows, the balance of payments, and budgetary allocations for foreign affairs and national security. Treasury has had a major responsibility for international monetary negotiations.

The Department of Commerce—Chiefly concerned with questions of international trade, including the ability of American firms to sell their products abroad.

The Department of Agriculture—Concerned, along with Commerce, with American agricultural trade abroad. Agriculture assumed a much more important role in foreign policy with the passage of P.L. 480 in 1954, establishing a program for the sale of American surplus food abroad. This program is administered by Agriculture and it is now being phased out.

The Department of Justice—Supervises immigration and naturalization, issues visas, and seeks to control the international traffic in "dangerous" drugs.

The Atomic Energy Commission—Supervises the transfer of nuclear materials and information on peaceful uses of atomic energy.

The United States Information Agency—Loosely attached to the Department of State, the USIA supervises American information efforts abroad, including information programs, cultural exchange, overseas libraries, and the like.

The Agency for International Development—Attached to State but with a degree of autonomy, AID supervises American economic aid programs abroad.

The United States Arms Control and Disarmament Agency—A Department of State organization with a key role in negotiations on weapons limitations.

Ideally, the participants listed above would be ranked according to their respective influence on United States foreign policy or, at least, on particular types of policy. To do so, however, would imply a degree of stability in individual and institutional relationships which does not exist. Even study of particular cases fails to reveal constancy in the relative importance of different "inputs" or participant voices in the making of foreign policy.[15] If it were possible to assume some controlling relationship between a particular administrative agency and a policy issue involving its major function, we would be well-situated to describe typical patterns of policy-making. Even this plausible simplification, however, encounters serious difficulties. It is not true, for example, that the military services usually have a preponderant voice in most questions of military policy. The tendency to gauge influence in quantitative rather than institutional terms helps to account for the oversimplified attribution of great influence to men in uniform.[16]

The foreign affairs bureaucracy should not be viewed as a group of cubbyholes on an organization chart with tidy lines of authority flowing from one box to another. When a President assumes office, he confronts a foreign affairs establishment in which dissension, inertia, and conflicting opinion are present to a degree seldom acknowledged by the public; an on-going panoply of foreign policies shaped in the past and little susceptible to rapid changes of direction; and a host of counter-part voices and wills in other states dependent on his influence to a much lesser degree than domestic groups. Within the Executive Branch, a new President occupies by tradition and law a primary position at the apex of a hierarchical decision-making pyramid, but must accept the fact that the hierarchy is a facade concealing a vigorous process, quite different from the electoral politics which has dominated his life for months prior to assuming office.

Coordination of Foreign Policy

A new President usually views the foreign affairs bureaucracy as a set of problems to be attacked, hopefully resolved, and, at least, managed. The overall problem is one of coordinating the disparate participants and their actions into a coherent policy. Presumably, a consistent and orderly foreign policy would be realized if the disparate views and actions within and between government agencies could be harmonized. And why, given the vast political resources of the President, particularly his constitutional role as Chief Executive, can he not achieve this? Once particular explanations for specific difficulties are set aside (such as the failure of a Department of State country director to obtain Pentagon clearance for a cable instructing an embassy to report on a controversial foreign military personality), there are four general reasons for officialdom's failure to reach the degree of coordinated response to presidential policy desired. In these four obstacles to a satisfactorily coordinated policy—obstacles when looked at from the perspective of the White House—we can begin to perceive the organizational limits to the primacy of the President in foreign policy-making.

The *first* of these limits is the *proliferation of participants* in the policy-making process. The time when two men, William Hunter and A. A. Adee, could draft most of the Department of State's outgoing telegrams and provide the basic continuity and coordination of American foreign policy in successive careers spanning nearly a century, can no longer be considered as anything but a quaint circumstance of an irretrievable past.[17]

It is essential to grasp the character of a problem that is easily misunderstood. Lack of coordination of foreign policy is partly a consequence of the proliferation of institutional and individual participants in the foreign policy process. Reform measures to structure and "improve" foreign policy often concentrate, therefore, on the need to reduce the participants involved in making decisions. By reducing personnel, it would then allegedly be possible to reduce the number of "clearances" in other offices, to reduce the number of committees and the number of meetings of remaining committees. The number of reports from the "field" (embassies and other official forms of American representation abroad) could be reduced.[18] Missing in this analysis, however, is an understanding of the transition of the United States to superpower status. Proliferation of participants in foreign policy-making stems from a structural change in the international position of the United States. Increases in personnel and agencies since World War II represent a government's necessary response to a complex world. Proliferation of participants in foreign policy-making creates a problem of coordination, but one which is not assuredly resolved *simply* by reducing personnel.

The *second* limitation on gaining a fully coordinated policy is the *differing constituencies and interests served by Executive Branch agencies.* Government departments do not have electoral constituencies in the same sense as Congressmen but they do develop interests related to the groups most affected by their action. In 1970-71, for example, State and Agriculture clashed over trade negotiations with the United Kingdom. State, wanting to ease Britain's negotiations for membership in the European Common Market, took the line that a temporary disadvantage to American farmers in the British market was a small price to pay for assisting British entry into Europe, from which the British would be better placed to plead for more liberal arrangements for all American trade. Agriculture, however, responding to farm pressures, favored a hard line demanding immediate concessions from Britain which would have complicated that nation's European negotiations. Though State eventually carried the day in this case, it required two White House decisions to make their position stick.

A *third* limitation inherent in the foreign affairs bureaucracy is the *sabatoge of presidential intent*. The undermining of presidential intent by a subordinate is rarely a purposeful act of defiance such as General MacArthur's challenge to President Truman concerning the conduct of the Korean War.[19] Customarily, the problem arises from a difference in perspective, a President addressing himself, for example, to a policy of détente with the Communist world, including increased trade, while an Embassy official in Moscow resists a Russian request to buy a type of precision instrument because the item had previously been placed on a list of goods subject to strategic embargo.

A *fourth* and final limitation is found in the *essential characteristics of bureaucracy*. In a classic essay on the relation of foreign policy to governmental structure and leadership patterns, Henry Kissinger asserts that "the purpose of bureaucracy is to devise a standard operating procedure which can cope effectively with most problems." The criterion of success for a bureaucracy is efficiency, again in the words of Kissinger, "if the matters which it handles routinely are, in fact, the most frequent and if its procedures are relevant to their solution."[20] Leadership is impeded when bureaucracy defines the wrong problems as routine, when it avoids decisions while seeking to make crisis routine, when the efforts of leaders are constantly diverted to internal problems of bureaucracy rather than the problems which bureaucracy cannot assimilate, and when bureaucratic procedures fail to adapt to changes in the events with which they deal. When bureaucracies deal with the unexpected or nonroutine, or when Presidents are compelled to busy themselves with routine problems that have been exacerbated by bureaucratic divisions, the reality of foreign policy-making departs sharply from the tidy administrative lines of authority that appear in organization manuals.

ASSERTING THE PRESIDENT'S POSITION

In reviewing the major organizational limits which inhibit a President from coordinating the foreign policy bureaucracy, we have adopted a perspective not too remote from that of recent incumbents. A President's attempts to deal with the limits set by proliferation of participants in policy-making, differing constituencies and interests of Executive agencies, sabotage of his directives, and the basic characteristics of bureaucracy must be viewed from a different perspective. This is necessary because his response to the foreign affairs bureaucracy has varied according to the office-holder's temperament, background, ambition, and personality; in short, what is so often referred to as a "President's style." A President with a lengthy career as an army general, the background of Eisenhower, for example, will be accustomed to the unique advantages and demands of large-scale organization and will naturally respond in a very different fashion to "staff" problems than a President accustomed to the intense small-group politics of the Senate, such as Lyndon Johnson.[21]

Despite the personal and widely divergent approaches of Presidents to the organizational limits set by the foreign policy bureaucracy, there are a few general responses which all Presidents have evidenced to some degree. Recourse to personal diplomacy, discussed in the previous chapter, or an appeal to public opinion, to be discussed in Chapter 8, are conventional methods by which Presidents can, through their own initiative, seek to reestablish direct control over a particular foreign policy issue. But there are others more directly related to the management of the Executive Branch.

The Presidential Clique

One method by which a President responds to the problems created by an enormous bureaucracy in the area of foreign affairs is to gather a small group or clique of advisors around himself, committed to his interests and ideas and personally loyal to him. The practice is similar to the more formal structuring of ministerial cabinets in France and several other European political systems whereby a newly designated minister appoints a group of aides to assist him in administering his department. The composition of the clique fluctuates in number and, of course, in composition from one administration to another and may even change while a President is in office. It is not a particularly recent innovation; cabals or camarillas or inner circles have long been associated with high levels of government. Its function has been served in monarchies for centuries by court favorites such as Essex or Buckingham or, in an example of the dangers of a total perversion of the advisor's role, by Othello's Iago. What is particularly striking about the existence of a presidential clique in recent years is the continuing need that it evidently fulfills, despite the astonishing growth of the foreign policy bureaucracy staffed with competent individuals to handle the nation's foreign policy. Large-scale organization, it seems, does not encourage the qualities of personal loyalty, confidentiality, and face-to-face relationships upon which the clique is based; in fact, the scarcity of these values in the large group tends to increase their value in the small one. The clique augments the President's "span of control," not in the sense the term is used by students of public administration to indicate the range of reporting subordinates, but rather in the sense of extending the President's voice through a number of individuals whose primary interest is to protect and extend the President's position, not to build or represent an independent base of power.

Within the presidential clique, there is often a single individual who attains a special preeminence in his dealings with the President. Colonel House, until his dismissal, attained this position in dealings with Woodrow Wilson. Among recent Presidents, Harry Hopkins clearly enjoyed the complete confidence of President Roosevelt and was often entrusted with extremely delicate diplomatic tasks, as well as serving as sounding-board and advisor. Theodore Sorensen in part played the role of alter ego to President Kennedy, although Robert Kennedy more effectively provided the President with an opportunity for the complete frankness conducive to a relationship of trust. Henry Kissinger has enjoyed a similar favored position vis-à-vis President Nixon; his diplomatic maneuvers in facilitating President Nixon's visit to mainland China are directly comparable to some of the missions undertaken by Harry Hopkins.

While the prominent position of single individuals in the official foreign-policy hierarchy has been apparent in a number of administrations, the tendency, nonetheless, is for a President to acquire a number of trusted confidants with whom he consults and discusses policy decisions without formal institutional rules or other institutional constraints. Composition of the group follows no regular pattern, although there has been an increased tendency since Franklin Roosevelt's Presidency for the White House staff to increase in size in the domain of foreign affairs and for members of the presidential clique to be formally connected to the President by their positions on this staff. Even this tendency requires qualification. It is especially significant that when the White House staff increased rapidly during the first Nixon administration, forfeiting some of the advantages of the clique, it was then cut drastically, presumably to restore the importance of personal relationships.

Practice has varied enormously. President Truman tended to find his most loyal and trusted advisors within the formal leaderships of old-line agencies, especially Dean Acheson, and his predecessor, General Marshall. On the other hand, Franklin Roosevelt hardly ever consulted with his Secretary of State, Cordell Hull, and was inclined to circumvent the Department of State whenever major decisions were made. President Eisenhower tended to seek advice from both his immediate staff members and the Secretary of State who, in many respects, served more as personal advisor to the President than manager of the traditional foreign affairs agency of the government.

While patterns differ, the extension of the President's influence by a small group of advisors seems to be an organizational constant of American foreign policy and to provide the President with a modicum of control over the sprawling network of agencies concerned with relations with other states.

Reorganization

The President's clique assists in defining, coordinating, and implementing foreign policy. It does not aid, except indirectly, in coping with the proliferation of institutional and individual participants in the policy-making process. The principal method by which a President seeks to cope with this problem as well as the vagaries, inertia, and resistance of bureaucracy is through organizational innovation. Organization "conforms to each President's experience, desires, and methods of work," as President Eisenhower recommended it should in his reflections on the office.[22] It should be viewed, therefore, less as a technique for progressively increasing efficiency than as a technique for asserting control.

A constant tension has existed between the President's desire to introduce coherence and responsiveness into his direction of foreign policy and the ostensible resistance of the bureaucracy to centralized direction. As a result, the hierarchy in the Executive Branch is often a facade disguising the reality of a political process *within* the Executive that undermines the command and consultative relationships fostered by each successive reorganization of functions and offices. Bureaucratic resistance to central direction is more often a product of the intractable problems encountered, the need for channeling difficulties into routine problem-solving procedures, the overlapping of jurisdictions, and a host of other environmental factors as well as organizational obstacles.

INSTITUTIONALIZING PRESIDENTIAL PRIMACY

The characteristics of the foreign affairs bureaucracy discussed in this chapter suggest continuing problems of coordination, cohesion, and coherence as well as continuing presidential efforts to ensure control. Although future Presidents will continue to depend on cliques and reorganization efforts because they alone provide the flexibility necessary to adapt bureaucracy to differing presidential "styles," the problems of control and coordination also lead to institutionalized steps to insure presidential primacy in foreign policy.

This has already occurred in the evolution of the National Security Council (NSC) machinery.[23] The National Security Council, established under the 1947 National Security Act, shifted from a primary position as the central policy-making organ of government in all matters involving national security under Eisenhower to near neglect under his successor, President

Kennedy. Originally, the Council was intended to bring together all administrative heads involved in foreign policy-making to advise the President on the nation's most important policy questions. Presidents Kennedy and Johnson, reacting in part to criticisms that the NSC under Eisenhower had placed an organizational straitjacket on policy-making, reverted to less formal administrative methods. Under President Nixon, the NSC has regained much of its former importance as the chief foreign-policy institution of the Executive Branch.

The NSC staff, headed by the Assistant to the President for National Security Affairs, is a part of the Executive Office of the President, the select appointed advisors to the President who safeguard his interests in working with Executive agencies and the Congress. These are the President's men, directed by the President's Special Assistant for National Security Affairs, who is also the chief staff officer of the NSC. Though the Special Assistant has long been a major part of the President's clique, the NSC staff has grown from a small, relatively obscure, essentially managerial group in the Truman days to the large and highly influential operation of the Nixon Presidency as successive Presidents have sought to cope with the problems of cohesion and control and have grappled with their inability to get what they considered acceptable performance out of the Department of State.

Under President Nixon, the NSC staff, formerly headed by Henry Kissinger, assumed a prominent role in the formulation of foreign policy.[24] The National Security Council has not played an important part in the design of policy. It had 37 full meetings in 1969; 21 in 1970; and only 10 in 1971. More important in the policy process has been its mechanism for developing National Security Study Memorandums (NSSMs) on matters requiring fundamental choices. Up to the end of 1971, 138 of these NSSMs were drafted, leading to 127 formal decisions.[25] The Council is intended to speed the production of an NSSM and facilitate a subsequent decision *and* oversee its implementation.

President Nixon's appointment in 1973 of Henry Kissinger as Secretary of State was an attempt to overcome the frustrations faced by successive Presidents when dealing with the Department of State; it indicated a desire to create a department that could at once respond to his policy prescriptions and efficiently direct and coordinate the foreign policy of the United States. As Special Assistant to the President for National Security Affairs, Mr. Kissinger had headed the largest and most influential staff in NSC history; he had helped to carry the institutionalization of presidential primacy to a point never before known. His appointment as Secretary of State (without being required to give up the NSC post) signaled a recognition of the need to exert both presidential control over the Department of State and State's control over foreign policy, if presidential primacy is to be insured in both the conception and implementation of foreign policy. It will not do to ignore or bypass State in institutionalizing presidential primacy because State's career Foreign Service Officers will still be involved in foreign policy after the incumbent President and his NSC staff have departed from the political scene. Thus, the creation of a "mini-State Department" within the White House may be temporarily necessary, but it is not sufficient to maintain continuing presidential primacy.

Kissinger described the situation very clearly in his first press conference as Secretary of State-designate:

> *. . . What we are going to try to do is to solidify what has been started . . . .*

> *Now, this requires that there will be a greater institutionalization of foreign policy than has been the case up to now. One of the challenges in going to the State Department will be the ability now to work with the great*

> *professionals in the Foreign Service who will be here after*
> *this administration has left and who, hopefully, will carry*
> *on the traditions that are valid and that will by then have*
> *been established.*[26]

The task is not an easy one; the many bureaucratic impediments to the assertion of effective presidential control over State and the primacy of State within the bureaucracy remain.

CONCLUSION

Bureaucracies are indispensable to the conduct of governmental business in complex societies; but they create problems of coordination and control. The growth of American involvement in world affairs and the resulting growth in size of the Department of State, the proliferation of agencies and departments involved in foreign policy, and the establishment of a career Foreign Service whose members place a higher priority on loyalty to institution than loyalty to any incumbent President have combined to make difficult the assertion of presidential primacy over foreign policy. Successive Presidents have tried to circumvent these problems in various ways. Informal cliques of presidential advisors have been augmented in the post-World War II era by an increasingly large and influential National Security Council Staff working in the White House. Reorganization of the bureaucracy has been regularly undertaken. The weakness of this as a permanent solution and the continuing need felt by Presidents to assert control over and improve the efficiency of the bureaucracy is illustrated by the decision of President Nixon to appoint Henry Kissinger as Secretary of State while retaining his services as Special Assistant to the President for National Security Affairs.

7. Congressional Resistance to Executive Primacy

*"In fact, I believe the
relationships between the Congress and
the President have never been better than
they have been in this remarkable period
in the postwar world."*
                    *—Under Secretary of State
                    N. Katzenbach, 1967*

From 1945-1965, congressional-Executive relations, intricate and often perplexing to students of American domestic politics, were relatively simple in the area of foreign policy. The President made foreign policy; Congress approved it, usually after consultation and rarely with any outward show of recalcitrance. That period of congressional deference and acquiescence in presidential foreign policy leadership has now ended. A stronger congressional role in the foreign policy process is vigorously advocated by representatives of both political parties. The purpose of this chapter is to review the main features of the relationship between President and Congress in the area of foreign policy and the rise of congressional resistance to the primacy of the President.

The Vietnam War was the catalyst for the change from the previously deferential attitude of Congress to the President; the change was signaled by congressional reexamination of the Gulf of Tonkin Resolution, originally passed on August 7, 1964, by 88 to 2 in the Senate and 416 to 0 in the House of Representatives.[1] This Resolution expressed congressional support of the President as Commander-in-Chief to do whatever was necessary to prevent aggression and stated that

> *the United States is...prepared,* as the President deter- *mines, to take all necessary steps, including the use of armed force, to assist any member or protocol state of the Southeast Asia Collective Defense Treaty requesting assistance in defense of its freedom....*[2]

It was subsequently argued by Administration officials that the Resolution was a "functional equivalent" for a declaration of war. Certainly, it operated as the principal legal basis for American escalation of the Vietnam War during the Johnson administration.[3]

The slippage of "war powers" from Congress to the Executive did not start with the Gulf of Tonkin Resolution. The process was under way in the nineteenth century and gathered momentum during World War II and thereafter, notably at the time of the Formosa and "Eisenhower Doctrine" Resolutions in 1954 and 1957 respectively. Slippage generally occurred after provocation from a foreign enemy, the most striking example occurring when the Japanese attacked Pearl Harbor in December 1941. An analogous situation appeared to prompt the Gulf of Tonkin Resolution. Congressmen, many of whom vividly recalled the attack on Pearl Harbor, were told that an attack on an American destroyer, the *Maddox*, had been perpetrated by North Vietnamese naval "vessels" on August 2, 1964, and that another attack had been launched on August 4, this time on the *Maddox* and another destroyer, the *C. Turner Joy.*

Congressional authorization for the prosecution of the Vietnam War, contained in the Gulf of Tonkin Resolution, was subsequently a matter of regret to individual Congressmen. It was not until February, 1968, however, that the added significance of the Resolution became apparent. At that time, after a meticulous investigation, the Senate Foreign Relations Committee conducted a hearing on the Gulf of Tonkin incidents.[4] The investigation and later testimony called into question whether a second North Vietnamese attack on the two American destroyers had actually occurred on August 4, 1964. Moreover, it became abundantly clear that the incident in the Tonkin Gulf was exaggerated and exploited by the President's advisors to intensify American participation in the Vietnam War.[5] With the recognition of the presidential abuse of Executive "war powers," spreading resistance to presidential predominance in all areas of foreign affairs developed and continues to the present. It is in Congress that the strongest challenge to the President's primacy in foreign affairs is now situated, with the outcome of the contest critical to the conduct of United States foreign policy as well as the country's constitutional development.

FROM BIPARTISANSHIP TO CONSTITUTIONAL STRUGGLE

The congressional challenge to the President's primacy in the making of foreign policy has its origins in the different character and functions of the two branches of government. These differences in the two branches were recognized early and intentionally designed by the framers of the Constitution. In the area of foreign affairs, John Jay argued, in *Federalist Paper*, No. 64:

> *The Constitution provides that our negotiations for treaties shall have every advantage which can be derived from talents, information, integrity, and deliberate investigations, on the one hand, and from secrecy and dispatch on the other.*[6]

Secrecy and dispatch were, of course, considered the province of the Executive, while integrity and deliberation were the qualities to be brought to foreign affairs by the Congress, especially the Senate. After two centuries of congressional-Executive relations and great efforts to reach a satisfactory division of labor, usually undertaken to conform in broad terms to Jay's prescription, no permanent equilibrium has been reached. In fact, tension between the two branches has never been higher.

In a ground-breaking essay on congressional-Executive relations, former Assistant Secretary of State Roger Hilsman appropriately commented that "the classic observations on the effects of the separation of powers are not completely satisfying." He added, "They explain the impasses in policy, perhaps, the arguments and rivalries, but not the achievements."[7] Hilsman's purpose was to describe the "achievements," which he did by constructing a "censensus-building model" that has successfully broadened our understanding of the making of foreign policy. Hilsman's "consensus-building model" was a particularly useful approach to the making of American foreign policy during a period in which consensus did, in fact, prevail on the threat posed by Communism to United States interests.[8] This same consensus supported the successful appeal by postwar Presidents for a bipartisan foreign policy. Except for sporadic dissidence and the long debate on the Bricker Amendment (an attempt to limit the treaty-making powers of the President, discussed in the concluding part of this chapter), bipartisanship dominated congressional participation in foreign policy during the two decades following the end of World War II.

Bipartisanship, however, is a term the meaning of which has not been generally agreed upon in political discourse.[9] On one level, bipartisanship is readily understood to describe unity among Democrats and Republicans on foreign policy issues in which the country confronts threatening adversaries. The elusiveness of the concept is related to the forms by which unity is attained. Does bipartisanship involve consultation by the President with the leaders of the opposing party before a decision? Does it simply refer to advance briefing of a decision to be announced? Does it mean that members of the party out of presidential office should be represented on delegations to international conferences? Does bipartisanship convey a tacit agreement to place foreign policy issues outside political campaigns; in the words of Truman, Vandenberg, and others, does it mean that "politics should stop at the water's edge"? Each of these and other interpretations have been supported and criticized by scholars and politicians.

While the forms of bipartisanship were disputed in the postwar period, the principle has remained relatively sacrosanct until recently. Ready acceptance of this principle, which appears to be in contradiction to established democratic norms, was a result of congressional agreement on the immediacy and gravity of the Russian threat and was influenced by consideration of the historical context in which the principle developed. Acquiescence to bipartisanship had its origin in the critical struggle between Woodrow Wilson and the Senate Republicans led by Henry Cabot Lodge over United States membership in the League of Nations. After World War II broke out, a war which the League had been designed to prevent, yet was powerless to deter with or without American participation, a *unified* national effort was repeatedly stressed by President Roosevelt. In the closing stages of the war, planning for the postwar world began among the Allied powers. Roosevelt, acutely aware of the Senate's rejection of the League, determinedly set out to avoid rejection of another international organization intended to safeguard the security of its members. He assiduously cultivated the support of both political parties in Congress for the United Nations. Significantly aided by the internationalist and anti-Communist outlook of the Republican Senate stalwart, Arthur Vandenberg, a bipartisan approach to foreign policy was established and extended through the Truman and Eisenhower administrations.

It was during this early period of the Cold War that bipartisanship often seemed to be a device employed by Presidents to gain their objectives with a potentially balky Congress. It was a tool of presidential primacy as well as a description of congressional-Executive relations. Even Senator Vandenberg, despite his preferential position, is reported on one occasion to have warned the Truman administration that he wanted to be in on the "take-offs" as well as the "crash landings" in foreign affairs.[10] Senator Robert Taft used the occasion of the Greek-Turkish aid program to complain that Republicans "were hardly called in" until "policy itself had been formulated and was ready to be announced. They were merely asked to go along."[11]

During the initial breakdown of the Cold War consensus, the principle of bipartisanship displayed remarkable resiliency. Bipartisanship probably delayed congressional opposition to the Vietnam War and, when opposition finally was voiced by Senators Wayne Morse, Ernest Gruening, and William Fulbright, criticism did not divide in any consistent manner along party lines. Policy differences did not converge with party divisions. Only during the first Nixon administration did congressional debate on foreign policy begin to overlap party affiliation. Thus, antiwar votes in three major roll-calls during the first Congress of the Nixon administration divided in the following proportion of total votes:[12]

Democrats	*78.3% antiwar votes*
Republicans	*31.4% antiwar votes*

Dissent over American foreign policy, initially sporadic, unorganized, and largely outside the party system, has now moved into the party system, yet it is articulated primarily in the constitutional setting of a division between Executive and Legislative institutions rather than according to party division. Because of the character of nonideological, loosely-structured parties, the American party system is not likely to reflect partisan differences as clearly as the Executive-congressional rivalry. Bipartisanship has now been superseded by a sharp, often caustic rivalry between the Executive and Congress in which the latter has demonstrated an unusual tendency to resist the customary preeminence of the Presidency.

PATTERNS OF CONGRESSIONAL INVOLVEMENT IN FOREIGN POLICY

Before describing patterns of congressional-Executive relations and weighing the direction of influence in their dealings with one another, it is imperative to restate an obvious but often neglected feature of congressional involvement in foreign policy. The Executive Branch seeks and sometimes achieves a coherent, unified formulation of policy. As we have seen, coordination of policy is a difficult problem for Presidents but it is a function of the Chief Executive's office which is accepted by all and constantly promoted by Presidents and their close advisors. One can correctly speak, therefore, of the foreign policy of the Wilson or the Truman or the Nixon administration, whereas it would be inaccurate to speak of the foreign policy of the 71st or 86th or 92nd Congress. In sharp contrast to the common interests of the Executive Branch, the heterogeneity in background and attitude of its members is the most salient characteristic of Congress. Thus, a constant reminder is needed in a discussion of Congress that some Congressmen dissent from their colleagues. The effort to mobilize support when it cannot be commanded is a major reason for the slow pace of congressional deliberation and the bias toward a conservative or noninnovative approach to political problems. We will, in the following pages, repeatedly allude to congressional preferences or attitudes, signifying, when no illustrative vote is cited, that the preference or attitude is sufficiently strong in contrast to the past to warrant special mention.

The role of Congress in the making of American foreign policy is joined to, not separated from, that of the President by the Constitution. The Senate consents to treaties that the Executive negotiates and ratifies; the Senate confirms appointments that the President makes; the Congress declares war—at least in principle—while the President, as Commander-in-Chief of the armed forces, deploys the troops. These *shared* responsibilities and numerous others, particularly the important functions of Congress related to its legislative prerogatives, place it in constant contact with the Executive Branch. A summary of the different forms which this relationship takes is depicted in Table 3.

TABLE 3
INVENTORY OF CONGRESSIONAL-EXECUTIVE CONTACTS IN FOREIGN POLICY

Nature of Contact	Participants
Constitutional and Statutory	
Treaty confirmation	Senate, after Executive negotiation
Approval of appointments	Senate, upon presidential nomination
Testimony in congressional hearings	Department and agency heads and staff (except White House staff)
Authorization and appropriations	Congressional committees, Senate, House, on Executive initiative
State of the Union (World) address	President, House, Senate

TABLE 3–Continued
**INVENTORY OF CONGRESSIONAL-EXECUTIVE CONTACTS
IN FOREIGN POLICY**

Nature of Contact	Participants
Customary	
White House briefings	Congressional leaders, Committee on Foreign Affairs, Committee on Foreign Relations
Congressional investigations	Appropriate House and/or Senate Committee
VIP tours	Invited Congressional leaders, committee members with Executive posts
Congressional participation in diplomacy	Senate and/or House leaders (normally with balance between parties)
Congressional resolutions	Senate and/or House directed to President
Occasional	
Social affairs	Senate and/or House leaders, friends of President
Correspondence	President, department heads to or from any Congressman

The inventory of contacts set forth in Table 3 is not exhaustive. It does not include, for example, the crucial factors of personality that play so large a part in congressional-Executive relations and affect so many of the contacts between the two branches. The differences between Representative Thomas Morgan, Chairman of the House Foreign Affairs Committee, who once described himself as "only the quarterback not the coach of the team," and Senator William Fulbright, Chairman of the Senate Foreign Relations Committee, whose reputation is based on his role as "the great dissenter," are not revealed in the inventory.[13] But there are two major problems which the table helps to crystallize; first, the direction of influence between Congress and the Executive Branch in each and all of the contacts described and, second, other types of congressional particpation in the making of foreign policy not dependent on contact with the Executive.

The second problem is by far the easiest to resolve. There is no congressional participation in the foreign policy process outside some relationship with the Executive Branch. It is true that Congress has a preponderant role in dealing with some foreign policy issues, notably immigration, but these issues are mostly minor and only serve to provide evidence of the occasional ascendancy of Congress in relation to the Presidency, illustrating the first problem mentioned concerning the direction of influence between the members of the two branches of government. While Congress or individual Congressmen do occasionally have independent views on foreign policy and may seek to influence American foreign policy in diverse ways that do not entail direct contact with the Executive Branch, there is no congressional participation in foreign policy that does not also ultimately involve Executive participation.

A CONGRESSIONAL-EXECUTIVE LEDGER

Before turning to an assessment of the direction of influence in congressional-Executive relations, it will be helpful to review the various advantages and disadvantages that Congress possesses in its dealings with the President, his advisors, and the agencies of the Executive. Most discussions of this subject focus on the disadvantages under which Congress labors, thus playing down or even excluding any mention of the very real advantages it enjoys. There are at least three major congressional advantages that merit consideration. The first, which stems from the heterogeneous composition of Congress and its modus operandi, is the capability of demanding public accountability from the Executive. Congress can summon any official of the Executive Branch (except those protected by Executive privilege—the President and members of the White House staff) to appear before its committees and, to a degree far beyond that of the courts, demand justification of agency activities and the policies of the President. No other public forum—certainly not the presidential press conference—so effectively scrutinizes and oversees Executive performance in foreign policy as congressional committee hearings. During the first five years of his tenure, Secretary of State Dean Rusk appeared in 129 formal committee meetings of Congress.[14] Add to these appearances others by the Secretary of Defense, both their Under Secretaries, a parade of Assistant Secretaries, sundry other aides, members of the Joint Chiefs of Staff, and other agency heads and advisors involved in national security affairs, and it is obvious that the power to require public accountability is a major political resource as well as a means for closing the distance between the two ends of Pennsylvania Avenue.

The demand for public accountability is not always an advantage pursued through congressional committee hearings. Joint resolutions, amendments to legislation, and various organizational requirements also strengthen the Congress in its dealings with the Executive Branch. Nevertheless, committees are the major instruments by which Congress expresses its claim on the Executive to justify its activity.

In the Senate, the prestigious Foreign Relations Committee is best known for its involvement in matters of foreign policy. Its membership has remained relatively stable during recent years and its members—who have included Senators Fulbright, Church, Muskie, Case, Mansfield, and Javits—are well-known and respected for their liberal "internationalist" orientation. On the House side, the Foreign Affairs Committee is less well-known and its membership fluctuates more rapidly, but its position is likely to be closer to the Administration. It captures fewer headlines than its Senate counterpart but plays a crucial role in bridging the distance that has developed in recent years between the Senate's administration critics and the Executive's determination to safeguard its prerogatives.

Besides the Senate Foreign Relations Committee and the House Foreign Affairs Committee, there are the less publicized but influential House and Senate Armed Services Committees whose purview extends to defense and other national security budgets and, therefore, policies; the Appropriations Committees of the two Houses and their various sub-committees whose responsibility has virtually no boundaries relative to policies in which funds are required (and virtually all foreign policy has funding implications); and other committees, such as Agriculture, in which foreign policy issues arise.

A second advantage of Congress is connected to its autonomy under the Constitution which authorizes its latent threat of not only defying, but actually sabotaging, the foreign policy of a President. Rarely does the Senate or House of Representatives take action totally contrary to a President's wishes. The reasons for this, however, are not wholly attributable to the advantages possessed by the Executive Branch, but are in large measure due to the Executive's anticipation of what is and what is not acceptable to Congress. In other words, the Congress derives some advantage from having certain limits beyond which an Executive cannot go and still expect to obtain a majority for a treaty, an appropriation, or an appointment. The classic instance of the failure to discern these limits was, of course, Woodrow

Wilson's submission to the Senate of the Treaty of Versailles creating a League of Nations. Congress has enormous potential power, even including the capability to impeach a President, which operates as a moderating force on the range of policy alternatives that can be seriously entertained by a President.

A third advantage, that belongs less to Congress as a whole than to certain individual Congressmen, is exceptional expertise. Congressmen, both in the House and Senate, who acquire continuing favor with their constituencies and thereby build up significant seniority on committees that deal with issues of foreign policy, are also in a position to acquire extensive knowledge of administration programs and problems, the personalities of responsible civil servants, and the internal organization of the agencies involved. Occasionally, they develop a knowledge of national defense policies, the organization of the State Department, the development of a particular weapons system, the intricacies of international finance, or some other matter that not only exceeds the experience of a President in this area, but also that of his appointed advisors. An abundance of examples of this phenomenon can be cited: Senator Henry Jackson's role in gaining support for the Polaris weapons system; Congressman Otto Passman's informed, if dreaded, annual assault on the foreign aid program; Congressman Henry Reuss' professional yet powerful involvement in international monetary affairs; Congressman Maloney's jealous guardianship of the Department of State's annual budget—in all these and numerous additional cases, Congress as a whole derives an advantage from the acquired expertise of certain of its members.

Other advantages besides those represented by the demand for public accountability, the latent threat to use sanctions accorded by the Constitution, and the expertise gained in the process of obtaining seniority by some individual Congressmen could undoubtedly be cited. When all are taken together, however, they still appear to be far short of offsetting the many substantial disadvantages experienced by Congress in its relations with the Executive Branch. Following James Robinson's division of the foreign policy decision-making process into seven functions (intelligence, recommendation, prescription, invocation, application, appraisal, and termination),[15] we will proceed by identifying the disadvantages experienced in the performance of each of these functions.

The most marked disadvantage of Congress in dealing with the Executive is in the performance of the *intelligence* function: gathering the information on which action can be based. The Executive Branch has available to it a number of specialized intelligence services comprising what is officially referred to as the "intelligence community" and in which information on all facets of American foreign relations is collected, analyzed, and disseminated to those with a "need to know." Not only does the Executive Branch, therefore, have access to information not available to the Congress, as well as access to all non-official information available to the Congress, it also has control through elaborate classification procedures over what official information is made available to Congressmen. What Congress obtains from the Executive Branch is interpreted information that normally leads to obvious policy choices.[16] The expertise of individual Congressmen contributes to the policy-making process but rarely enters into the initial stage of decision-making.

If Congress does not have adequate information, it cannot satisfactorily participate in the *recommendation* of various policy alternatives. Accounts of White House briefings generally substantiate the disadvantage of congressional leaders in recommending alternatives, most of which are set forth in the early moments of a briefing. Congress has, on occasion, amended legislation, which has the effect of a policy recommendation. Such was the case in the unrequested appropriation of funds for the B-70 supersonic bomber which, however, were then impounded by President Kennedy.[17] The principal difficulty experienced by Congress in recommending alternatives is the inaccessibility of planning documents or "internal working papers" which, if ever submitted to Congress at all, are passed on with the greatest reluctance. Consequently, Congress rarely enters into the policy process until a course of action has already been determined.

Congress would appear to have a major role in fulfilling the *prescription* function of the policy process but, in determining the choice among possible policy alternatives, it still labors under severe disadvantages. First of all, it seldom is given a series of alternatives to decide among, receiving instead a neatly packaged and strongly advocated policy prescription from the White House. In the appropriations process, the initial request for funds, justification for their expenditure, and the overview of the relationship among expenditures are all uniquely in the hands of the Executive Branch. Congress can reduce expenditures on foreign policy requests. Staff resources and congressional organization, however, are simply not adequate to determine a choice among alternatives, a function quite different from raising questions about choices made by the President supported by his extensive staff and information resources.

In the *invocation* of a selected alternative, the decision to call upon a policy choice already made, in other words, to do something rather than nothing, Congress is not burdened by any particular disadvantage unless it be a difficulty in getting the Executive to execute. Congress has no responsibility, and hence no disadvantage, in the *application* of a decided course of action; that function is customarily and through administrative necessity an Executive responsibility.

In the sixth and seventh stages of the decision-making process, *appraisal* of the effectiveness of a prescribed course of action and *termination* of the initial policy, Congress continues to work under severe handicaps: lack of information, lack of consultation in the planning stage, lack of organizational capability to prepare independent policy prescriptions. In addition, a policy once applied that advances to the appraisal stage of the decision process forces upon Congress the responsibility of diverging from the Executive in an area where national unity is assumed to be desirable. Dissident Congressmen do not become traitors by adversely criticizing United States foreign policy; they do, nonetheless, incur the problems that arise in setting their individual views in opposition to those that have been expressed by the "President of all the people" and a policy that has presumably been perceived abroad as the policy of the United States. From this perspective, those early voices of dissent against the escalation of the Vietnam War by Senators Ernest Gruening of Alaska and Wayne Morse of Oregon can be better appreciated for the courage they required and the political liabilities attached to their utterance. It is interesting to note that neither Senator was returned when he next stood for re-election.

Given the disadvantages of Congressmen in appraising policy already implemented, the preference for examining the organization of the policy-making process rather than the substance of foreign policy is more readily understood. There may also be a factor of national style which inhibits Congress from devoting more time to appraisal of policies already in force. The major critical assessments of recent years, the Senate Foreign Relations Committee Hearing on Vietnam in 1966, the same Committee's analysis of the Dominican intervention, and the investigation into the circumstances resulting in the Gulf of Tonkin Resolution have had substantial impact on academic and congressional attitudes toward events in these instances of American foreign policy. Each assessment, however, has been primarily dependent on cooperative spokesmen from the Executive Branch. More symptomatic of the disadvantaged position of Congress is the scarcity of such reports.

Congress can be a dominant actor in the termination of a policy. Its major disadvantage in performing this function is the difficulty in acting with dispatch, a corollary to the natural advantages associated with deliberative bodies. It is just as easy to exercise initiative in terminating a policy as in prescribing one, but by not acting quickly, Congress relinquishes the initiative in foreign policy (as in domestic policy) to the President.

When the debits and credits of congressional-Executive relations in foreign policy are set alongside each other, most careful observers see the ledger greatly unbalanced in favor of the Executive Branch. This judgment is obviously not a straight-forward arithmetical operation; discretion and judgment are important components in reaching such a conclusion. Among the more persuasive arguments which support the preponderance of Executive influence in relation to congressional influence in making foreign policy is the comparison and analysis of twenty-two foreign policy decisions in James Robinson's book, *Congress and Foreign Policy Making.*[18] Beginning with Neutrality legislation in the 1930's and proceeding to other areas such as Lend Lease in 1941, the Truman Doctrine, the Korean decision, the Formosan Resolution, and others, Robinson notes that most were decided over a relatively long period of time, a factor which tends to favor congressional involvement by permitting a "deliberative" body the opportunity to debate without the necessity of rapid decision. On the other hand, he also notes that his sample of cases includes few in which Congress assumes the initiative, whereas prevailing influence seems to be strongly related to the initiation of a policy.

Despite these qualifications, Robinson's analysis shows that Congress tends to be more influential in nonviolent compared to potentially violent foreign policy decisions, tends to prevail when it takes the initiative, but does not tend to take the initiative nearly as often as the Executive.[19] In summary, the evidence seems to corroborate the view that the Presidency is usually the primary and predominant policy-making institution in American foreign relations, particularly as the urgency or crisis character of the policy process displaces routine governmental activity.

REDRESSING THE IMBALANCE

Coincident with the de-escalation of the Vietnam War, Congress has increasingly sought to redress the perceived "imbalance of power" between itself and the Executive Branch in the making of foreign policy. This congressional assertiveness, stronger in the Senate but developing support in the House of Representatives, can be seen in specific substantive areas of policy such as the effort to curtail bombings in Cambodia after the signing of the initial Paris Peace Accords. Its more general importance, however, is in the basic procedural changes in congressional-Executive relations that it has set in motion.

There are numerous precedents for congressional resistance to presidential primacy originating in the "silences of the Constitution."[20] Washington's assertion of neutrality in the war between France and Britain in 1793 led Congress to its own neutrality act the next year. Through successive administrations and changing patterns of congressional-Executive relations, Presidents tended to assert their prerogatives in foreign affairs only to meet subsequent congressional resistance. Seldom, however, was congressional reaction successful in recouping all of the initiative and range of responsibility exercised in presidential action. The net result was a slow accretion of power and authority by Presidents until the wartime administration of Franklin Roosevelt, when the Executive power in foreign affairs expanded at an unprecedented pace by means of wartime conferences of the main allied powers and the imperatives of rapid wartime decision-making.

Presidents of the post-World War II period have consolidated and sought to further extend Executive primacy in foreign affairs. They have been aided by a generally quiescent Congress, in turn sharing the pervasive domestic consensus that prevailed during the Cold War. A brief congressional reaction occurred during 1950-51 over the question of President Truman's dispatch of troops to Europe. The debate was a partial response to

Truman's commitment to send troops to Korea (a decision taken with only informal consultation of congressional leaders). The debate failed to lead to any genuine limits on the President's war powers.

The most forceful resistance to presidential primacy in the postwar period, prior to the reaction begun with the re-examination of the Gulf of Tonkin Resolution, also occurred in the early 1950's, reaching its climax in February, 1954, during the congressional debate on the Bricker Amendment.[21] The Bricker Amendment (named for its author and chief sponsor, Senator John Bricker, Ohio Republican and vice-presidential candidate in 1948), and the various other similar proposals made at the time, were designed to limit the Executive's power to enter into treaties and Executive agreements which have the legal force of treaties but do not require the "advice and consent" of the Senate.[22]

Under the terms of the amendment, Congress was to have the "power to regulate all Executive and other agreements with any foreign power or international organization," a proviso that would have resulted in a major incursion by Congress into the traditional freedom of the Executive. Presidents would have been hobbled in negotiating any agreements with foreign powers unless there had been the certainty of congressional approval. The challenge to the President was obvious and forceful, unquestionably drawing on the sense of affront and impropriety generated in the conservative sector of Congress by memories of the Yalta pacts and the earlier bases-for-destroyers agreement with Britain negotiated by President Roosevelt.

The Bricker Amendment was defeated in the Senate on February 25, 1954; the next day, a compromise offered by the more prestigious Senator from Georgia, Walter George, failed of the requisite two-thirds majority after the tally showed 60 "for", 30 "against" and Senator Kilgore marched into the Senate and shouted "No!" Certainly support for the Bricker, later George,

Amendment was compounded of a variety of motivations. Probably at the forefront of these was dissatisfaction with the new global responsibilities of the United States; a nostalgia for an earlier "isolationist" period. Institutional hostility to the assertion of power by the President was present but not dominant.

Similar motivations have been present since the demonstration of congressional resistance to the Executive in the early 1950's. The revelations accompanying the conduct of the Vietnam War, however, greatly reinforced the institutional hostility of Congress to the Executive. The Nixon administration has been the target of this hostility because of its conduct of foreign affairs and, equally important, because of the accumulated resentment from past administrations which the Nixon administration inherited. While partisanship along party lines is obviously related to increasing congressional hostility to the Executive's primacy in foreign affairs, it is primarily an institutional cleavage between Congress and the Presidency, often paralleling the attitudinal cleavage on whether the American role in global affairs should be severely circumscribed or not, which has provided the momentum for congressional action.

The National Commitments Resolution, passed by the Senate in June, 1969, by 70 to 16, contributed to changing the mood of the Senate toward presidential primacy in foreign affairs by calling for a treaty or legislative act by both Houses of Congress before an American commitment was made to a foreign government or people. By itself, it did little more than help to signal the changed national attitude toward the decelerating Vietnam War. It soon became evident, however, that the National Commitments Resolution was part of an evolving pattern of congressional assertiveness in the conduct of foreign affairs.[23] Soon after the dispatch of troops into Cambodia by President Nixon in May, 1970, without any prior authorization from Congress, Senators Cooper (Rep., Kentucky) and Church (Dem., Idaho) proposed an amendment to the Foreign Military Sales Act, designed to limit any further military involvement in Cambodia through the denial of funds. After lengthy debate, the Cooper-Church Amendment finally passed the Senate overwhelmingly by 75 to 20, only to be rejected later by the House.

Following on the Cooper-Church Amendment was the repeal of the Gulf of Tonkin Resolution on July 10, 1970, by a roll-call vote. An ambitious but unsuccessful attempt to cut off funds for U. S. military activities, if prisoners of war were released, was contained in the McGovern-Hatfield Amendment (Senator George McGovern, Dem., South Dakota and Senator Mark Hatfield, Rep., Oregon) to a draft extension bill. Variations on this bill were proposed by Senator Mike Mansfield (Dem., Montana) and adopted by the Senate in June and September, 1971. Slowly seeking to nibble away at presidential powers in the area of foreign affairs, Congress finally settled on the question of the President's war powers.

Passage of the War Powers Bill, adroitly maneuvered through Congress by Senator Jacob Javits (Rep., New York), was the culmination of recent attempts to restrict the power of the President in the use of American armed forces and thereby to reassert a stronger congressional role in foreign policy.[24] War Powers legislation was introduced in the Senate in 1970 but was displaced from center stage by debate on the Cooper-Church and McGovern-Hatfield amendments. In 1971, a spate of war powers bills was introduced in both House and Senate, including a revision by Senator Javits of the bill which he offered the prior year. A compromise bill (widely known as S.440) was finally agreed upon by Senators Javits, Stennis, and Eagleton. After extensive hearings, this bill was passed by the Senate in April, 1972, by a vote of 68 to 16. A weaker bill was passed in the House but the conference committee, formed to resolve the differences between the two versions, met only once, inconclusively, before Congress adjourned. The same Senate bill was introduced in the next session of Congress. In the House of

Representatives, however, the bill (sponsored by Representative Clement Zablocki, Dem., Wisconsin) was considerably stronger than the earlier version. It passed the House on July 18. Two days later, S.440 passed the Senate by a vote of 72 to 18.

The Senate version of the war powers legislation specified in fairly concrete terms those situations in which the President could commit American troops abroad. The Zablocki bill was less detailed in its approach and was the basis for the eventual House-Senate Conference Committee's compromise War Powers Bill, finally sent to the President in October, 1973. In its final form, the bill presented a constitutional interpretation by Congress which authorized the President to commit U. S. armed forces to hostilities, or to situations where hostilities might be imminent, only after a declaration of war; specific legislative action; or a national emergency created by an armed attack on the United States, its territories, possessions, or armed forces. The bill also urged the President "in every possible instance" to consult with Congress before committing troops as well as to consult after such a commitment.

The bill, in addition, required the President to report within 48 hours to the House Speaker and President pro tempore of the Senate in the event of a commitment or escalation ("substantial enlargement") of American combat forces, and to submit supplementary reports every six months thereafter. The bill further required termination of a troop commitment within 60 days after the President's initial report unless supported by Congress or if Congress was unable to convene because of an armed attack on the United States. A 30-day extension of this period remains possible if the President so determines on grounds related to the safety of American troops. Added provisos authorized the reconvening of Congress when not in session, congressional direction to the President to disengage troops when there was no congressional authorization, and resort to priority procedures in Congress for consideration of bills designed to achieve a troop disengagement.

On October 27, 1973, President Nixon vetoed the War Powers Bill, as he had previously indicated he would, on the grounds that the 60-day limit on authorized troops commitments and the authority assumed by Congress to disengage troops and, in effect, end a commitment by concurrent resolution, were unconstitutional. At the time of the veto, few if any observers had any doubts that the Senate would override the veto; yet the same preponderance of opinion felt exactly the opposite about the House where little chance was seen for successfully voting the bill in with a two-thirds majority. On November 7, 1973, however, the House rejected the President's views and responded to its critics with a resounding vote of 284 to 135, four votes greater than the requisite two-thirds majority. A few hours later, the Senate passed the same legislation by 75 to 18. After a prolonged effort to curb the President's war powers, the congressional rebellion had finally succeeded.

Did the war powers legislation voted by Congress redress the balance between Congress and the President, at least in this one crisis-ridden area of foreign policy? Few commentators or Congressmen viewed the legislation as an assertion of congressional equality with the Presidency in foreign policy or national security policy. Legislation certainly contributed to redressing the balance but not to restoring it as the framers of the Constitution had conceived of "balance" in the area of war powers. The legislation, therefore, contributed to reshaping the ambience of foreign policy-making; it was a strong reminder to the Executive that presidential powers in foreign affairs were not totally free from legal restraints and that the acquiescence of Congress in the Executive's accretion of authority was not automatic. The War Powers Bill was also a sign of congressional resentment over the tangled and disastrous revelations of Executive imprudence associated with Watergate. Passage of the War Powers Bill did not signal, however, any serious curtailment in the overall primacy of the President in the conduct of American foreign policy. In fact, some argued that it strengthened the President's powers by providing prior congressional sanction for presidential dispatch of troops, for however short a period, where none had existed before. President Nixon's opposition, rather than the substantive provisions of the bill, is what made the issue one of congressional vs. Executive power.

CONCLUSION

In retrospect, conduct of the Vietnam War can easily be seen as the stimulus for congressional resistance to the primacy of the President in foreign affairs. Prior to the war, the post-World War II period was one of regular congressional acquiescence to the President's policies, often manifested in the Executive's successful appeal for bipartisanship. Prior to World War II, the record of congressional-Executive relations was uneven but tended toward an accretion of power to the Executive branch.

While Congress and the President are required under the Constitution to share responsibilities in foreign affairs, even the most far-reaching of recent measures toward congressional assertiveness, the war powers legislation, does not appear to have restored balance between the two branches. The President still has the power to initiate an American military response (albeit with the expectation now of prior consultation with Congress) and, in other areas of foreign policy, he and his advisors enjoy a wide latitude of discretion. Thus, Congress can continue to exercise restraints on the conduct of America's foreign policy, but it cannot wrest the main functions of policy-making from the Executive Branch. When determined to act, Presidents may confront congressional resistance but are not likely to experience an effective counter-weight to their traditional primacy.

8. Public Opinion, Press, and Pressure Groups

*"For among the means of power which
now prevail is the power to manage
and to manipulate the consent of men."*
—C. Wright Mills

According to the traditional theory of representative government, opinions of private citizens are represented by those directly responsible for governmental decisions, including decisions related to foreign relations. The theory aids in understanding public indifference and ignorance of foreign affairs, widely documented by survey research.[1] These attitudes can also be partially attributed to public awareness of the impracticality of direct popular participation in foreign policy decisions. As we observed in Chapter 2, there has always been greater respectability for elitism in foreign policy than in domestic policy. On the other hand, the accountability of Presidents and Congressmen to the public in elections, combined with the democratic belief that public officials should act as "servants of the people," allows a role for the public in the foreign policy process. This is true at least for an interested and informed citizenry, and justifies the influence attributed to public opinion in the conduct of United States foreign relations. In this chapter, we will shift from an examination of the way the President uses and is restrained by the foreign policy bureaucracy and the Congress to those strengths and restraints that originate in the private sector of the American political system. We will first examine the roles played by public opinion or, more accurately, an attentive public opinion, and then turn to the mass media, the major expression of public opinion. Pressure groups, those organizations associated with American business and labor, religious life, education, and other facets of American society, do not play as strong a role in foreign policy as in domestic policy. Since these groups do have access to the Executive Branch and often to the President himself, and since they frequently develop views about foreign policy, they will also be examined as elements of the foreign policy-making process. In particular, we will stress the development of that aggregate of pressure groups collected in the notion of the military-industrial complex.

THE PUBLIC: PRESIDENT'S DICTATOR, ACCOMPLICE, OR CRITIC

No subject in the study of American politics has received more scholarly attention during the past three decades than public opinion: its sources, characteristics, and content.[2] One generally accepted result of this research is recognition of the need to differentiate between different 'publics.' The distinction made by Gabriel Almond in 1950 between a mass public and an attentive public, with an elite group more involved in the formulation than in the reception of opinion, still remains useful.[3] There is considerable evidence that the mass public, including a heavy majority of the adult population, is neither well-informed nor especially interested in foreign affairs. This is not a special insight of social scientists. Bill Moyers, one of President Johnson's closest associates, has written:

At the White House, for example, we were impressed and discouraged by reliable studies which indicated how poorly informed many Americans really are.

One study by the Survey Research Center of the University of Michigan, made for the Council on Foreign Relations, revealed that one-forth of the respondents were not aware that Mainland China was ruled by a communist government. A Gallup poll in 1964 revealed that two-thirds of the American people had paid little or no attention to developments in South Viet Nam, although the United States had been involved there for ten years.[4]

Until recently, it was believed that public indifference to foreign policy contributed to wild fluctuations in public attitudes, particularly in times of crisis. A recent study convincingly challenges this "conventional wisdom" and suggests that public opinion is characterized "by a *strong* and *stable* 'permissive mood' toward international involvements."[5] Whichever interpretation is adopted, there is no reason to discount the mass public entirely. To do so runs the risk of overlooking a decline in its number if more people become more concerned with foreign affairs or, more likely, if a specific issue becomes so widely and intensely discussed and debated that the attentive public is enlarged by recruits from the mass public. Vietnam was an obvious illustration of the latter possibility. Moreover, at election time the mass public, though continuing to be uninformed, may take on a crucial role and become the target for a variety of attempts at manipulation. Normally, however, public opinion is an expression of the attentive public.

Sophisticated methods make it possible not only to sample and ascertain public opinion on particular questions but to examine its components in the familiar categories of pollsters: age, sex, political party preference, education, income, and region of residence in the country. Whether the public, or certain segments of it, approves of the conduct of a war or the efforts made for peace, negotiations with the Russians, the sale of arms to Israel, withdrawal of troops from Europe, or other policy alternatives can be determined with findings that are remarkably precise. Polling has attained the status of a scientific enterprise. There remain, however, two basic problems in relating public opinion to foreign policy. The first is a general problem of survey research: the measurement of intensity of opinion. While this measurement is possible to some extent, the results are extremely costly to attain and less reliable than measuring the range of opinion. Moreover, it is crucial to a policy-maker to have some anticipation of whether an unpopular decision will meet with hostile indifference or street demonstrations. Such a calculation is rarely aided by polls that do not discriminate among the mass public and the attentive public nor among the intensities of opposition within the attentive public.

A second fundamental problem is the reciprocal relationship between national leaders, especially the President, and public opinion in the area of foreign policy—the linkage between policy and opinion. It is easily assumed that national leaders adapt their behavior to the public will in the fashion of the oft-quoted French parliamentarian who noticed the crowd running through the streets, quickly ran outside, and announced, "I am their leader; I must follow them." On reflection, we realize that public opinion is not likely to take shape without interaction with political and other national leaders. While there are some excellent studies of "opinion-makers,"[6] too few explore the critical relationship between opinion-makers and the public to describe adequately the intricate linkage between them. What we can do is contrast differing interpretations of the public's role in the foreign policy process and assess the general inhibitions placed by public opinion on the President.

The Public as Dictator to the President

Walter Lippmann, not alone but more eloquently than others, has contributed to the notion that public opinion is a dictator to government officials. In a provocative book entitled *Public Opinion*, first published in 1922, Lippmann touched on most of the theoretical ideas concerning the formation and political significance of public opinion, later investigated in more rigorous studies by social scientists.[7] In this early work, Lippmann was remarkably sensitive to the problematic aspects of public opinion. He foresaw that the "manufacture of consent" would involve knowledge that "will alter every political calculation and modify every political premise." He acknowledged that "leaders often pretend that they have merely uncovered a program which existed in the minds of their public."[8] Despite these concerns about what leaders might do, Lippmann was sensitive to the limitations of public opinion. These limitations ensue from the information and intellectual capabilities of the mass public, however, not from a lack of influence. The ability of the public to determine policy in its broad outlines, when simple dichotomous choices are at hand, is not doubted by Lippmann and, in fact, repeatedly becomes the object of censure in later writings.

In his *Essays in the Public Philosophy*, published thirty-five years after *Public Opinion*, Lippmann is no longer concerned about the "manufacture of consent" but focuses on the subservience of leaders to led, what he describes as the "derangement of powers."[9] In his view, public opinion is a stalemating force in society since it cannot substitute for a governing power. Where public opinion does decide, it "has been destructively wrong at the crucial junctures," compelling governments which usually know better "to be too late with too little, or too long with too much, too pacifist in peace and too bellicose in war, too neutralist or appeasing in negotiation or too intransigent." Finally, "it has shown itself to be a dangerous master of decision when the stakes are life and death."[10] Always, for Lippmann and others of his persuasion, notably George Kennan and Hans Morgenthau, the pressure of public opinion that forced McKinley's hand in bringing the United States into the Spanish-American War and the public's role in the experiences of the McCarthy period were precedents that justified distrust of the mass public.

Lippmann's strong criticism of the "mounting power" of public opinion, and its capability to decide, is obviously not shared by all or perhaps even a majority of observers of American foreign policy. We single it out here because it is a typical view of the public as a dominant, even dictatorial, force in the making of foreign policy. It is an explicit contradiction of the notion that the Presidency is preeminent in making important decisions in the area of foreign policy. Lippmann's description of a "derangement of powers" suggests that the President and his advisors are buffeted about in the winds of public opinion, always seeking to appease a majority—for electoral reasons—and incapable of initiating the necessary dialogue between governors and governed which is at the heart of successful constitutional government.

Public Opinion: Accomplice to the President

A view sharply at odds with Lippmann's situates public opinion in a supportive role in the making of foreign policy, one in which it is generally acquiescent, susceptible to persuasion, and open to appeals for support. According to this view, the public plays the role of an accomplice to the President once it is persuaded or manipulated to show its support. It aids him, once he can demonstrate its support, in dealing with Congress and other governments. President Johnson, for example, would carry a sheaf of newspaper clippings with the latest poll results in his pocket which he proudly displayed when they worked in his favor.

Stanley Hoffmann metaphorically refers to the American public as a "sea on which various, connected rafts float and try to chart their course."[11] Hoffmann cites V. O. Key, one of the early and most influential theorists of public opinion, in describing a consensus of decision which "is so closely articulated with governmental action as to appear to be decisive if not directive."[12] Hoffmann's view that the public is to be cultivated and that its support is of major assistance in the conduct of foreign policy is not totally irreconcilable with the judgment of Lippmann, that the Executive has become subordinated to shifting whims of public opinion. Hoffmann acknowledges that a President's behavior is in some measure conditioned by the needs of appealing to the public for support.

The role of public opinion as accomplice to the President in foreign policy suggests a consensus model of foreign policy-making with the Executive situated at the controls or, to adopt Hoffmann's metaphor, at the helm of the "connected rafts." There is strong support for this consensus view of American foreign policy, the results of which have already been discussed above.[13] But a major qualification needs to be added. The President's relationship with the public is not entirely a dialogue *à deux*; important leadership groups may intervene whose influence is not easily measurable, yet is certainly capable of limiting the President's power of mobilizing public opinion. Their influence adds a dimension of complexity to the notion of public support which should not be ignored. Acknowledging the existence of an "opinion-making public," which may affect certain policy alternatives or lend crucial support to national leaders in crisis situations, accurately directs attention to the intricate *process* of opinion formation.[14] If the formation of opinion is viewed as a process rather than as a fixed attitude on one or another policy, the President's position no longer appears subordinate to the public but, instead, one major influence—perhaps *the* major influence, but not a controlling one—in an extremely complex interaction of presidential attitudes and policy choices, the preferences of diverse leaders of opinion who speak for their own constituencies and, finally, the general ambience of popular opinion.

While all the details of this process are not known, some of the basic elements by which the President seeks to shape public opinion can be identified. He uses his staff, particularly his press secretary and speech writers, to communicate with the public through prepared press releases or speeches. White House press releases in the Kennedy administration ran at roughly three times the annual rate of those issued during the Roosevelt administration.[15] The President's press conference in various forms has evolved into a major platform from its curious origins as an "audience" granted by Theodore Roosevelt to a few reporters in the afternoon while he was being shaved.[16] Equally important to the development of slick public relations techniques for communicating Executive views is the now common awareness of Presidents that they can make news whenever they wish and, by doing so, shape or test public opinion. President Johnson repeatedly sought, with considerable success, to upstage vigorous criticism of the Vietnam War by press conferences, speeches, and, on one occasion, a quick round-the-world trip including a visit to the Pope.[17]

Presidents do, then, seek to persuade, manipulate, or even manufacture supporting opinion. But this does not mean they are totally free of the "will of the people." The compulsive interest of nearly all Presidents in the "feedback" of any and all opinion—demonstrated through a resort to scientific survey research during the Roosevelt, Kennedy, and Johnson years; the analysis of mail; voracious press reading; and in the case of Franklin Roosevelt, frequent use of his wife, Eleanor, as a reflection, however imperfect, of public views—reveals that the relationship between President and public is neither simple nor unidirectional.

Public Opinion:
Presidential Critic

One other view of the relationship between President and public opinion merits serious consideration. This is the conception of the public as a critic of the President and his policies. According to this interpretation, generally implicit in the

TABLE 4
RESPONSES TO QUESTIONS ABOUT THE BOMBING OF HANOI AND HAIPHONG, 1965-66

	% of those with opinion	
	Favor bombing	Oppose bombing
Do you think the administration is more right or more wrong in not bombing Hanoi or Haiphong?		
September 1965	30	70
February 1966	42	58
May 1966	50	50
— — — — Bombing begun — — — —		
Do you think the administration is more right or wrong in bombing Hanoi and Haiphong?		
July 1966	85	15

Source: Harris Poll, *Los Angeles Times,* June 13, 1966, and July 11, 1966.

frequent polls about presidential popularity or "conduct-in-office," the President's foreign policy is not a result of popular whim but a fitting object of public approval or disapproval. Thus, the Executive is relatively free to formulate and implement any policy he chooses with public opinion—and the electoral sanction it implies—judging, rather than directing, the office-holder. Convincing evidence for this viewpoint is found in the successive shifts of attitude on the bombing of North Vietnam in 1965-66.[18] The data tend to show public opinion as an approving critic of presidential policy, thus supporting the notion of the public's generally "permissive mood" toward any foreign policy action. It is much more difficult to find disapproving criticism among the mass public. Only small minorities tend to articulate criticism of the President in matters of foreign policy.

In the three strongly contrasting relationships between the Presidency and public opinion: as dictator, accomplice, and critic, there is no obvious and simple synthesis or "underlying factor" that favors one interpretation of the public's role over the others. Each interpretation seems to provide the "best" description depending on which event is being analyzed. Sometimes all three interpretations are appropriate to the same event. Such was the case in the sequence of decisions during which President Nixon ordered troops in and out of Cambodia in the spring of 1970. Prior to the decision, public opinion tended to serve as an accomplice to the President's Vietnam policy of troop reduction, intensive negotiation, and strengthening of the South Vietnamese regime. After the decision to send American troops, with those of South Vietnam, into Cambodia in order to "clean out major enemy sanctuaries," a remarkable public outroar spilled over from the campus onto nearly every town, business, profession, and group activity in the country. Most Americans cannot remember public opinion being a more hostile critic of presidential action than at this time. The consequent decisions by the President—first, to limit the territorial extent of American involvement, and then the duration of American participation—provide substantial evidence for the view that Presidents act in response to the dictates of public opinion.[19]

The troops-to-Cambodia episode does not allow any single interpretation of the public's relationship with the President. In this respect, the episode, although more dramatic, is similar to other crisis situations in showing that the relationship between President and public is not a simple one, but rather, one determined by numerous inter-related factors: what is at stake, whether the policy can be presented to the public in understandable terms, the antecedent events, the political skill of the President in gauging the limits of public interest and support, the mode of expression employed by the public, and the range of support within the opinion-making public. One cannot justifiably conclude that the opinion of the public is insignificant as a restraint on the preeminent position of the President in foreign affairs. The problem is one of determining on what issues and by what methods an attentive public can participate in the making of foreign policy, and, on this, there is no conclusive judgment. In sharp contrast to earlier judgments on the role of public opinion dating from the Spanish-American War, many leaders of opinion have recently advocated limiting the primacy of the President by compelling him to respond more readily to public opinion. How this would be done is rarely discussed; whether it is desirable usually turns on one's appreciation of whether a given policy is correct or not.

THE PRESS: VOCAL BUT FEEBLE RESTRAINT

We are all familiar with the theory of a free press serving as a means of enlightening the public which will then restrain Presidents and Prime Ministers from acting arbitrarily. Journalists rarely take exception to the notion of the press as a "fourth branch of government" and probably most believe Oscar Wilde's comment, "In America, the President reigns for four years, but Journalism governs forever."[20] The press is unquestionably a major formative influence on public opinion (in common parlance, it is often identical with public opinion) and is ostensibly a serious limitation on the discretion of the Chief Executive in the making of foreign policy.

If the testimony of Presidents is taken literally, the press is indeed a formidable restraint on a Chief Executive's freedom of action. Scarcely a single President has left office with a much different opinion than Thomas Jefferson's that, "The man who never looks into a newspaper is better informed than he who reads them" (a striking change from his earlier attitude that he would prefer "newspapers without a government" rather than the reverse.)[21]   No President, including the remarkably popular President Kennedy, has escaped criticism from the press nor the impression of being unfairly treated, an impression no doubt partly true.

While Presidents may justifiably perceive the press as a carping and often unfair critic of their policies, there is abundant evidence that this point of view has little bearing on any evaluation of the actual influence of the press as a restraint. Although a vocal critic, the press is nonetheless a relatively feeble voice in the making of policy. James Reston, columnist, Washington bureau chief of the *New York Times*, and as close to the exercise of presidential power as any journalist since World War II, has emphasized the primacy of news over opinion as one reason for this state of affairs. According to Reston, headlines displace editorial opinion and, since a President can usually dominate headlines at his pleasure, thus introducing his own bias into a newspaper's columns, he can overwhelm the critical, opinion-making function of the press.[22]   The news, in other words, is "manageable," even if the opinions of the press are not.

In managing the news, the President has enormous advantages. He can produce information or withhold it; he can lay claim to the media whenever he feels events justify the request for air-time; he can call press conferences when and if he desires and, once they are called, he can assume all the advantages that the podium offers any speaker; he can reward some journalists with interviews and "inside information" and punish others by exclusion or insult; he can "leak" information to the public by floating "trial balloons" (leaks which are able to be denied later or used as weapons in inter-departmental battles and in dealings with the Congress); he can appeal for self-censorship and chide dissenting opinion. In short, the President has the upper hand with the press in almost every respect but the expression of editorial opinion. Since American newspapers only give 3 to 8 percent of their general newsspace to "foreign affairs" and adult readers only read on the average about half a column of this material,[23] the actual influence of the press in moulding an active public opinion capable of restraining the Chief Executive should not be overrated.

Editorials, which are even less heeded than news by the average reader, do acquire considerable importance in the major newspapers, especially the *New York Times* and *Washington Post*. These papers have a direct influence on the Executive Branch and Congress, not just as a conveyor belt of news to an attentive public, but also as a sounding board of public opinion. Their editorials are part of an informed opinion "feedback" system and thereby constitute a daily measure of opinion very distinct from general newsspace which transmits or relays opinion.[24]

It is quite true that the *Times* and *Post* form the early morning reading of a large majority of officials responsible for foreign policy; it is equally true that the "prestige papers" such as these help to "define for the policy-makers the current political universe."[25] Yet the press remains dependent on the Chief Executive for most of its foreign policy news; its influence is almost always after the fact; and its editorial criticism is as likely to be an object of Executive scorn as dismay, an opinion to be changed rather than a voice to be followed.

The electronic media—television and radio—warrant separate discussion because of the quite different impact they have on foreign policy news. The audience for the electronic media is potentially larger than for the press. Each of the three major networks count their viewers in the millions whereas large-circulation newspapers count their readers in hundreds of thousands. More important than the difference in audience size is the difference in news presentation. Rigid time limits on the electronic media force the compression of news into a series of headlines with few if any qualifications or nuances. News on the electronic media is usually a gross distortion of reality compared to the printed word. Simplification of the news is often furthered by the demands of the medium. For example, reporting of the Vietnam War rarely employed the use of a satellite relay because of the costs involved. As a result, emphasis was placed on reporting the routine aspects of the war rather than the unexpected occurrences which would already have been reported by the press.[26] The monotony of the reporting on the war was largely a consequence of the economic and time limitations peculiar to television.

Is television and radio news less easily "managed" because of its directness? There is little more than speculation on this question and a few examples, largely drawn from political campaigns, of news manipulation. In the CBS documentary, "The Selling of the Pentagon," the network producers criticized the Department of Defense for staging or "reconstructing" military actions for the benefit of cameramen. Yet, evidently it was common operating procedure for troops to simulate battle for the benefit of cameramen.[27] News is, on occasion, "managed" or "reconstructed" or "staged," but it is certainly not completely manipulated to the benefit of policy-makers. The more disturbing feature of the electronic media is the impact it has in distorting perceptions of citizens and policy-makers alike from the realities of international politics. Important facets of American foreign policy—activities of an Embassy abroad, negotiations among high-level officials, the influence of business groups and leaders on foreign policy—are generally deleted from the presentation of "news" by the electronic media simply because they are difficult or impossible to report.

No discussion of the role of the press in foreign policy is complete without reference to *The Pentagon Papers*, published in mid-1971 by the *New York Times* and, subsequently, other national newspapers. This collection of documents, comprising a history of United States involvement in Indochina from World War II to May, 1968, when peace talks were opened in Paris, was commissioned by former Secretary of Defense Robert McNamara. The documents fill 4,000 pages and the narrative history, written by more than thirty government officials serving as historians and a handful of intellectuals involved in various consulting positions, fills an additional 3,000 pages. The entire collection offers a remarkable "inside view" of the making of foreign policy over a period of time, as well as an indispensable source of information for citizens troubled and concerned with the participation of the United States in that war.[28]

Our interest here in the *Pentagon Papers* is related to what the facts of their publication convey about the role of the press in its relations with the Chief Executive. After the first three installments were published by the *Times*, the Attorney General of the United States sought and obtained a temporary restraining order barring any further publication of the *Papers*. The collection had been, of course, classified "top secret" and was intended only for dissemination within the Executive Branch on the grounds that it included material whose publication would possibly jeopardize national security. Very rapidly, the legal conflict between the Executive Branch (the Attorney General) and the *New York Times* proceeded through the lower courts to the Supreme Court which held, by a vote of 6 to 3 on June 30, only seventeen days after initial publication, that sufficient justification for prior restraint on the publication of the *Papers* did not exist. Unquestionably, the Supreme Court's decision was an exceptionally powerful confirmation of the freedom of the press. But was it also supportive of the direct participation of the press in making foreign policy or in restraining the actions of the President? The answer is clearly presented in the opinion which concurs with the Court's decision written by Justice Stewart and to which Justice White joined his approval. It merits lengthy quotation:

In the absence of the governmental checks and balances present in other areas of our national ife, the only effective restraint upon executive policy and power in the areas of national defense and international affairs may lie in an enlightened citizenry—in an informed and critical public opinion which alone can here protect the value of democratic government. For this reason, it is perhaps here that a press that is alert, aware, and free most vitally serves the basic purpose of the First Amendment. For without an informed and free press there cannot be an enlightened people.

Yet it is elementary that the successful conduct of international diplomacy and the maintenance of an effective national defense require both confidentiality and secrecy. Other nations can hardly deal with this nation in an atmosphere of mutual trust unless they can be assured that their confidences will be kept. And within our own executive departments, the development of considered and intelligent international policies would be impossible if those charged with their formulation could not communicate with each other freely, frankly and in confidence. In the area of basic national defense the frequent need for absolute secrecy is, of course, self evident.

I think there can be but one answer to this dilemma, if dilemma it be. The responsibility must be where the power is. If the Constitution gives the executive a large degree of unshared power in the conduct of foreign affairs and the maintenance of our national defense, then under the Constitution the executive must have the largely unshared duty to determine and preserve the degree of internal security necessary to exercise that power successfully. . . .[29]

According to Justice Stewart, the Executive possesses both the authority and the power to determine the degree to which information regarding foreign policy is or is not released to the press. When failures occur in exercising that responsibility, i.e. when internal security measures break down, the political price must be paid since no other institution has the requisite knowledge nor procedure to substitute its own judgment. While another section of this opinion accords a role to Congress and the courts in protecting government secrets, the central thrust of the opinion remains a corroboration of the legal and political prerogatives of the Executive in its dealings with the press in matters of foreign policy. Although the government is technically the loser in this case, the primacy of the Executive is reasserted insofar as it is capable of controlling its own members.

PRESSURE GROUPS

We arrive at a more realistic understanding of the role of the Presidency in the conduct of American foreign policy when we recognize the restraints placed upon the office by the foreign affairs bureaucracy, Congress, public opinion, and the press. Yet, with these limitations on presidential power acknowledged, we do not find any decisive reason to adopt the thesis that the President is a beleaguered, disadvantaged official vis-à-vis other political institutions and interests.[30] Still to be considered, however, are the many interest groups whose pressure on public officials is often crudely portrayed as a determining influence. Some people readily accept as direct relationships: the United States' foreign policy toward the Arab world and the presence of American oil companies in the Middle East, the policy toward Israel and an influential Jewish community in the United States, and the authorization for grain shipments to Communist countries and the lobbying of farm organizations such as the American Farm Bureau. Troublesome questions arise, however, in making these facile judgments about the direction of influence. What happens, for example, when there are conflicting pressures from opposing groups, which is almost always the case? How are pressure groups able to influence the Executive? Are all issues subject to pressure-group activity?

Frequently, it is helpful to address questions like these by thinking of American government as a pluralist political system in which competing groups vie in the political process for their own ends. Common among the views of political scientists in explaining domestic politics, this pluralist conception of American democracy has rarely been extended to explain foreign policy formulation.[31] One reason it is less applicable to foreign policy is that the President and other officials do not act only in the role of arbiter, reconciling the competing claims and pressures of private groups in dealing with other countries. In certain categories of issues which are remote from direct group influence —most military questions and the handling of the United States' position in international crises in which national ideological factors tend to overshadow the interests of particular groups—the President does much more than arbitrate. He defines the issue and decides United States policy with little more than a backward glance at the probable attitudes of interested groups. But, in other areas of foreign policy decision-making, especially economic and monetary questions, the President is subjected to significant pressures from groups, indirectly through the Congress or directly through lobbying and informal approaches made by group representatives in the Executive Branch.

If we tentatively adopt the pluralist position, the first problem that confronts us is identification of contending groups. The conventional approach to this problem is to make a prior determination of an issue or set of issues and then investigate the participation of interested groups. An issue area such as foreign aid, for example, would show that pressures on policy are exerted by trade unions, the large industrial organizations such as the

National Association of Manufacturers, religious associations, shipping concerns, taxpayers' groups, and numerous others.

If we confine ourselves only to those groups whose *scope of interest* is likely to involve them in a wide variety of foreign policy issue areas, we find that in addition to the press, Congress, and other agencies of government, there is only one group, American business, whose interests are sufficiently broad to be treated separately. As economic issues become increasingly prominent in international affairs, the concern of American business with foreign policy increases and their attempts to influence policy become ever more vigorous. The spread of multinational American firms overseas, the role played by oil companies during the energy crisis, the movement of large firms into agriculture, and the evident connection between the rise of food exports and the increase in domestic prices of food all contribute to the easy judgment that American business is a dominant, if not controlling, force in the foreign policy-making process. Influence of multinational corporations may also be exerted on foreign governments, thereby posing difficult foreign policy issues for American officials, as in the case of ITT Corporation in Chile.[32]

Obviously, American business interests do have a formidable impact on certain types of foreign policy, not confined to financial and trade areas. It is inaccurate, however, as well as difficult, to establish any generalized cause-and-effect relationship between business interests and foreign policy.[33] "American business interests" are, to begin with, divided into a large number of sub-groups, such as producer and consumer, importer and exporter, manufacturing and marketing, and retail and wholesale. Even when many of these groups are joined together, as in the large multinational corporations—General Motors, Dupont, the large oil companies, and others—there is little evidence that common interests exist within the firms, much less among other firms dealing with different products and different types of economic problems. Controls on overseas investment may damage the interests of some large multinational firms but aid other competitors situated in the United States. Inflationary government spending may aid some enterprises and prove disastrous to others.

It is much more accurate to pinpoint the influence of business on foreign policy through an analysis of particular economic sectors or firms. That the influence exists is certain, but it varies widely depending on how large the foreign operations of the firm may be, its reliance on supplies from abroad, its relation to domestic employment, and a host of other factors. One area where the influence of business on foreign policy decisions appears plausible and consistent is in the development of a so-called military-industrial complex.

The Military-Industrial Complex

Since the mid-1960s, a renewed interest has developed in the relationship between the military supply side of American business and foreign policy. Business interests, principally those involved in producing and selling armaments, are claimed to be in alliance with military interests in the national defense establishment, forming what is labelled the military-industrial complex. This "complex" is presumably not a single, identifiable group in the sense of the Chamber of Commerce or the American Legion. Instead, it is a composite of various groups or interests whose influence is considered either considerable or controlling by various observers.[34] Its importance in recent interpretations of American foreign policy justifies according it separate attention.

Ironically, support for the view that industry and the military are joined in a powerful if informal alliance with a capability for "misplaced power" was furnished by a past Commander-in-Chief of the Armed Forces, President Eisenhower, in his "farewell" address. The phrase, "military-industrial complex," was coined in this address in a context which still deserves to be quoted:

This conjunction of an immense Military Establishment and a large arms industry is new in the American experience. The total influence—economic, political, even spiritual—is felt in every city, every statehouse, every office of the Federal Government. We recognize the imperative need for this development. Yet we must not fail to comprehend its grave implication. Our toil, resources, and livelihood are all involved; so is the very structure of our society.

In the councils of government we must guard against the acquisition of unwarranted influence whether sought or unsought, by the military-industrial complex. The potential for the disastrous rise of misplaced power exists and will persist. [35]

Although President Eisenhower bequeathed an authoritative warning to the American public about the rise of a military-industrial complex, concern about the relationship between munitions makers and the military establishment is not new. In 1934, Senator Gerald Nye of North Dakota held a series of congressional hearings based on the assumption that enormous profits made by arms manufacturers before and during World War I were an incentive for business leaders to pressure United States entry into the war. These hearings failed to establish any causal relationship of the kind anticipated or any evidence of conspiracy between the armaments industry and military leaders. The Nye Hearings are today only a distant memory and probably should remain so. The circumstances of superpower status combined with the prolonged existence of a large-scale military establishment suggest that the results of the Nye Hearings should only serve as a caution against a too facile assumption that the use of military hardware is intended by manufacturers and desired by the military.

There is abundant evidence that a military-industrial complex exists in the United States. A defense budget which hovers at $80 to $90 billion annually, with approximately one-third of this sum ear-marked for procurement of military goods, provides *prima facie* evidence for the view that there is reciprocal dependence on the part of industry and the military. The question, then, is not whether the complex exists but in what way it is organized and, as corollaries, whether there is any centralized control of it and, most importantly, to what extent, if any, it influences the conduct of American foreign policy. Does the existence of a military-industrial complex undo the constitutional position of presidential primacy in the conduct of American foreign policy and weight that policy in favor of military solutions to international problems?

Some controversial answers to these questions are supplied in *Pentagon Capitalism*, a potent indictment by Seymour Melman of the military-industrial complex and its role in American foreign policy.[36] Melman claims that a new institution has succeeded the loose collection of groups formerly labelled the military-industrial complex. He calls this new institution the "state-management" and dates its origins to the tenure of Robert McNamara as Secretary of Defense under President Kennedy. The "state-management" is a centralized, managerial institution headquartered in the Pentagon; it is "the most powerful decision-making unit in the United States government."[37] It has a propensity to expand, the criterion of its success. Whereas the military-industrial complex was characterized by "an informality of relationships" with the understanding "that the main interest groups concerned tend to move together, each of them motivated by its own special concerns, but with enough common ground to produce a mutually reinforcing effect," the "state-management" is "clearly structured and formally organized."[38]

Unfortunately, Melman does not make any serious effort to link the "state-management" to the conduct of American foreign policy. He assumes a "pattern of exploitative imperalism" abroad on the parts of both business and military leaders but focuses his attention on "an institutional network that is parasitic at home."[39] By failing to address the foreign-policy objectives by which political leaders have justified the growth of a large military establishment, Melman has overlooked many of the conventional reasons for the existence of military forces. In addition, there are substantial difficulties in Melman's analysis, such as his assertion of a tendency for the defense budget to decline as a proportion of the overall federal budget, and in absolute terms, if inflationary factors are discounted. Many readers of Melman, and virtually all responsible officials in government, would consider his views misguided at best and, in private conversations, nonsensical. Yet the plausibility of some of the argumentation as well as the extensive research which supports Melman's view of "state-management" is too reminiscent of the attitude expressed in Calvin Coolidge's aphorism that "the business of America is business," to be dismissed cavalierly. Without any agreed-upon measure of the influence of the military-industrial complex on American foreign policy, we have no convincing reason for assuming the primacy of the President has been supplanted by this composite pressure group. We have compelling reasons, however, for developing and insisting upon procedures that will insure awareness of alliances between military and business leaders and assure countervailing voices and pressures.

CONCLUSION

In our survey of those flexible limits on the primacy of the President in foreign policy which originate in the private sector of American society, we have encountered the same ambiguity as in previous discussions of the foreign affairs bureaucracy and Congress. On the one hand, the President is subject to the constraints and influence of an attentive and informed public opinion; of the press, which all Presidents see at varying times as being critical and even hostile to official policies; of pressure groups in at least the economic areas of foreign policy; and finally, of the military-industrial complex, with its high concentration of resources and interests. On the other hand, each of these elements of the private sector, and their related organizations, offers the President a means of strengthening his hand toward opposition in the domestic political system or in dealings with other countries. Presidents often seem to prevail when opposed by various groups or a vocal segment of the public; more often, they prevail by gaining the support of the public, the press, or other competing influential groups in American society. Despite some contrary evidence (perhaps President Johnson's decision not to run for a second term, announced in March, 1968, or President Nixon's decision on Cambodia), and with the realization that foreign policy decisions rarely are reached in conformity with a tidy allocation of responsibility within a carefully controlled chain-of-command, there is ample reason to accept the previously quoted statement of President Truman, "I make foreign policy." [40]

We turn to the concluding chapter, in which some of the future issues of American foreign policy are discussed, with the understanding that the primacy of the President in the making of foreign policy has been only slightly, if at all, eroded by the competing forces of the American political system.

9. *Conclusion*

> *"If all mankind minus one, were of*
> *one opinion, and only one person were*
> *of the contrary opinion, mankind would*
> *be no more justified in silencing that*
> *one person, than he, if he had the*
> *power, would be justified in silencing*
> *mankind."*
> —John Stuart Mill

In this final chapter, we shall present some of the broad conclusions which emerge from our description of American foreign policy. In addition, we will comment on the specific issues discussed in Chapter 1, and then seek to present a general position or perspective to the intelligent citizen committed to democratic principles suggesting how he might approach these issues. In so doing, we will comment directly on citizen responsibility in the development of American foreign policy.

We begin by acknowledging the enormous complexity of foreign policy and the foreign policy-making process, and the ultimate responsibility formally borne by the President in these areas. The President carries responsibility for foreign policy in ways he does not for domestic policy, and he possesses constitutional, institutional, and political resources incomparably superior to those he wields in the domestic sphere. Yet, these resources are not sufficient to enable him to impose his will regularly on the policy-making process. In addition to the limitations of experience and environment, the foreign affairs bureaucracy and Congress, parties, interest groups and public opinion, all described in earlier chapters, the President is inhibited from fully controlling foreign policy by competing demands on his time and the need to avoid "presidential overkill."

Competing demands on the President's time is the most self-evident of these limiting factors. No President is able to devote equal personal attention to all foreign policy issues, nor should he. No President is able to insure that his closest advisors devote their time appropriately to the variety of issues which confront the American government at any given time. The problem for all Presidents is to use their time, and that of their principal advisors, optimally. The optimal use of presidential time means not only attending to the most pressing issues—all Presidents do this—but also to attend to those issues which will be tomorrow's crises if they are not dealt with today. Presidents almost always find that they do not have time to do that with any consistency. President Eisenhower learned that the time required to attend to the election of 1956, to the problems created by his Secretary of State's serious illness, and to his own recuperation from a serious heart attack left no opportunity to give unambiguous signals to our closest ally, the British, in time to prevent the Suez crisis of 1956. President Kennedy found that the time required to get his administration in working order deprived him of time to study and evaluate the policies already being implemented, such as the one which led to the Bay of Pigs disaster. President Nixon found that the time required to deal with Vietnam made it impossible for him to pay sufficient attention to the necessity of reversing the deterioration of the Atlantic alliance. Of course, when a President has time to examine an issue carefully, there is no guarantee that he will make appropriate decisions, nor is the lack of attention to a policy area synonymous with bad policy, a condition which may have been demonstrated by the "benign neglect" of Latin America by the Nixon administration. Still, the analyst of foreign policy finds case after case in which Presidents and their top advisors are unable to work their will because of competing demands on their time and attention.

"Presidential overkill" is a more subtle concept, but equally limiting. It suggests that presidential resources need to be used prudently. A President may, as we suggest in Chapter 5, create a crisis or raise an issue to the level of crisis in order to increase his freedom to maneuver, but he cannot raise every issue to the level of crisis. If he does, he will find that crises no longer free him from the "prison" of past policies or the "prison" of bureaucratic politics or any of the other "prisons" which ordinarily limit his freedom of action. He may use his position to take a case to the people, in ways we described in Chapter 8, but if he does so too often, he will find the people no longer listening. He may commit the Congress to his program by presenting it forcefully in person, as Harry Truman did with the Truman Doctrine in 1947, but if he appears before too many joint sessions of the Congress, he will find the effect of such appearances subject to the law of diminishing returns. If he neglects domestic policy he may find that his low reputation in that field spills over onto the foreign policy field as well. In short, the President must use his resources judiciously and expend them on issues of highest priority only. Otherwise, he will lack the resources to overcome the myriad other institutional and political restraints on his freedom of action and discover that he must bow to policies determined, not by presidential decision, but by international circumstance, by congressional or popular whim, and by bureaucratic bargaining.

Presidential resources cannot be measured in a fixed way as though they are savings in a bank account where a dollar spent is a dollar unavailable for future expenditure. They are more flexible. They may be expanded by the successful use of presidential power or they may contract through presidential ineptitude. They are found in presidential charisma as well as in the statute books, in presidential personality as much as in his role as commander-in-chief, in his ability to persuade as much as in his power of patronage. Controlling their use and their availability is the essential skill of the Presidency. Mastery of this skill differentiates the "strong" President from the "weak."

The resources of the Presidency are sufficient, when judiciously and skillfully used, to overcome most limitations. It is in this sense that we asserted in Chapter 5 that the President makes foreign policy. He can overcome the weight of history as Presidents Roosevelt and Truman did in taking the United States into the United Nations and into the long-term postwar alliances; he can dominate the Congress as President Truman did in enunciating the Truman Doctrine; he can mobilize the slow-moving and internally divided bureaucracy as President Nixon did in the aftermath of his visit to China; he can galvanize and unite public opinion as President Kennedy did in the Cuban missile crisis; he can even muzzle the press—at least temporarily—as President Kennedy did in the Bay of Pigs; he can persuade, blackmail, or force foreign powers to support his action, as President Johnson did in the Dominican crisis and President Nixon did with the British in Vietnam.

There are innumerable other foreign policy issues which the President is not forced to, or does not choose to, make his own. How are they made or changed in the American setting? No simple answer can be given since the complexities of the American government, the fragmentation of power in the American system, and the influence of experience and culture contrive to give varying importance to different individuals and groups, both within and outside the government, on different foreign policy issues. A few general conclusions resulting from our analysis can be confidently stated about the handling of this multitude of disparate issues which, except for brief appearances on the stage of international politics, fall outside the panorama of sustained public and presidential attention.

1. *Issues will be defined differently by different groups, and will be seen from different perspectives by them.* There are two aspects to this divergence of perspectives. First, there is the

difference in perspective which results from the divergent institutional needs of various agencies of government. Thus a foreign policy issue will be perceived in one way by one department of government and in quite a different way by another department. Some departments will have domestic constituencies which will be important factors in their consideration of issues. Others will have no such constituencies. Some will have easy relations of mutual support with the Congress; others will not. Some will be led by a Secretary who is a close confidant of the President; others will not. All of these factors and more make for conflicting perceptions of foreign policy issues and their solutions among departments. Within the American government (or any government for that matter) people and agencies rarely, if ever, adopt a policy position solely because of an abstract or even concrete conception of some national interest. That is not to say they oppose the national interest; rather, they tend to see policy prescription more as being in the interest of the Departments of State, Treasury, Agriculture, or Defense, the CIA, or any one of the myriad other agencies involved in foreign policy-making. The concept of the national interest is sufficiently broad and ambiguous to easily accommodate such divergent policy positions.

The second aspect of divergent perceptions involves the national interest itself. Conflicting perceptions of the national interest may be related to differing agency affiliations, but this will not necessarily be the case. It is also possible for the highest ranking decision-makers to have basically different views about the national interest, quite apart from any institutional interests. An official who believes it is America's primary interest to foster national self-determination will take a quite different view of the Dominican crisis of 1965 than one who places a high priority on the resistance to Communist expansion. A similar divergence of views was apparent in the Cuban missile crisis of 1962 when Attorney General Robert Kennedy resisted the military recommendation for a surprise air strike and invasion of Cuba on the grounds that the national interest would be ill-served by a policy which would be remembered as a "Pearl Harbor in reverse." Others, like former Secretary of State Dean Acheson found this conception of the national interest inappropriate and emphasized the need to redress the military balance which the Soviets, he argued, had upset by installing offensive missiles in Cuba.[1]

Conflicting institutional interests and perceptions of the national interest will mean that a clear definition of the issue at hand will not be easy to come by. Different spokesmen will emphasize different aspects of the problem, reflecting differing perceptions. Both within and outside the government, conflicting definitions of the issue will complicate the search for solutions and will condition the solutions advocated by various officials.

2. *Policy choice will tend to be the result of bargaining.* As each participant in the decision-making process brings his own perception of the issue to bear on the making of policy, it will be hard to find readily agreeable policy choices. Since most foreign policy issues now involve several departments and agencies of government, as we noted in Chapter 6, each official tends to bring to the decision-making process a separate set of interests. Departments are theoretical equals, although each has a set of resources which makes some, like Orwell's farm animals, more equal than others. The distribution of resources, however, is not fixed; it will vary from issue to issue and from one period to another. Despite hierarchical organization (the President being uninvolved, or only tangentially involved, in most issues) the decision-making process takes on the character of bargaining.[2] The result will ordinarily be compromise on a policy choice which all participants can accept. Although many participants will possess an effective veto power over decisions, and failure to agree will push the issue to the next level of the hierarchy and, ultimately, to the President himself, this sequence of events is

avoided because it removes individuals from the decision-making group and increases the risk that a strongly held position will be overruled.[3] Thus, there is a tendency to settle at the point of the least common denominator through a bargaining process unless policy positions are completely irreconcilable. Irreconcilable issues are passed up to the next level of the bureaucratic hierarchy where perceptions of institutional and national interests may again differ and encourage a solution by bargaining. Ultimately, failure to bargain effectively means the issue lands on the President's desk where, as Truman noted, the buck stops! But Truman was wrong in one sense. If the President is unable or unwilling to decide, the issue is apt to go unresolved, each agency possessing sufficient resources to prevent a solution it does not want, but none possessing resources sufficient to impose its will on others. An unresolved issue permits each agency or department to act on the basis of its own desired solution, which gives foreign policy its often noted character of confusion, poor coordination, or disorder.

3. *Policy will not be clearly defined.* Since most foreign policy results from a bargaining process in which compromise is reached at the lowest common denominator, or a failure to resolve divergent policy positions at all, it is not surprising that the definition of policy is far from clear, either within the government, to the public, or to foreign powers. Failure to resolve an issue, as we have just noted, leaves each agency free to try to do all it can to implement its desired policy. But even when policy has been agreed upon, it is up to separate departments and agencies to implement it, and thereby to emphasize those aspects of the agreed policy decision which are most in line with its preferred solution. Government agencies at home and abroad often seem to be working at cross purposes; United States policy seems contradictory; there seem to be (and the appearance is fact) foreign *policies* rather than a single American foreign policy. Control of policy implementation, the maintenance of unity and

cohesion, and the imposition of order become central problems in the foreign policy process. The involvement in foreign affairs of agencies and institutions not even legally subject to administration control—the Congress, trade unions, American based multinational corporations, and other private groups—only adds to the fragmentation of policy and the multiplication of foreign *policies*.

4. *Policy change will be slow and incremental.* Like all large organizations, governments tend to devise new policies by making minor, incremental changes in existing policies. Policy-making is rarely conceived of as an exercise in choosing from among an exhaustive list of alternative policies, but is rather an adjustment in existing policy. This tendency is clearest in budgeting, where organizations rarely begin by asking how best to divide the funds available but, more typically, begin by asking what adjustments are appropriate in the items in last year's budget. Less precisely, but with equal significance, the same tendency can be seen in other aspects of policy-making.[4]

Furthermore, large organizations are characterized by a tendency to focus attention on present rather than on potential problems. So long as a policy *seems* to be working successfully, there will be little inclination to examine it systematically or to assess its future implications. Such changes as are required will tend to be minor adjustments rather than wholesale re-evaluations. Only the dramatic, clearly apparent failure of a policy will call forth the kind of analysis required to develop major policy changes. The world-view of policy-makers changes slowly (if at all) in the absence of *dramatic* evidence of changed conditions. Thus, there is a tendency for policy to perpetuate itself until crisis forces thorough reconsideration.[5]

5. *Immediate issues will get prime attention; long-range planning will be neglected.* Another characteristic of all large organizations, reinforced in the case of foreign policy by certain traits of the American character discussed in Chapter 4, is the inclination to focus on immediate policy questions to the neglect

of long-range planning. There are many reasons for this tendency. First there is the simple problem of competing pressures. Busy officials have little time to contemplate long-range issues, pressed as they are for immediate answers to immediate questions. Moreover, they have little time for other officials who are specifically charged with long-term planning and who are seen by their busy operational colleagues as divorced from the real world of immediate considerations. Long-range planning is the one task which large organizations can put off with no immediate ill effects. Long-range planning can be done tomorrow or next week or next month because the "long-range" can always be postponed; today's crisis has to be dealt with today. Furthermore, the immediate problems are "where the action is" and, therefore, where the promotions and the psychic satisfactions are. The astute and the ambitious will naturally gravitate to them, avoiding long-range issues and leaving them to less action-oriented colleagues or to academic analysts who do not have to accept the consequences of their recommendations or analyses.

AMERICA IN THE LAST QUARTER OF THE TWENTIETH CENTURY

If we return now to the major areas of debate discussed in Chapter 1, it is evident that the evolution of American foreign policy is not likely to conform to a well-ordered plan, to demonstrate much consistency, or to help restore a consensus on objectives. The areas of debate which we described earlier: identification of major forces of change in the world; United States responsibility to other states; the role of the United States in maintaining order; and the critical controversy of urgent domestic significance, who should make foreign policy; will continue as basic dimensions of a continuing debate on American foreign relations. There is no apparent possibility of restoring a consensus on foreign policy such as existed during the period

1945-65, nor is there any prospect for a new substantive consensus.

While debate on foreign policy continues, the major problems (identified earlier in issue clusters attached to the four major areas of debate) will not be fully resolved and will be only tentatively managed or postponed, subject to cautious approaches, but, generally, poorly defined and resistant to long-range planning. Dramatic initiatives may be expected from time to time—initiatives which will break the hold of past dogmas and open a new range of options. Specific predictions of the outcome of these issues cannot be made with any confidence in view of the nature of the policy-making process and the context for policy described in earlier chapters. Even in that issue cluster attached to the debate on the role of the United States in maintaining order, a set of issues where there would appear to be ample basis for reducing the degree of ambiguity, no clear direction is discernible. It appears likely that support for the United Nations will continue but without enthusiasm and, despite occasional pleadings for a stronger United Nations police force, no agreement seems likely on extending the role of the United Nations in the maintenance of international peace, except in specific situations such as Cyprus. The issue of alliances and alliance management, especially NATO, would seem to be beyond dispute. NATO at least has been one of the most enduring and respected features of American foreign policy since its inauguration. Whether this will continue depends on the actions of the Europeans, notably in economic relations with the United States, and the result of bargaining among administration, congressional, and Executive agency representatives on the future size of the American commitment of troops and resources to the alliance. The issue of overseas bases remains unclearly defined and intertwined with numerous other issues in other areas of debate, particularly, the types and amounts of military expenditures. The same is true of military assistance programs. Finally, the problem of reaching agreement on criteria for military intervention, despite the general disenchantment following United States participation in the wars of Indochina, appears much less susceptible to solution than during the period of consensus politics and will likely remain so.

Inability to reach any clear agreement on the probable outcome of most major issues of American foreign policy during the next decade or two should not prove troubling to students or policy-makers. The foreign policy-making process in the United States does not work to produce "grand designs" or a genuinely coherent policy. Even if it appeared to do so, actions of other nation-states would constantly interfere with the realization of any "grand design" that might be followed, causing national frustration. Debate is, therefore, a desirable as well as an inevitable feature of foreign policy-making in the United States, once the failings of a consensus on the substance of policy are recognized. Debate is not, however, a decision on policy but only a means to that decision. Responsibility must still be assumed for decisions, the subject to which we now turn.

THE RESPONSIBILITY OF AMERICANS: THE FUTURE OF CONSENSUS POLITICS

A wise man once said, "The only dogma of democracy is that there is no dogma." This is true to the extent that democratic theory emphasizes procedures for decision but no independent criteria for judging the rightness of decisions. American democracy, however, has occasionally tended to sacrifice procedures for the pursuit of specific objectives, notably in the area of foreign policy. Consensus politics, as it has been practiced in the United States, is characterized by the imposition of a dogma which stifles foreign policy debate and dictates foreign policy perspectives.

The deleterious effects of consensus politics on the substance of foreign policy can best be seen in the ways that limits
on American intervention were cast off (described in Chapter 3).
Consensus politics is also evident in American attitudes toward
the European unification movement in general, and the Common
Market in particular. The consensus in the United States which
viewed federal unity as one of the keys to the nation's success led
Americans to prescribe similar solutions for Europeans. Such a
prescription was actually inserted into the Marshall Plan act by
Congress. When the European Common Market was established in
1958, American policy-makers rushed to support it as a step
toward fulfillment of the American federalist dream for Europe.
With similar devotion to the dogma of federalism, Americans
actively supported British membership in the Common Market in
the 1960s, support which was partly responsible for American
troubles with General de Gaulle who was opposed to British
entry. Throughout this period, dogmatic support for European
unity was based, not on a continuing analysis of American
interests, but on the nostalgic reading of the American experience. Only on the eve of British entry, in the early 1970s, did the
general breakdown of consensus politics permit a more sophisticated analysis of the effect of European unification on American
interests. A change in policy dependent on consensus is usually a
traumatic occurrence. Change would also occur in policy which
emerged from a deliberative process dependent on a reasoned
choice among carefully analyzed and debated alternatives, one in
which policy prescriptions would not depend primarily on easy
assumptions to which all policy-makers adhered. Policy which
departed from the comfortable reassurance of consensus and was
the result of constant analysis and reappraisal should be at once
less traumatic and more understandable abroad.

The sweeping away of consensus politics is not a panacea
for the problems that beset American foreign policy. One result
of a complete disappearance of consensus would be to give free

rein to the advocates of divergent foreign policies. Fragmentation of policy could be greater than ever. This is the most serious threat created by those who currently engage in the battle to "restore" the role of Congress in foreign policy-making. Interestingly enough, they are often the same people who, little more than a decade ago, were campaigning for ways of strengthening the President's ability to overcome a reluctant and recalcitrant Congress. The reason for this contradictory behavior is that they are looking in the wrong places for solutions to problems. The question is not whether the Congress or the President is endowed with sufficient statutory or constitutional authority. For the critics of the Kennedy Congresses and of President Nixon, the central question is really one of which policy they supported. In the earlier period, it was the policy of the President, and they wanted his hand strengthened; later it was policies advocated by some articulate members of Congress, and they sought to strengthen Congress at the expense of the President on the assumption that the entire Congress would follow their policy preference. (As an old mountain man in Kentucky used to say, "When people say, 'It ain't the money, it's the principle;' it's the money!") One reason confusion abounds in proposals for congressional reform is that people seem to be trying to strengthen Congress when what they are really trying to do is change the President's policies. The reverse is equally true, of course. Such efforts are not totally misplaced, for they are one way of bringing political pressures to bear on a President to change his policies.

Nevertheless, it is clear that in the mid-1970s, the President, and only the President, can bear the final responsibility for foreign policy. The factors described in Chapter 5 simply cannot be reversed. Unity, secrecy, speed, information—all of these mean that the President, ultimately, must make foreign policy. A *procedural* consensus which represents agreement on this central point is essential to an effective foreign policy. But a procedural consensus should go farther; it should include an acceptance by all—the President as well as the Congress—of the legitimacy of foreign policy debate, a debate which seeks to identify, explain, and question the fundamental assumptions of foreign policy, the method by which it is carried out, and the competence of those responsible for it.

Such a procedural consensus would be a radical departure from the one which informs much of foreign policy debate today and has done so throughout the postwar era. It suggests a more restricted view of the requirements of secrecy than has usually been displayed by the Executive Branch. A President who accepts this kind of procedural consensus will try to keep press, public, and Congress as fully knowledgeable as possible so that debate over substantive foreign policy may be informed. Specifically, this requires a much more restricted view of Executive privilege than has characterized recent administrations, especially that of President Nixon; greater availability of the President and other administration officials to the press; and a much more limited view of what information must be kept secret. Above all, a President must recognize that criticism, far from being seditious or treasonous, as some recent Presidents have implied, is essential to a healthy foreign policy.

The Congress, too, must accept a new procedural consensus. It requires, in the first instance, that Congressmen accept restraint on the use of executive sessions by committees, a device which indicates that Congress prizes secrecy fully as much as the President does. Furthermore, if a healthy foreign policy debate is to be fostered, members of the Congress must begin to understand the British notion that the function of the opposition is to oppose—not to obstruct. Such a practice cannot be simply transplanted from Westminster to Capitol Hill, for the American Chief Executive, unlike his British counterpart, is not a creature of the legislature. Since Congress is often controlled by the opposition, American legislators will have to pay particular attention to the fine but crucial distinction between opposition and obstruction. If they recognize the first principle of our new procedural consensus—that the President bears ultimate responsibility for foreign policy—that distinction should be easy to keep clearly in view.

We conclude, therefore, that there should be an end of bipartisanship in foreign affairs. In our view, it has not served the nation well. If the function of party politics in the United States is, among other things, to provide alternatives for public choice, the effect of bipartisanship is to deny such a choice. If the function of party politics is, among other things, to enable the electorate to hold officials responsible, the effect of bipartisanship is to remove that ability. The decline of bipartisanship in foreign policy is not something to be decried; its complete demise is something to be devoutly hoped for. Politics should not stop at the water's edge.

This prescription for a new procedural consensus in foreign policy implies the hope (and it is only that) that press and citizenry will become more active and more sophisticated participants in foreign policy debate. There are features of our new procedural consensus which should encourage such a development—greater availability of information, greater participation by Congress in debate on fundamental issues, greater openness of the policy process to informed opinion. On the other hand, the evidence of overwhelming public apathy on most foreign policy issues in the past and sporadic and oversimplified press coverage does not engender confidence in predicting change. But even if greater participation is not generated, the new procedural consensus—one which prizes and encourages serious debate about fundamental issues in the context of an awareness of ultimate presidential responsibility—should improve the formulation and execution of foreign policy.

Such a procedural consensus would imply a far greater tolerance of fundamentally divergent views within our own society. That, in itself, is no small benefit. One can also expect related principles to spill over onto American behavior in world affairs, as the principles on which the substantive Cold War consensus did. The new procedural consensus should stimulate greater tolerance for diversity in an increasingly pluralistic world. This represents a direct attack on the past rigidities of American policy. A President and a people who do not feel threatened by internal dissent should feel less threatened by criticism and cultural and political diversity abroad. The incentive to intervene to make the world over in the American image—often characteristic of the Cold War consensus—would be diminished. American intervention, indeed, all features of American policy, would no longer take off from the dictates of an oversimplified consensus that too easily identified friend and foe, assumed the rightness and wrongness of various courses of action, and celebrated American interests in universal terms. Instead, policy would be nonideological, constantly subject to reappraisals of basic assumptions as well as particular courses of action. There would be a consistency to such policy based on continuing debate and gradual changes, rather than a consistency stemming from reflexive responses to the actions of other states. The goals of such policy would be less grandiose but more clearly understood by all. There would be a surer sense of what was possible gained by policy-makers who would become accustomed to analyze and deliberate rather than to respond with the "quick draw."

To urge a new procedural consensus and the abandonment of a substantive one is no panacea. There are no genuine panaceas in the making of foreign policy. Certainly, our prescription does not guarantee correct choices but only increases the possibility of minimizing error. It is our conviction that in a world of political conflict and cooperation, the more demanding effort of making foreign policy on the basis of a reasoned and debated analysis of basic assumptions, as well as immediate events, is preferable to a substantive consensus.

Notes

Chapter 1

1. *United States Foreign Policy for the 1970's: A New Strategy for Peace: A Message from the President of the United States* (Washington: Government Printing Office, 1970), p. 1.
2. Seyom Brown, *The Faces of Power: Constancy and Change in United States Foreign Policy from Truman to Johnson* (New York: Columbia University Press, 1968), p. 378.
3. For a supporting assessment of the continuing hold of the postwar consensus as well as an alternative formulation of the assumptions upon which it was based, see Lincoln Bloomfield, "Foreign Policy for Disillusioned Liberals," *Foreign Policy,* No. 9 (Winter, 1972-73), pp. 55-68.
4. See Zbigniew Brzezinski, "How the Cold War was Played," *Foreign Affairs,* 51 (October, 1972), p. 183.
5. See Brown, *op. cit.,* for a history of postwar policy based on security and balance of power themes.
6. Harry S. Truman, *Memoirs,* Vol. 2, *Years of Trial and Hope* (Garden City, N.Y.: Doubleday, 1956), p. 513.
7. Walter Lippmann, *The Cold War: A Study in U.S. Foreign Policy* (New York: Harper, 1947).
8. See Lloyd Gardner, "Mr. Truman and the Revisionists: Beyond the Devil Theory of the Cold War," (Paper presented to the Vassar College Cold War Conference, April 26, 1968).
9. See the comments of former Vice President Agnew, reported in *New York Times,* June 4, 1970, p. 35; June 21, 1970, p. 39.
10. For some historical comparisons which support this conclusion, see Robert L. Beisner, "1898 and 1968: The Anti-Imperialists and the Doves," *Political Science Quarterly,* LXXXV (June, 1970), pp. 187-216, and Samuel Eliot Morison, Frederich Merk, and Frank Freidel, *Dissent in Three American Wars* (Cambridge: Harvard University Press, 1970).
11. See Robert W. Tucker, *The Radical Left and American Foreign Policy* (Baltimore: The Johns Hopkins Press, 1971).
12. Significant literature on this includes Leslie H. Gelb, "Vietnam: The System Worked," *Foreign Policy,* No. 3 (Summer, 1971), pp. 140-167; Richard M. Pfeffer (ed.), *No More Vietnams?* (New York: Harper and Row, 1968), pp. 44-114; and James C. Thomson, "How Could Vietnam Happen? An Autopsy," *The Atlantic Monthly,* 22 (April, 1968), pp. 47-53.

13.   The major re-evaluations of the Cold War are Lloyd Gardner, Arthur Schlesinger, Jr., and Hans Morgenthau, *The Origin of the Cold War* (Waltham, Mass.: Ginn-Blaisdell, 1970); Gar Alperovitz, *Atomic Diplomacy: Hiroshima and Potsdam* (New York: Random House, 1965); Martin F. Herz, *The Beginnings of the Cold War* (Bloomington: Indiana University Press, 1966); D. F. Fleming, *The Cold War and Its Origins, 1917-1960,* 2 vols. (New York: Doubleday, 1961); Joyce and Gabriel Kolko, *The Limits of Power: The World and United States Foreign Policy* (New York: Harper and Row, 1972); on the Korean War, I. F. Stone, *The Hidden History of the Korean War* (New York: Monthly Review Press, 1952); on the Dominican invasion, Theodore Draper, *The Dominican Revolt: A Case Study in American Policy* (New York: Commentary, 1968); on the Third World, Richard J. Barnet, *Intervention and Revolution: America's Confrontation with Insurgent Movements Around the World* (Cleveland and New York: World Publishing Co., 1968).

14.   This perspective on congressional-presidential relations may be gleaned from Arthur Schlesinger, Jr., "Congress and the Making of American Foreign Policy," *Foreign Affairs,* 51 (October, 1972), pp. 78-113, and above, Chapter 7, pp. 181-204; on the military-industrial complex from John Kenneth Galbraith, *How to Control the Military* (New York: New American Library, 1969); Seymour Melman, *Pentagon Capitalism: the Political Economy of War* (New York: McGraw Hill, 1970); and Mark Pilisuk and Thomas Hayden, "Is There a Military-Industrial Complex Which Prevents Peace?: Consensus and Countervailing Power in Pluralistic Systems," *Journal of Social Issues,* XXI (1965), pp. 67-117; on American corporate power in the international arena from the review article by Robert Keohane and V. Ooms, "Multinational Enterprise and the World Political Economy," *International Organization* (Winter, 1972), pp. 84-120, and the works cited therein.

15.   For another exposition of these different schools and some examples of the analysis of each, see Howard Bliss and M. Glen Johnson (eds.), *Consensus at the Crossroads: Dialogues in American Foreign Policy* (New York: Dodd, Mead, 1972).

16.   More extensive expositions of traditionalist views can be found in almost any major foreign policy address of the postwar Presidents and Secretaries of State. A particularly good source is the Department of State *Bulletin* which prints such speeches and many other relevant documents depicting official positions. The memoirs of Presidents Truman, Eisenhower, and Johnson and Secretary of State

Dean Acheson are also useful sources. Some of President Kennedy's foreign policy pronouncements suggest a move away from the traditionalist view and these have been emphasized by his major biographers. See Arthur Schlesinger, Jr., *A Thousand Days* (Boston: Houghton Mifflin, 1965) and Theodore Sorensen, *Kennedy* (New York: Harper and Row, 1965). For a useful analysis which emphasizes the foreign policy traditionalism of the Kennedy Presidency, see Richard J. Walton, *Cold War and Counter-revolution: The Foreign Policy of John F. Kennedy* (New York: Viking, 1972).

17. A more extensive treatment of the limitationist critique of American policy may be found in Charles Gati, "Another Grand Debate? The Limitationist Critique of American Foreign Policy," *World Politics,* XXI (October, 1968), pp. 133-151; Robert W. Tucker, "The American Outlook," in Robert E. Osgood et al., *America and the World: From Truman Doctrine to Vietnam* (Baltimore: The Johns Hopkins Press, 1970), pp. 27-78; and Robert W. Tucker, *Nation or Empire?: The Debate over American Foreign Policy* (Baltimore: The Johns Hopkins Press, 1968). Also interesting expressions of the limitationist perspective are George F. Kennan, *Memoirs: 1925-1950* (Boston: Little, Brown, 1967) and *Memoirs: 1950-1963* (London: Hutchinson, 1973); and J. William Fulbright, *The Arrogance of Power* (New York: Random House, 1966). Much of the congressional criticism of American foreign policy after the escalation of the Vietnam War falls into the limitationist category.

18. The revisionist literature has become quite voluminous in recent years. An excellent analysis of this critique can be found in Robert W. Tucker, *The Radical Left and American Foreign Policy* (Baltimore: The Johns Hopkins Press, 1971). See also his *A New Isolationism: Threat or Promise* (New York: Universe Books, 1972). The main inspiration of recent revisionist writing is D. F. Fleming, *op. cit.* The reader is also urged to consult the writings of William Appleman Williams, Gabriel Kolko, Gar Alperovitz, David Horowitz, and Carl Oglesby.

19. See, for example, William Appleman Williams, *The Tragedy of American Diplomacy* (New York: Dell, 1962).

20. See, for example, Michael Parenti (ed.), *Trends and Tragedies in American Foreign Policy* (Boston: Little, Brown, 1971).

21. Gabriel Kolko, *The Roots of American Foreign Policy* (Boston: Beacon Press, 1969), pp. 14-26, 140-142; and G. William Domhoff, "Who Made American Foreign Policy, 1945-63?" in David Horowitz,

(ed.), *Corporations and the Cold War* (New York: Monthly Review Press, 1969), pp. 24-48, 64-7.

22. There is an immense literature on nationalism. Among the best treatments of its nature and its role in international affairs are Carelton J. H. Hayes, *Essays on Nationalism* (New York: Macmillan, 1926); Hans Kohn, *The Idea of Nationalism: A Study of Its Origins and Background* (New York: Macmillan, 1944); Boyd C. Shafer, *Nationalism: Myth and Reality* (New York: Harcourt, Brace, 1955); Elie Kedourie, *Nationalism* (New York: Praeger, 1960); Barbara Ward, *Nationalism and Ideology* (New York: Norton, 1966); and Anthony D. Smith, *Theories of Nationalism* (New York: Harper, 1971).

23. Among the best expositions of Marxism as an ideology is R. N. Carew-Hunt, *The Theory and Practice of Communism* (New York: Macmillan, 1957).

24. John H. Kautsky, *Communism and the Politics of Development* (New York: Wiley, 1968).

25. See especially, the perceptive critique by Fulbright, *op. cit.,* pp. 76-78.

26. For a fuller explanation of the term and an examination of its meaning for international politics, see Hans J. Morgenthau, *Politics Among Nations,* 5th ed. (New York: Knopf, 1973), pp. 40-44.

27. A much clearer view of international affairs and American foreign policy is gained by considering the concept of "intervention" in other than purely military terms.

28. An earlier example of roughly the same imagery can be found in President Franklin D. Roosevelt's "Quarantine the Aggressor" speech of 1937.

29. See, for example, Hans J. Morgenthau, *In Defense of the National Interest* (New York: Knopf, 1951).

30. For important examples of this concern see George F. Kennan, *Memoirs, 1950-1963, op. cit.,* pp. 134-144, 327-351.

31. See Harold D. Lasswell, *National Security and Individual Freedom* (New York: McGraw Hill, 1950), chapter II; and Harold D. Lasswell, "The Garrison-State Hypothesis Today," in Samuel P. Huntington (ed.), *Changing Patterns of Military Politics* (New York: 1962), pp. 51-70.

32. Interesting tentative assessments of the long-term implications of the current debate can be found in each of Robert W. Tucker's works cited above. See also Stephen A. Garrett, "The Relevance of Great

Debates: An Analysis of the Discussion over Vietnam," *The Journal of Politics*, 33 (May, 1971), pp. 478-508.

Chapter 2

1. See Joseph Frankel, *The Making of Foreign Policy* (London: Oxford University Press, 1963), pp. 20-24. An interesting and more extensive discussion of the nature of foreign policy and a summary of the literature may be found in William Wallace, *Foreign Policy and the Political Process* (London: Macmillan, 1971).

2. See, for example, Richard E. Neustadt, *Alliance Politics* (New York: Columbia University Press, 1970). For an interesting attempt to analyze one incident—the Cuban missile crisis—from these two perspectives as well as an analysis of the perspectives themselves, see Graham T. Allison, *Essence of Decision: Explaining the Cuban Missile Crisis* (Boston: Little, Brown, 1971). Allison divides the domestic perspective into two separate parts: the bureaucratic (emphasizing standardized patterns of behavior in decision-making) and the bargaining.

3. Cited in Walter LaFeber, *America, Russia and the Cold War, 1945-1966* (New York: Wiley, 1967), p. 256.

4. See James Rosenau, "Foreign Policy as an Issue Area" and Herbert McClosky, "Personality and Attitude Correlates of Foreign Policy Orientation" in James N. Rosenau (ed.), *Domestic Sources of Foreign Policy* (New York: Free Press, 1967).

5. For a summary of some of the empirical evidence on this point see Kenneth W. Terhune, "From National Character to National Behavior: A Reformulation," *The Journal of Conflict Resolution*, XIV (June, 1970), especially pp. 216-232.

6. Barbara Tuchman, *Stilwell and the American Experience in China, 1911-45* (New York: Macmillan, 1971).

7. Roberta Wohlstetter, *Pearl Harbor: Warning and Decision* (Stanford: Stanford University Press, 1962).

8. Louis J. Halle, *The Society of Man* (New York: Dell, 1969), chapter 1, pp. 17-32.

9. On these points, see William N. Turpin, "Foreign Relations, Yes; Foreign Policy, No," *Foreign Policy*, No. 8 (Fall, 1972), pp. 50-61; and Richard N. Cooper, "Trade Policy is Foreign Policy," *Foreign Policy*, No. 9 (Winter, 1972-73), pp. 18-36.

10. John Franklin Campbell, *The Foreign Affairs Fudge Factory* (New York: Basic Books, 1971), pp. 83-84.

11. Alexis de Tocqueville, *Democracy in America* (trans. by George Lawrence) (New York: Harper and Row, 1966), p. 211. Similar views have been expressed by some of America's most distinguished diplomats including George F. Kennan and Charles Bohlen.

12. Kenneth Waltz, *Foreign Policy and Democratic Politics* (Boston: Little, Brown, 1967), p. 311. See also Lester Pearson, *Democracy in World Politics* (Princeton: Princeton University Press, 1957), especially chapter vii, pp. 96-123.

13. F. S. Northedge, "The Nature of Foreign Policy," in F. S. Northedge (ed.), *The Foreign Policy of the Powers* (New York: Praeger, 1969), p. 14.

14. See Herbert Feis, *The China Tangle* (Princeton: Princeton University Press, 1953); Tang Tsou, *America's Failure in China, 1941-1950* (Chicago: University of Chicago Press, 1963); and John King Fairbank, *The United States and China*, 3rd ed. (Cambridge: Harvard University Press, 1971).

15. John E. Mueller, "Trends in Popular Support for the Wars in Korea and Vietnam," *American Political Science Review,* LXV (June, 1971), pp. 358-375.

16. For a more thorough discussion of the level of analysis problem, see J. David Singer, "The Level-of-Analysis Problem in International Relations," in Klaus Knorr and Sidney Verba (eds.), *The International System: Theoretical Essays* (Princeton: Princeton University Press, 1961), pp. 77-92. See also James N. Rosenau (ed.), *Linkage Politics* (New York: Free Press, 1969).

17. The systems approach has become very prevalent in the social sciences in recent years. Though quite complicated in many of its most sophisticated forms, it is really quite simple when stripped to its basic components. Fundamentally, it suggests a way of looking at something. A system is a unit of observation (for our purposes, foreign policy-making) which has (at least, analytically) definable boundaries. It exists in and receives inputs from an environment external to itself. It has an internal pattern of action which differs from that of other systems. It produces outputs (in our case, foreign policies) which in turn feed back as inputs into the system in their effects on both the system itself and its environment. Outputs can be analyzed in terms of their effects on maintaining, transforming, or destroying the system. One of the major strengths of systems analysis is that it focuses attention on the inter-relationships between different parts of the system and their impact on one another.

The fundamental work on systems theory in the social sciences is Talcott Parsons, "An Outline of the Social System," in T. Parsons, E. Shils, K. Naegle, and J. Pitts (eds.), *Theories of Society* (New York: Free Press, 1961), pp. 30-79. In political science see David Easton, *The Political System* (New York: Knopf, 1953).

Chapter 3

1. Stanley Hoffmann, *Gulliver's Troubles: or the Setting of United States Foreign Policy* (New York: McGraw Hill, 1968), p. 110.

2. Arthur Schlesinger, Jr., "Congress and the Making of Foreign Policy," *Foreign Affairs,* 51 (October, 1972), p. 106.

3. Two of the best histories of the pre-World War II period in American foreign policy are Alexander De Conde, *A History of American Foreign Policy,* 2nd ed. (New York: Charles Scribner's, 1971) and Julius Pratt, *A History of United States Foreign Policy* (Englewood Cliffs, N.J.: Prentice Hall, 1955). From the early 1960's, an interpretation of the United States as an imperial power has become increasingly prevalent. See Walter LaFeber, *The New Empire: An Interpretation of American Expansion 1860-1898* (Ithaca: Cornell University Press, 1963); and William Appleman Williams, *The Roots of the Modern American Empire* (New York: Random House, 1969). For further bibliography, see Lloyd Gardner et al., *Creation of the American Empire* (New York: Rand McNally, 1973).

4. Quoted in Julius Pratt, "The Origins of Manifest Destiny," *The American Historical Review,* XXXII (July, 1927), p. 795.

5. T. Roosevelt to Congress, December, 1904, cited in De Conde, *op. cit.,* pp. 387-388.

6. De Conde, *op. cit.,* p. 389. Data on U. S. intervention is from J. Terry Emerson, "A Chronological List of 199 U. S. Military Hostilities Abroad Without a Declaration of War, 1798-1972," in U. S. Senate, Committee on Foreign Relations, *Hearings, War Powers Legislation,* 93rd Cong., 1st Sess., 1973, pp. 137-142.

7. Cited by George F. Kennan in "Supplemental Foreign Assistance, Fiscal Year 1966," *Hearings before the Senate Foreign Relations Committee,* 89th Cong., 2nd Sess., p. 336.

8. See Chapter 4, pp. 102-7, for a discussion of the unique sense of political virtue possessed by Americans.

9. See Robert Tucker, *The Radical Left and American Foreign Policy* (Baltimore: The Johns Hopkins Press, 1971), pp. 34, 96-7.

10. For a slightly different interpretation, see John G. Stoessinger, *The U. N. and the Superpowers* (New York: Random House, 1965); and

Inis L. Claude, Jr., *The Changing United Nations* (New York: Random House, 1967).

The transformation of the wartime alliance into the Cold War is a story too intricate to be told in detail here. Some of the most interesting aspects of this story are cited in reference 13, Chapter 1. See also Herbert Feis, *From Trust to Terror: The Onset of the Cold War, 1945-1950* (New York: Norton, 1970); and John Lewis Gaddis, *The United States and the Origins of the Cold War: 1941-1947* (New York: Columbia University Press, 1972).

Some of the participants have recorded their observations: Dean Acheson, *Present at the Creation* (New York: Norton, 1969); George F. Kennan, *Memoirs, 1925-1950* (Boston: Little, Brown, 1967); Harold Nicholson, *Diaries and Letters of Harold Nicholson*, Vol. III, *The Later Years, 1945-1962* (New York: Atheneum, 1968); Harry S. Truman, *Memoirs,* 2 vols. (New York: Doubleday, 1955-1956); Arthur Vandenberg, Jr. (ed.), *The Private Papers of Senator Vandenberg* (Boston: Houghton Mifflin, 1952).

11. For an interesting demonstration of this, see the story of how the zonal boundaries of Germany were set and how Berlin came to be deep inside the Soviet zone. Two interesting accounts are in Cornelius Ryan, *The Last Battle* (New York: Simon and Schuster, 1966), pp. 140-162, and Herbert Feis, *op. cit.,* pp. 27-34.

12. For an insider's account of the process by which this and the Marshall Plan decisions were reached within the government, see Joseph M. Jones, *The Fifteen Weeks* (New York: Viking, 1955).

13. The full text of Truman's speech may be found in *Vital Speeches of the Day,* XIII (March 15, 1947), pp. 322-324.

14. Note, for example, the similarity of the oft repeated explanation by the former Secretary of State Dean Rusk in the 1960s that the United States was in Vietnam to teach the North Vietnamese to "leave their neighbors alone."

15. "X" (George F. Kennan), "The Sources of Soviet Conduct," *Foreign Affairs,* 25 (July, 1947), pp. 566-582. There is much dispute over the interpretation of this article and over its influence on American foreign policy. For Kennan's own assessment, see George F. Kennan, *Memoirs, op. cit.,* pp. 313-324, 357-366. See also the contemporary criticism of Kennan's analysis by Walter Lippman, *The Cold War: A Study of U. S. Foreign Policy* (New York: Harper, 1947) and the subsequent assessments by Herbert Feis, *op. cit.,* pp. 221-224 and

Charles Gati, "What Containment Meant," *Foreign Policy*, No. 7 (Summer, 1972), pp. 22-40.

16. See Harry Bayard Price, *The Marshall Plan and Its Meaning* (Ithaca: Cornell University Press, 1955).

17. Greece and Turkey adhered to the Treaty in 1952 and West Germany became a member in 1955, bringing the total membership to 15.

18. See, for example, William G. Carleton, *The Revolution in American Foreign Policy* (New York: Random House, 1963).

19. Cited in Walter LaFeber, *America, Russia and the Cold War, 1945-1966* (New York: Wiley, 1967), p. 100.

20. *Ibid.,* pp. 91-92.

21. See Chalmers Roberts, "The Day We Didn't Go to War," *The Reporter*, 11 (September 14, 1954), pp. 30-35.

22. For a more extended discussion of NSC 68, see Chapter 5, pp. 138-39.

23. These speeches have provided the data for many of the pro-Kennedy liberal interpretations written by those close to Kennedy. See especially Arthur Schlesinger, Jr., *A Thousand Days* (Boston: Houghton Mifflin, 1965) and Theodore Sorensen, *Kennedy* (New York: Harper and Row, 1965). For a contrary assessment of Kennedy which picks out the globalist, unilateralist statements by him and members of his administration, see Richard Walton, *Cold War and Counter Revolution* (New York: Viking, 1972).

24. On the Laotian crisis see Roger Hilsman, *To Move a Nation* (Garden City, N. Y.: Doubleday, 1967), pp. 91-155.

25. The Cuban missile crisis has generated a spate of studies. The most important are Robert F. Kennedy, *Thirteen Days* (New York: Norton, 1971); Elie Abel, *The Missile Crisis* (Philadelphia: J. B. Lippincott, 1966); Graham Allison, *Essence of Decision: Explaining the Cuban Missile Crisis* (Boston: Little, Brown, 1971); and Albert and Roberta Wohlstetter, *Controlling the Risks in Cuba* (London: Adelphi Papers, April, 1965).

26. The best brief summary of the Nixon Doctrine is in *U. S. Foreign Policy for the 1970s II: A Report to the Congress by Richard Nixon,* February 25, 1971 (Washington: Government Printing Office, 1971), pp. 10-21.

27. *United States Foreign Policy for the 1970s: Annual Reports to the Congress by the President of the United States* (Washington: Government Printing Office, 1970, 1971, 1972, 1973).

28. For some further reflections on changes in power factors, see Chapter 4, pp. 120-21.

Chapter 4

1. For evidence of this see Hadley Cantrill and William Buchanan, *How Nations See Each Other* (Urbana: University of Illinois Press, 1953).

2. A useful summary of national character studies in the social sciences may be found in Kenneth W. Terhune, "From National Character to National Behavior: a Reformulation," *The Journal of Conflict Resolution*, XIV (June, 1970), pp. 204-206 and the works cited therein.

3. Alexis de Tocqueville, *Democracy in America* (trans. by George Lawrence) (New York: Harper and Row, 1966).

4. Terhune, *op. cit.*, p. 204. He also summarizes other definitions which have been applied to this concept. See especially Table 1 on p. 210. See also H. C. J. Duijker and N. H. Frijda, *National Character and National Stereotypes* (Amsterdam: North Holland Publishing Co., 1960); and Alex Inkles and Daniel J. Levinson, "National Character: The Study of Modal Personality and Sociocultural Systems," in Gardner Lindzey and Elliot Aronson (eds.), *The Handbook of Social Psychology*, 2nd ed., Vol. 4 (Reading, Mass.: Addison-Wesley, 1969).

5. Terhune, *op. cit.*, p. 231.

6. *Ibid.*, pp. 211-216.

7. For reflections on some of these problems, see *ibid.* See also James N. Rosenau, *Public Opinion and Foreign Policy* (New York: Random House, 1961); and Herbert McCloskey, "Personality and Attitude Correlates of Foreign Policy Orientation," in James N. Rosenau (ed.), *Domestic Sources of Foreign Policy* (New York: Free Press, 1967), pp. 51-109.

8. Stanley Hoffmann, *Gulliver's Troubles: or the Setting of American Foreign Policy* (New York: McGraw Hill, 1968).

9. Among the best sources on the American national character are Geoffrey Gorer, *The American People: A Study in National Character* (New York: Norton, 1948); Henry Steele Commager (ed.), *America in Perspective* (New York: Random House, 1947); Margaret Mead, *And Keep Your Powder Dry: An Anthropologist Looks at America* (New York: W. Marrow and Co., 1942); D. W. Brogan, *The American Character* (New York: Knopf, 1944); David Riesman, *The Lonely Crowd: A Study of the Changing American Character* (New Haven: Yale University Press, 1952); Max Lerner, *America as a Civilization* (New York: Simon and Schuster, 1957); and Richard M. Pfeffer (ed.), *No More Vietnams?* (New York: Harper and Row, 1968), pp. 7-19.

10. Gabriel A. Almond, *The American People and Foreign Policy* (New York: Praeger, 1960). This book was first published in 1950.

11. In fairness, it should be noted that the quote, although usually repeated in this way, is not really accurate. What Wilson actually said was in response to a question from a member of the Senate at his confirmation hearing. The questioner wanted to know whether he could take a decision as Secretary of Defense "extremely adverse to the company, in the interests of the United States Government." He replied, "Yes, sir; I could. I cannot conceive of one because for years I thought what was good for our country was good for General Motors and vice versa."
The actual quote is perhaps even more revealing than the apocryphal one. Note the way in which it reflects the notion of identity of interests between business and national security. See *Hearings before the Committee on Armed Services*, U. S. Senate, 83rd Cong., 1st Sess., January 15, 1953, p. 26.

12. We have not attempted to give a comprehensive discussion of the characteristics of American culture as they affect general American behavior or even political behavior, but only as they affect foreign policy. The interested reader may find broader treatments in the sources cited in reference 9.

13. An interesting example of differences between nations on this point can be found in the controversies surrounding the drafting of the U. N. Universal Declaration of Human Rights. The United States wanted to emphasize the rights of the individual and some other countries wanted to emphasize the rights of the collectivity—state, trade union, corporation, etc.—or the obligations of the individual to the collectivity. For interesting reflections on this, see Joseph P. Lash, *Eleanor: The Years Alone* (London: Andre Deutsch, 1973), pp. 55-81.

14. Hoffmann, *op. cit.*, pp. 100-102.

15. James Bryce, *The American Commonwealth* (edited and abridged by Louis Hacker) 2 Vols. (New York: G. P. Putnam Sons, 1959), p. 306.

16. Grenville Clark and Louis B. Sohn, *World Peace through World Law*, 3rd ed. (Cambridge: Harvard University Press, 1966).

17. De Tocqueville, *op. cit.*, pp. 506-507.

18. The full text of the inaugural address may be found in *Vital Speeches of the Day*, XXVII (February 1, 1961), pp. 226-227.

19. The notion of oscillation of moods is popular with writers in American foreign policy. Gabriel Almond, *op. cit.*, is among the

foremost contemporary exponents of such an interpretation and our analysis relies heavily on his work. See also the recent essay by Zbigniew Brzezinski, "How the Cold War Was Played," *Foreign Affairs,* 51 (October, 1972), pp. 181-209. For an empirical test of the Almond hypothesis, see William R. Caspary, "The 'Mood Theory': A Study of Public Opinion and Foreign Policy," *APSR,* LXIV (June, 1970), pp. 536-547. See also Dexter Perkins, *The American Approach to Foreign Policy* (Cambridge: Harvard University Press, 1952).

20. Andrew Hacker, "Britain's Political Style Is Not Like Ours," *New York Times Magazine* (September 20, 1964), pp. 118, 120.

21. Margaret Mead, *op. cit.*

22. Hoffmann, *op. cit.,* p. 179.

23. *Ibid.,* pp. 180-200.

24. Many of the writers on American national character note the role of pragmatism, but two of the best treatments of this phenomenon are Henry Kissinger, *American Foreign Policy* (New York: Norton, 1969), pp. 29-34; and Hoffmann, *op. cit.,* pp. 143-175. We have relied heavily on these two sources for our treatment of pragmatism.

25. Kenneth Keniston, *The Uncommitted: Alienated Youth in American Society* (New York: Dell, 1965), p. 254.

26. Hoffmann, *op. cit.,* p. 148.

27. An interesting model of how such characteristics are reflected in American organizational behavior can be found in Graham T. Allison, *Essence of Decision: Explaining the Cuban Missile Crisis* (Boston: Little, Brown, 1971), pp. 78-96.

28. See, for example, John Franklin Campbell, *The Foreign Affairs Fudge Factory* (New York: Basic Books, 1971).

29. Hoffmann, *op. cit.,* pp. 160-161.

30. The interested reader should consult the writings of Barbara Ward, especially *The Rich Nations and the Poor Nations* (New York: Norton, 1962). See also Zbigniew Brzezinski, *Between Two Ages: America's Role in the Technetronic Age* (New York: Viking Press, 1970).

31. Scholars continue to dispute the extent to which the colonial system was an economic gain or drain for the "mother" country and for the colony. What matters for international politics, however, is not the truth—whatever that may be—but the fact that economic exploitation is widely believed to have characterized the relationship. The reader may sample the dispute in Kenneth E.

Boulding and Tapan Mukerjee (eds.), *Economic Imperialism* (Ann Arbor: University of Michigan Press, 1972).

32. See the works cited in reference 31, Chapter 1.

33. See Mao Tse-tung, *On Guerilla Warfare* (trans. by Samuel B. Griffith) (New York: Praeger, 1962); and Che Guevara, *Guerilla Warfare* (New York: Random House, 1968).

34. For a fuller exposition of this thesis, see John Herz, "Rise and Demise of the Territorial State," *World Politics*, IX (1957), pp. 473-493 and his "The Territorial State Revisited: Reflections on the Future of the Nation-State," in James N. Rosenau (ed.), *International Politics and Foreign Policy*, revised ed. (New York: Free Press, 1969), pp. 76-89.

35. For some more extensive thoughts on this, see Kenneth Waltz, *Foreign Policy and Democratic Politics* (Boston: Little, Brown, 1967).

36. See the summary of this argument in William Wallace, *Foreign Policy and the Political Process* (London: Macmillan, 1971), pp. 10, 39-40).

Chapter 5

1. These categories are discussed in Theodore Sorensen, *Decision-Making in the White House* (New York: Columbia University Press, 1963), chapter 3.

2. This is one of the guiding themes in his *Presidential Power* (New York: Wiley, 1960).

3. Excellent examples of this perspective come from President Kennedy who was perhaps more candid about his problems than some other Presidents (or perhaps inspired more candor among the ambitious intellectuals who recorded his views). Numerous examples of his frustrations can be found in Theodore Sorensen, *Kennedy* (New York: Harper & Row, 1965); and Arthur Schlesinger, Jr., *A Thousand Days* (Boston: Houghton Mifflin, 1965).

4. Quoted in Louis Koenig, *The Chief Executive* (New York: Harcourt, Brace & World, 1964), p. 211.

5. Quoted in W. H. Harbaugh, *The Life and Times of Theodore Roosevelt* (New York: Colliers, 1963), p. 204.

6. Quoted in Schlesinger, *op. cit.*, pp. 818-19.

7. Margaret Leech, *In the Days of McKinley* (New York: Harper, 1959), pp. 181-82, 463.

8. Roger Hilsman, *The Politics of Policy Making in Defense and Foreign Affairs* (New York: Harper, 1971), p. 17.

9. The phrases are in Hilsman, *ibid.*, pp. 18, 20, 21.

10. John Miller, *Alexander Hamilton and the Growth of the New Nation* (New York: Harper "Torchbooks," 1959), pp. 369-72.

11. See Chapter 3, pp. 56-58.

12. "Banco Nacional de Cuba v. Sabbatino," *International Legal Materials* (Supplement), March, 1964, p. 393. A fuller exposition of the constitutional position of the President can be found in Louis Henkin, *Foreign Affairs and the Constitution* (Mineola, N.Y.: Foundation Press, 1972).

13. *United States* v. *Curtiss-Wright Export Corp.*, 299 U. S. 304 (1936).

14. *Zemel* v. *Rusk*, 381 U. S. 1, 17 (1963).

15. "Banco Nacional de Cuba v. Sabbatino," p. 394.

16. "Apologia Pro Libro Hoc," *Present at the Creation* (New York: Norton, 1969).

17. *Ibid.*, pp. 373-77.

18. The justification for appropriations still includes the Soviet threat but is shifting to other grounds related to the preservation of global security. See the presentations of Secretary of Defense James Schlesinger and Chairman of the Joint Chiefs of Staff, Admiral Moorer, before The Senate Armed Services Committee (February 5, 1974) reported in the *New York Times,* and subsequent discussions of the military budget reported in the *New York Times* and news journals.

19. Pertinent passages of the Eisenhower Doctrine are quoted and discussed in Seyom Brown, *The Faces of Power* (New York: Columbia University Press, 1968), p. 128.

20. *Ibid.*, pp. 135ff.

21. Elmer Plischke, *The Conduct of American Diplomacy*, 3rd ed. (Princeton: Van Nostrand, 1967), chapter 2.

22. For a critical assessment of "democratic diplomacy," see Harold Nicholson, *Diplomacy* (New York: Oxford University Press, 1964), pp. 41-54.

23. For an introduction to this large literature, see Erik Hoffmann and Frederic Fleron, Jr. (eds), *The Conduct of Soviet Foreign Policy* (New York: Aldine-Atherton, 1971).

24. Donald Robinson, "The President as Commander-in-Chief," *Center Magazine*, 4 (Sept./Oct., 1971), pp. 58-67. The military draft ended January 27, 1973.

25. James MacGregor Burns, *Roosevelt: The Soldier of Freedom* (New York: Harcourt, Brace & Jovanovich, 1970), pp. 490 passim.

26. Theodore White, *The Making of the President 1964* (New York: Atheneum, 1965), pp. 293-300.
27. This concern runs through both volumes of George F. Kennan's *Memoirs* (Boston: Little, Brown, 1967, 1972) and is also reflected in David Halberstam, *The Best and the Brightest* (New York: Random House, 1972).
28. See the discussion in Chapter 7, pp. 181-83.
29. Quoted in Sidney Warren (ed.), *The American President* (Englewood Cliffs: Prentice Hall, 1967), p. 33.
30. James Richardson (ed.), *A Compilation of the Messages and Papers of the Presidents,* Vol. 1 (by authority of Congress, 1902), pp. 194-95.
31. For the reporting by Anderson, see *The Washington Post,* December, 1971, January, 1972.
32. *Constitutional Government in the United States* (New York: Columbia University Press, 1961), pp. 77-78.
33. An elaboration of this problem is contained in Graham Allison, *The Essence of Decision: Explaining the Cuban Missile Crisis* (Boston: Little, Brown, 1971), chapters 3, 5.
34. Dean Rusk, "The President," *Foreign Affairs,* (April 1960), pp. 353-69; George Ball, "Nixon's Appointment in Peking: Is This Trip Necessary?" *New York Times Magazine* (February 13, 1972), pp. 11ff.
35. Plischke, *op. cit.,* pp. 49-50.
36. *Alliance Politics* (New York: Columbia University Press, 1970).
37. Kenneth Waltz, *Foreign Policy and Democratic Politics* (Boston: Little, Brown, 1967), pp. 274-75.
38. Koenig, *op. cit.,* p. 354.

Chapter 6

1. James MacGregor Burns, *Roosevelt: The Soldier of Freedom* (New York: Harcourt, Brace & Jovanovich, 1970), pp. 33-63.
2. Arthur Schlesinger, Jr., *A Thousand Days* (Boston: Houghton Mifflin, 1965), p. 406. Kennedy's comment is not a direct quote.
3. Quoted in Richard Neustadt, *Presidential Power* (New York: Wiley, 1960), p. 9.
4. *Waging Peace 1956-1961* (Garden City: Doubleday, 1965), p. 630.
5. *Ibid.* Eisenhower's views remain highly controversial.
6. For a predominantly institutional focus, see Burton Sapin, *The Making of United States Foreign Policy* (New York: Praeger, 1966).

7. The question of experts versus generalists is endlessly debated. Basic terms of the debate were long ago set forth. *Cf.* H. H. Gerth and C. Wright Mills (eds.), *From Max Weber: Essays in Sociology* (New York: Oxford University Press, 1958), pp. 232-9.

8. A good but uncritical description of the contemporary Foreign Service is W. Wendell Blancke, *The Foreign Service of the United States* (New York: Praeger, 1969).

9. John Campbell (New York: Basic Books, 1971), p. 230.

10. Quoted in Schlesinger, *op. cit.*

11. *New York Times,* June 29, 1964.

12. *Ambassador's Journal* (New York: Houghton Mifflin, 1969).

13. The effort to extend the DOD programming system to the entire area of foreign affairs did not succeed. See Frederick Mosher and John Harr, *Programming Systems and Foreign Affairs Leadership* (New York: Oxford University Press, 1970).

14. A brief and informed overview of the Intelligence Establishment is Roger Hilsman, *To Move A Nation* (Garden City: Doubleday, 1967), Part 3. See also Lyman Kirkpatrick, *The Real CIA* (New York: Macmillan, 1968); and Patrick McGarvey, *C.I.A.: The Myth and the Madness* (Baltimore: Penguin, 1973).

15. Case studies do not thereby lose their value: they suggest regularities in the policy-making process and often deal with events such as the Cuban missile crisis, the Marshall Plan, and the TFX decision which have a permanent impact on subsequent policy-making.

16. This point is concisely made by Samuel Huntington, "Power, Expertise, and the Military Profession," *Daedalus* (Fall 1963), pp. 793-801, reprinted in Douglas Fox (ed.), *The Politics of U. S. Foreign Policy Making* (Pacific Palisades: Goodyear, 1971), pp. 203-9.

17. Thomas A. Bailey, *A Diplomatic History of the American People* 5th ed. (New York: Appleton-Century-Crofts, 1955), p. 427.

18. See Zbigniew Brzezinski, *Between Two Ages* (New York: Viking, 1970), p. 292.

19. John Spanier, *The Truman-MacArthur Controversy and the Korean War* (Cambridge: Belknap, 1960).

20. "Domestic Structure and Foreign Policy," *American Foreign Policy* (New York: Norton, 1969), p. 18.

21. Awareness of these differences has led to much discussion on the relative merits of differing careers as preparation for the Presidency. Even if agreement were reached on what is and is not a desirable

background, it is doubtful that the agreement would have much practical effect.

22. *Waging Peace,* p. 638.
23. A good survey of the evolution of the national security machinery and a discussion of alternative organizational schemes may be found in Keith Clark and Laurence Legere (eds.), *The President and the Management of National Security* (New York: Praeger, 1969).
24. For the operation of the NSC under Kissinger, see J. Leacacos, "Kissinger's Apparat," pp. 3-27; and I. M. Destler, "Can One Man Do?" *Foreign Policy* (Winter 1971/72), pp. 28-40.
25. Leacacos, p. 3.
26. *Department of State Bulletin* (September 17, 1973), pp. 368-9.

Chapter 7

1. Discussion of the Resolution and related events is based on Anthony Austin, *The President's War* (Philadelphia: J. B. Lippincott, 1971).
2. *Ibid.,* pp. 9-10.
3. *Ibid.,* chapter 1.
4. *Ibid.,* chapter 11.
5. *Ibid.,* chapter 10.
6. *The Federalist Papers* (New York: Mentor Books, 1961), p. 393.
7. "Congressional-Executive Relations and the Foreign Policy Consensus," *American Political Science Review* (September, 1958), p. 731.
8. See Chapter 1, pp. 3-7.
9. Cecil Crabb, Jr., *American Foreign Policy in the Nuclear Age,* 1st ed. (New York: Harper & Row, 1960), chapter 6; and Cecil Crabb, Jr., *Bipartisan Foreign Policy: Myth or Reality?* (Evanston: Row, Peterson and Co., 1957).
10. Crabb, *Bipartisan Foreign Policy,* p. 60.
11. *Ibid.,* p. 61.
12. Barbara Hinckley, *Stability and Change in Congress* (New York: Harpers, 1971), p. 145.
13. The "role" of the Chairman of the Senate Foreign Relations Committee has not normally been a dissenting one.
14. Francis Wilcox, *Congress, the Executive and Foreign Policy* (New York: Harpers, 1971), p. 67.
15. *Congress and Foreign Policy Making,* 2nd ed. (Homewood: Dorsey, 1967). This division of the policy process is presented in various ways throughout the book.

16. A reaction to this is found in *U. S. Foreign Policy for the 1970's: A Comparative Analysis of the President's 1972 Foreign Policy Report to Congress* (Washington: G.P.O., 1972), a document prepared by the Congressional Research Service of the Library of Congress for the Committee on Foreign Affairs.

17. Richard Kaufman, *The War Profiteers* (Garden City: Doubleday "Anchor", 1972), p. 98.

18. Robinson, *Congress and Foreign Policy Making*, p. 65.

19. *Ibid.*, p. 67.

20. These precedents are reviewed in Arthur Schlesinger, Jr., "Congress and the Making of American Foreign Policy," *Foreign Affairs,* 51 (October, 1972), pp. 78-113.

21. Much of the following discussion is based on Stephen Garrett, "Foreign Policy and the American Constitution: The Bricker Amendment in Contemporary Perspective," *International Studies Quarterly,* 16 (June, 1972), pp. 187-220.

22. Under the proposed constitutional amendment, treaties would have no effect as domestic law except through legislation "which would be valid in the absence of treaty." This clause was intended to reassert the rights of states earlier undermined by the decision of the Supreme Court in *Missouri* v. *Holland.*

23. For specific events in this pattern and the chronology, *Congressional Quarterly* provides an excellent source.

24. Among the congressional documents, see especially, U. S. Congress, Senate, Committee on Foreign Relations, *Hearings, War Powers Legislation,* 93rd Cong., 1st Sess., 1973. See also Jacob Javits with Don Kellermann, *Who Makes War: The President versus Congress* (New York: Morrow, 1973).

Chapter 8

1. Hadley Cantril and Lloyd Free, *The Political Beliefs of Americans* (New York: Clarion, 1968); John Robinson, *Public Information about World Affairs* (Ann Arbor: Survey Research Center, 1967).

2. Useful introductory works are Robert Lane and David Sears, *Public Opinion* (Englewood Cliffs: Prentice Hall, 1964); and V. O. Key, *Public Opinion and American Democracy* (New York: Knopf, 1961).

3. *The American People and Foreign Policy* (New York: Praeger, 1960), especially chapter 7.

4. "One Thing We Learned," *Foreign Affairs* (July, 1968), p. 658.

5. William Caspary, "The 'Mood Theory': A Study of Public Opinion and Foreign Policy," *American Political Science Review* (June, 1970), p. 546.

6. One excellent study from which the phrase "opinion-maker" is borrowed is James Rosenau, *National Leadership and Foreign Policy* (Princeton: Princeton University Press, 1963). See also James Rosenau, *Public Opinion and Foreign Policy* (New York: Random House, 1961).

7. (New York: Macmillan, 1956).

8. *Ibid.*, pp. 248, 243.

9. (Boston: Little, Brown, 1965), chapter 3.

10. *Ibid.*, p. 20.

11. *Gulliver's Troubles* (New York: McGraw Hill, 1968), p. 234.

12. *Ibid.*

13. See Chapter 1, pp. 7-10.

14. Rosenau's "Opinion-making public" is similar to Almond's "elite."

15. Exact annual figures are furnished in Elmer Cornwell, Jr., *Presidential Leadership of Public Opinion* (Bloomington: Indiana University Press, 1965), p. 232.

16. *Ibid.*, p. 18.

17. The trip occurred in December, 1967, and is traced in *Keesing's Contemporary Archives*, pp. 22450, 22503.

18. This table and a discussion of the data are found in the provocative study of John Mueller, *War, Presidents and Public Opinion* (New York: Wiley, 1973), p. 70 passim.

19. The Cambodian episode can be followed in the press during the spring of 1970. For an analysis, see Peter Poole, *Expansion of the Vietnam War into Cambodia* (Athens: Ohio University Center for International Studies, 1970).

20. Quoted in James Reston, *The Artillery of the Press: Its Influence on American Foreign Policy* (New York: Harper, 1967), p. 43.

21. *Ibid.*

22. *Ibid.*, pp. 48-51.

23. Bernard Cohen, *The Press and Foreign Policy* (Princeton: Princeton University Press, 1963), pp. 115, 251.

24. *Ibid.*, pp. 233-4.

25. *Ibid.*, p. 139.

26. Edward Jay Epstein, *News from Nowhere* (New York: Random House, 1973), p. 33.

27. *Ibid.*, p. 158.

28. Various parts of the "Pentagon Papers" appear in editions of varying completeness and emphasis. A convenient collection is *The Pentagon Papers as published by the New York Times* (New York: Bantam, 1971). A more complete collection is *The Pentagon Papers* (Boston: Beacon "Senator Gravel Edition", 1971-72).

29. Bantam edition of *The Pentagon Papers,* app. 2, p. 657.

30. See Chapter 5.

31. There are, of course, exceptions. See Theodore Lowi, "Making Democracy Safe for the World: National Politics and Foreign Policy," in *Domestic Sources of Foreign Policy* (ed.), James Rosenau (New York: Free Press, 1967).

32. Anthony Sampson, *The Sovereign State of ITT* (New York: Stein and Day, 1973).

33. See especially, Raymond Bauer, et al., *American Business and Public Policy,* 2d ed. (New York: Aldine, 1972).

34. There is an enormous literature on the so-called military-industrial complex, most of it polemical. A hastily assembled but somewhat balanced introduction to some of the issues is available in a reader, *The Military and American Society,* Martin Hickman (ed.), (Beverly Hills: Glencoe, 1971).

35. The entire speech is available in Seymour Melman, *Pentagon Capitalism* (New York: McGraw Hill, 1970), app. A.

36. A large excerpt from the first chapter of Melman's book is available in Howard Bliss and M. Glen Johnson (eds.), *Consensus at the Crossroads: Dialogues in American Foreign Policy* (New York: Dodd, Mead, 1972), pp. 261-83.

37. Bliss and Johnson, p. 262.

38. *Ibid.,* p. 268.

39. *Ibid.,* p. 282.

40. Chapter 5.

Chapter 9

1. For an analysis of the missile crisis which emphasizes some of these characteristics of policy making see Graham T. Allison, *The Essence of Decision: Explaining the Cuban Missile Crisis* (Boston: Little, Brown, 1971).

2. An important formulation of some of these aspects may be found in Allison, *ibid.* On bargaining specifically, see Thomas Schelling, *The Strategy of Conflict* (New York: Oxford University Press, 1963).

3. Allison suggests that even when a President is prepared to take a decision (especially in the military field) which overrules a strongly advocated position of a department or agency, there will be delay while a record is prepared to demonstrate that the department or agency concerned was given the fullest possible opportunity to state its case at the highest possible level. See Allison, *op. cit.*, p. 181.

4. *Ibid.*, pp. 91-92.

5. For a fuller treatment of this tendency see Aron Wildawsky, "The Analysis of Issue-Contexts in the Study of Decision-Making," *The Journal of Politics,* XXIV (November, 1962), pp. 717-732.

Chronology

Events Relating to Post-World War II American Foreign Policy

The Truman Administration—1945-1953

1945	*February*	Yalta Conference
	June	United Nations Conference
	Jul./Aug.	Potsdam Conference
1946	*March*	Iranian Crisis
1947	*March*	Truman Doctrine Speech
	March	National Security Act creating National Security Council, CIA, and a unified Department of Defense
	April	Failure of the Moscow Foreign Ministers Conference
	April	Creation of the Department of State's Policy Planning Staff
	June	Marshall Plan proposed
	July	"X" article published in *Foreign Affairs*
	September	Rio Pact for regional collective self-defense in the Western Hemisphere
	December	European Recovery Act (Marshall Plan) adopted by Congress
1948	*February*	Coup d'état in Czechoslovakia
	March	Organization of American States (first meeting)
	June	Selective Service (draft) reinstituted in the U. S.
	June	Berlin blockade and airlift
	June	Vandenberg Resolution supporting U. S. participation in collective defense arrangements in Europe

1949	*January*	Point IV offering technical assistance to developing nations included in Truman's inaugural address
	January	COMECON established as Soviet-East European response to the Marshall Plan
	April	North Atlantic Treaty signed
	July	North Atlantic Treaty approved by the Senate
	September	First Soviet atomic bomb
	October	Communist victory in China
1950	*April*	NSC 68 approved by Truman
	June	Korean War begins
1951	*April*	U. S. agrees to integrated NATO command and American troops stationed in Europe
	September	ANZUS Pact (Australian, New Zealand, U. S. Defense Alliance)
	September	Japanese Peace Treaty
	October	Mutual Security Act approved (global assistance program)

The Eisenhower Administration—1953-1961

1953	*January*	Secretary of State Dulles calls for liberation of Eastern Europe
	March	Stalin dies
	March	Berlin uprisings suppressed by Soviet Union
	August	Congressional resolution supporting liberation of Eastern Europe
1954	*February*	Bricker Amendment fails Senate by one vote
	April	Geneva Conference on Indo-China
	June	U. S. refuses to aid French in Indo-China with air or troop support

	June	U. S. aids overthrow of "leftist" Guatemalan regime
	September	SEATO Treaty signed
	October	Paris Agreements allowing German rearmament
	December	U. S.-Republic of China mutual defense treaty
1955	*January*	Formosa Crisis and congressional resolution
	February	Bagdad Pact (U. S. not a formal member)
	July	Geneva Summit Conference—Open Skies Plan
	October	Germany admitted to NATO
1956	*October*	Suez Crisis
	November	Soviet intervention in Hungary
1957	*March*	Eisenhower Doctrine
	April	IKE uses Sixth Fleet to support King Hussein of Jordan
	August	Soviets fire first ICBM
	October	Sputnik
1958	*January*	Explorer I
	April	Nixon tour of Latin America
	July	Eisenhower sends Marines into Lebanon
1958-59		Berlin Crisis
1959	*January*	Castro comes to power in Cuba
	March	Iraq withdraws from Bagdad Pact following coup (CENTO [Central Treaty Organization] formed)
1960	*February*	France tests A-bomb in Sahara
	March	CIA training of Cuban exiles
	May	American U-2 plane shot down over USSR
	May	Collapse of Paris summit
	September	Act of Bogata (U. S. offers $500 million for "social development" in Latin America)

	September	First French thermonuclear device exploded
1961	*January*	U. S. breaks diplomatic relations with Cuba

The Kennedy-Johnson Administrations – **1961-1969**

1961	*March*	Alliance for Progress proposed
	April	Bay of Pigs invasion fails
	June	Vienna summit between Kennedy and Khrushchev
	July	Berlin Crisis (U. S. reserves called up and Congress approves appropriations and shelter program)
	August	Alliance for Progress created and funded
	August	Berlin Wall (U. S. reinforces Berlin garrison)
	October	Taylor-Rostow mission to South Vietnam (500 advisors)
1960-62		Laos Crisis
		Congo Crisis
1962	*April*	Kennedy orders U. S. nuclear test series
	July	Kennedy Declaration of Interdependence speech
	July	Geneva accords on Laos signed
	October	Trade Expansion Act (Kennedy Round legislation)
	November	Cuban missile crisis
	December	Kennedy-McMillan Nassau Conference– Skybolt issue
1963	*January*	10,000 advisors in Vietnam
	January	De Gaulle vetoes U. K. EEC membership
	June	Kennedy American University conciliatory speech on peace
	June	*Ich bin ein Berliner* speech in Berlin; Kennedy takes hard line

	July	Test Ban Treaty
	November	Kennedy assassinated
1964	*August*	Tonkin Gulf incident and resolution
	October	First Chinese atomic bomb
1965	*January*	Panama Crisis (riots in Canal Zone; pressures for new treaty)
	February	Bombing of North Vietnam begins
	February	White Paper on aggression from the North in Vietnam
	April	Johnson speech at Johns Hopkins—why we are there, peace overtures, and offer of development aid
	April &	
	May	Dominican Republic intervention
1966	*Jan./Feb.*	Senate Foreign Relations Committee Vietnam Hearings
	May	First Chinese thermonuclear bomb
1967	*June*	Arab-Israeli Six-day war
1968	*January*	Seizure of *Pueblo,* U. S. intelligence ship, by North Korea
	May	Johnson peace appeal and announcement he will not run again
	May	Vietnam peace talks open in Paris
	July	Nuclear Non-proliferation Treaty opened for signature

The Nixon Administration—1969-1974

1969	*June*	National Commitments Resolution passed by Senate
	July	Nixon Doctrine announced in Guam
1970	*May*	Cambodian invasion
	July	Gulf of Tonkin Resolution repealed
1971	*Mar./Dec.*	Bangladesh Crisis culminating in Indo-Pakistani War

	June	Supreme Court Decision in *Pentagon Papers* Case
	August	Nixon suspends convertibility of the dollar
1972	*February*	Nixon trip to China
	May	Nixon trip to USSR
	May	SALT agreements (first round)
	December	Paris Peace talks suspended; heavy bombing of North Vietnam
1973	*January*	Vietnam Peace Accords signed in Paris
	January	Preliminary talks on Conference on European Security in Helsinki
	February	Preliminary talks in Vienna on Mutual and Balanced Force Reduction (MBFR) in Europe
	May	Nixon proclaims Year of Europe
	August	Kissinger appointed Secretary of State
	October	Yom Kippur Arab-Israeli War
	October	Congress passes and Nixon vetoes War Powers Bill
	November	Congress overrides Nixon's veto of War Powers Bill
1974	*May*	Kissinger successfully completes negotiation of Middle-East disengagement
	June	Nixon visits USSR; Nixon-Brezhnev summit
	August	Nixon resigns